Lessons From A Tour Bus Presents
THE ACTION SANDWICH

Alan Frew
with Sharon Brennan

Binea Press

*For my beloved wife Marcy whose love and friendship has been
the perfect support for an imperfect man.*

Published in 2007 by
Binea Press, Inc.
512-1673 Richmond Street
London, Ontario, Canada N6G 2N3

Tel: 519.660.6424
Fax: 519.660.4449

E-mail: bineapress@bellnet.ca
www.bineapress.com

Distributed by:
Binea Press Inc.
519.660.6424

Library and Archives Canada Cataloguing in Publication
Frew, Alan
The Action Sandwich
A Six Step Recipe For Success By Doing What You're Already Doing
Alan Frew, Sharon Brennan
Foreword by Tim Long
ISBN 978-0-9736863-9-5
1. Success.   I. Brennan, Sharon, 1961-   II. Title
BF637.S8F69 2007   158.1   C2007-903120-X

11 10 09 08 07   1 2 3 4 5
First Edition

Design by Response Generators
London, Ontario, Canada
Tel: 519.432.4932
www.rgdirect.com

Printed in Canada by Friesens Corporation
Altona, Manitoba

"There is no worse place out of hell than that neighbourhood."
A writer's description of
Coatbridge, Scotland, (My hometown).

A SPECIAL THANKS:

With Tony Robbins I hit the goalpost, with Napoleon Hill I was leading at halftime, but with Jack Canfield's, *The Success Principles* I won the Cup! It's a basic, fundamentally sound, honest, practical book filled with truth and commonsense. Thanks Jack, you're the Paul McCartney of all of them.

"I want to sing my song, for you, for everyone."
Alan Frew, lyrics from Glass Tiger's *My Song*.

ACKNOWLEDGEMENTS

This book is the result of the RECEPTIVITY, DESIRE, BELIEF, INTENTION and ACTION of my business partner, co-author and loyal friend, Sharon Brennan. Thank you for your dedication, PASSION and perseverance in getting me to do this. It would never have happened without you. You never faltered, not a single time in staying true to our purpose. This is only the beginning.

A special thank you to all of the musicians that I have worked with professionally in the making of my favourite band, *Glass Tiger*, especially Wayne, Al, Sam and Michael. Without all of you I have no Rock 'n Roll tales to tell.

And so to my wife and munchkin thank you for making each day richer and richer still.

A special thank you to my dear son Gavin, who has walked by my side through many of these stories and so much more. Much love to Ryan whose journey is only now beginning and to my brother Gordon and sister Christine, our family is truly an "original." I always knew our wackiness meant something. To my dear parents Gracie and Hughie who are at last, together again.

Finally to Scotland for "your wee bit hill and glen" gave me my gift of the blether.

Sharon would like to thank her brilliantly gifted husband Peter and beautifully spirited daughter Jessica for their patience and support, and her parents and friends who have been so lovingly interested in every step of this process. Thank you Alan for giving me the chance to craft these precious stories with you, for unlimited access to the renewable resource of your enthusiasm and for the daily opportunity to be who I am called to be. We are creators. That's what we do.

Together, Alan and Sharon would like to thank the amazing Tim Long, our publisher, Richard Bain, of Binea Press for his guidance and wisdom, Peter Watson, Amanda Jean Francis and the team at Response Generators, Cynthia O'Neill, Deane Cameron, Wayne Gretzky, Rod Knight, Jacques Villeneuve, Keith Pelley and our dear friend and fellow-thug "Manchester Dave" Nolan who gave us the mighty UK stamp of approval.

TABLE OF CONTENTS

MY SONG – *Opus 6*

FOREWORD

Here's how you know you've made it in life – the guy whose music you failed to get laid to in high school asks you to write the foreword to his book.

I first encountered Alan Frew whilst sprawled on my parents' couch in Exeter, Ontario, in the mid-'80s, watching MuchMusic. The video was, of course, *Don't Forget Me (When I'm Gone)*, and I instantly recognized Alan as handsome, charismatic, and wildly talented. The kind of person who really gets on my nerves.

Cut to some eighteen years later, and I meet Alan at a late-night party at the Canadian Comedy Awards. It soon becomes clear that in addition to the aforementioned talent and charisma, Alan is also friendly and thoughtful. Plus he dresses well, smells great, and really seems to care what I have to say. By now, this guy is totally starting to piss me off.

Three more years pass, and Alan calls and asks if I would read his upcoming book and write the foreword. I agree instantly, because a) he's Alan friggin' Frew and b) I am a whore. But soon I'm gripped by an overwhelming fear: What if the book he's written is really, really good? As a professional writer and a fantastically small-minded person, how will I deal with that?

Not well, it turns out. As I drain the remnants of my third gin and tonic, it gives me no pleasure to report that the book you hold in your hand is – *sigh* – wonderful, full of hilarious anecdotes and priceless wisdom.

It turns out Alan Frew is one of those people who just sort of has things figured out: he knows what it takes to rise from hardscrabble Coatbridge (like him) or not-so-hardscrabble Exeter, Ontario (like me), achieve everything you've ever dreamed, and have fun doing it. What's more, he's generous enough to share that knowledge with the rest of us.

So read the damn book – it's great. Now, if you'll excuse me, I'm going to go fix another drink (my fourth) (okay, tenth) and start teaching myself how to write songs and play the guitar. Hear that, Frew? If you're gonna move onto my turf, I'm gonna move onto yours. You're a wonderful man... and you've written a gem of a book... but you're going *down*.

Tim Long
Executive Producer, *The Simpsons*
Former Head Writer, *David Letterman*
Los Angeles
April 2007

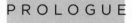

PROLOGUE

When it was announced that Deane Cameron was to become the President of EMI (Capitol) Music Canada, I was happy for him. He surely deserved it more than most. Deane literally knows the business inside out, for back in the '70s he started out as a warehouse employee packing vinyl albums into sleeves and driving the fork lift truck to load vast quantities of product onto skids that were on their way to the nation's record stores and eventually into the homes of music lovers all across the country. So here was a true rags to riches tale of a young man working his way up to becoming the man in charge, the President. My happiness for his success was also a little self-serving, for I knew that as the President of the label he would have the opportunity to meet all of the stars who were signed to his company including of course, *him.* GOD... ok, not The God, but my favourite, my idol. And there was no doubt in my mind that as President, Deane would actually meet him in person, shake his hand and actually, speak to GOD.

Being a so-called Pop Star in my own right carried with it a few perks, one of which was that I had managed to score second row floor seats to see him in concert in Toronto the following month. To say I was excited about attending his concert would be a bit of an understatement but actually meeting him, well now, THAT would be out of this world, no wait, THAT is another galaxy entirely and Deane, I knew would get to do just that...the lucky sod!

So the next time I was in his office I asked if and when the time came to meet GOD, would he be kind enough to get me an autograph signed to yours truly. I couldn't help it, I would not normally do something as contrary as this, but after all it was GOD, and I was helpless to resist the temptation. Deane said he would be glad to and I left it at that. The day of the concert came and I was surprised to receive word from EMI that there was going to be a press conference and an invitation had been put aside for me to attend and listen-in as GOD answered questions from the media. I thought I'd died and gone to, well, heaven, I guess, and so with a childlike skip in my step I headed down to the stadium.

The room was jammed, the atmosphere palpable as he entered the pressroom. Was there a living soul among this throng that was NOT a fan? Impossible! I had caused a tiny stir myself when I had entered earlier because *Glass Tiger* at the time was at the peak of its success and many, if not all, recognized me and enjoyed the novelty of having a so-called celebrity in the room with them waiting for GOD to enter. When he did, I was soon forgotten, but quite frankly I didn't care. He answered any and all questions, carefully, playfully and with the ease of a well-seasoned veteran. In what seemed like the blink of an eye I heard a woman say, "Last question please!" and then in a flash, it was over and he was gone.

Suddenly, I became fodder again for the attention of many of the reporters who wanted my take on all of it. I couldn't answer them, I did not wish to answer them, for I wanted to sit and bask for a moment in the fact that I had been in the same room as GOD and that answering their questions was just not something I wished to do. Then someone came to my rescue. A short, well-dressed woman, "Miss Last Question Please", with a clipboard in hand. She cried out in a very strong English accent, "Capitol Records, party of six and an Alan Frew!" I remember thinking, "What's an Alan Frew?" But wait! That was me! What the hell did she want with me?

"I...I'm an Alan Frew," I said, swallowing the large lump that had just leapt into my gaping mouth.
"Come on then," she said authoritatively.
"Where?" I asked.
"Where else, but to meet HIM of course?" she answered turning on her heel and leading the way.
My mind was a blur. How could I possibly meet HIM? What would I say to HIM?
I began to rehearse in my mind, "Errr, thanks a lot for being, well, you know...you. I am such a fan of, you know, HIM, well you are HIM, and I'm

sure you know that, but thanks a lot anyway." I was in trouble, but my legs seemed to be moving and I was indeed making my way down a long corridor following "Miss Last Question Please" at a rapid pace.

It seems that Deane had gone well above and beyond the call of just getting me an autograph and had made arrangements for me to go back to a secluded little room with the others from his company and have a private audience with, "Oh my God... GOD!"

No money, no accolades, no amount of record sales, could have replaced that moment in time for me, for I had dreamed of this since I could remember the sound of his voice blasting on the tiny transistor radio that sat beside the kitchen sink in our old prefabricated post-war home back in Scotland.

My dad was hilarious on these cold mornings, getting dressed in the kitchen, by the oven. I remember the time when singer-songwriter Jose Feliciano's version of "Light My Fire," originally written by Robby Krieger and Jim Morrison of *The Doors*, crackled out of our little radio.

"In the name of the wee man, who the hell is that?"
"Jose"
"Whoosee?"
"No Jose! Jose Feliciano, Dad, isn't he fab?"

In his version, at the end Jose would repeat over and over almost ad nauseam the line "Light My Fire, Light My Fire, Light My Fire..."
Causing my dad to inevitably say, "For Christ's sake will somebody light that laddie's fire and while yer at it...light ours!"

We'd be huddled at the oven or the little kerosene heater because coal was expensive and would never be burned for something like getting dressed in the morning.

"Fab? Turn that bloody rabble off!"
"But Dad, he's brilliant," I would plead.

"Brilliant my arse!" he'd reply.

How ironic this was, for by 1986 he would live vicariously and passionately through his son's pop-fame, and would become well versed, and learned regarding the world of pop music.

As I walked down that hallway towards the legend, my mind searched for an appropriate opening line but nothing would come to me. I knew that my wits had never let me down in the past and I was sure they wouldn't here, so I decided to just let providence guide me. "I'll bet it's easier meeting the Queen or the Pope!" I thought to myself.

Suddenly the door opened and he was the first one in front of me, his back turned, facing one of Capitol Record's representatives, who upon seeing me spoke up.

"Ah, here he is, this is one of our nation's top recording artists. Please let me introduce you both. Alan Frew meet…"

"It's About The Performance, Not The Applause"
ALAN FREW

THE MAN WHO WOULD BE BING

My life is a true success story. This book is a true success story. Last night's dinner is a true success story, as was that hug my baby girl just gave me. Come to think of it, just getting up this morning was a true success story, for let's face it, there are many who did not. The completion of any desired outcome, attaining that which you set out to attain, no matter how small or seemingly insignificant at the time is, again, a true success story.

Does it sound like I am oversimplifying? Perhaps. But then again, perhaps not, for life cannot possibly be all about the toys, the accolades, the houses, cars and the money, can it? I pray not. Surely it is not about who has the most. If that were so then would it not follow that Bill Gates is a success and everyone below his net worth is a failure? A preposterous notion I know, but what then would you call success, a million dollars? Fifty million? Three billion?

Let me ask you this. Is the dude who is pulling in a high seven-figure salary from Wall Street, who owns a Donald Trump condo and is driving to work in his special edition Lamborghini while making a call to his personal pilot to ready-up the Gulf Stream jet that will scoot him to his second home in the Turks and Caicos Islands a success, just because of the money and goodies he has?

Conversely, is the guy who is presently deep in a forest somewhere in Northern British Columbia living in a turn of the century shack that leaks like a bugger with no running water and no electricity and who still has to "snag" dinner if he intends to eat that night, not caring about money or the toys of life -- is he a failure because of his lack of material and financial abundance?

The answer of course is too diverse and has too many variables for us as outsiders to decide. But let's suppose for argument's sake that the Wall Street dude is addicted to cocaine, stressed out to the point of having blackouts and is separated from his wife and children due to his anger and violent outbursts. Jeremiah Johnson on the other hand is there in the Canadian wilderness eating organic food and vegetables living meditatively with his wife of thirty years eagerly awaiting the arrival of his children and grandchildren who make him happier than any job ever could. So now, if asked to decide, who would you say is the success and who's the failure?

I believe that living a truly successful life centres around one major factor: control. How much say do you have over your life and its outcome? How much control do you have over where you work, how you work, why you work at what you do, where you live, how you live, where you go, how much free time you have, how active or inactive you DESIRE to be, how much money you have and any number of the endless events that make up your life? Do you control these things, or do they control you?

Oh don't kid yourself. I love the bells, whistles and the trimmings of success. However, they are simply the by-products of achievement. Successful people know this. They know it's about the journey and not the destination. They know it's all about the performance and not the applause.

Oh yes indeed. I have always loved toys, why as a matter of fact...

Wavy lines, wavy lines...waaaavvvyy llliiiiinnnes....

Once upon a time, my mother took me shopping into the city centre of Glasgow, some nine miles and a bumpy double-decker bus ride away from my hometown. I was all of five years old, two feet tall and toothless. My baby teeth had fallen out when I was fifteen to eighteen months old, and by age five, my new ones had yet to grow in. The song "All I Want For Christmas Is My Two Front Teeth" is something that to this day I equate to finger nails being scratched across the full length of a chalk board, though perhaps the Walt Disney tune, "It's A Small World After All" is even more unbearable, for I would rather take a stick in the eye than have to listen to that bugger ever again. Perhaps one day I will tell you why.

The bus ride into the centre of Glasgow was uneventful, other than the performance put on by the token drunkard at the back of the upper deck of the bus. A bus ride to and from Glasgow without a drunk on board is like a scruffy dog without a flea. Scolding and singing, singing and scolding, that is their forte.

"SEE YOOOZE PEOPLE," he says, squinting as though he can't decipher if there are two or twenty-two on board.

"Yooooze people think yooooze are better than me...don't yooooze?"

This is always followed up with a little expletive.

"Well ....PISS OFF THEN!"

Now comes the song, usually a little Bing Crosby, Al Martino, Englebert Humperdink or if you're really lucky, some Jolson.

The Scots, especially those that are from the city of Glasgow (known as Glaswegians), are a breed unlike any other. Poets who can fight like lions, drunkards who can sing like larks, dropouts who can solve problems like Pythagoras, and wasters who can debate like Churchill, they are human encyclopedias. Walking libraries of information ranging from the mundane to the extraordinary. To this day I am fascinated by the fact that you can walk into any one of hundreds of pubs and see that same, wee scruffy drunk bastard, who is nothing short of a master in the art of debating. And yes, he's in EVERY single one of them. I kid you not. It's like cloning at its finest, and no matter how drunk, incapacitated or mentally challenged he may appear, he is a walking literary enigma, stacked to the hilt with facts and answers to questions ranging from "What was Plato's real name?" to "Which character has been on Coronation Street longer than any other?" Then, just for good measure, he'll give you a wee lecture on how Einstein got it wrong in his theory of relativity just before telling you what Geronimo had for breakfast prior to the battle of Little Big Horn.

Of all the races of people on this earth that I have had the fortune to come across, the Glaswegians stand out as a people who seem to know exactly who they are, and what they are doing here, even when they are talking a load of shite.

"SEE YOOOZE PEOPLE...yoooze people think am drrrrunk, don't yoooze? Well I'll show yoooze who's drunk!"

He then proceeds to tell you name for name, every member of the Scottish Football Team that beat England at Wembley in 1928!!!

As a matter of fact, the whole trip into and (for my mother), out of the big city that day was insignificant and uneventful right up until the moment when she arrived back at the house with bags in hand, only to be greeted by my father with an urgent question.

"Where's Alan?"
"Christ almighty!" I'm sure she said, "I forgot him! He's still in the store!"

And indeed I was, even after the manager had closed it up for the night, and headed home for a well-deserved fish supper with his wife and kids. For me there were two significant reasons why I didn't give a flying duck that I had been locked in a large department store all alone, at the tender age of five and-a-bit.

The first was the fact that a light had been left on in the back storage room. The second was that the back storage room was where the toys were kept. My mother had to contact the police (by going to the police station in person since we had no phone), who in turn found the manager, who grumpily re-opened the store, amidst quite a bit of huffing, puffing and panic. Totally oblivious to this was a boy at peace, a boy in bliss, a boy who at times had a voice loud enough to take the ears off a donkey. Yet here he was quietly playing with a toy farm set that featured a plastic farmer, a barn and fence, and cows, sheep, horses, ducks. And yes, a donkey. No panic. No fuss. No fear.

At no other time was it more apparent that I was destined to find the fortitude to take care of myself in this world than at that moment.
"He doesn't seem very worried, does he?" observed the police officer.
"No, he gets very focused on things he likes… as if nothing else exists," replied my mother, somehow distant.
"I could have finished my dinner by now!" grumbled the store manager.
"Come on then sonny, let's go home," said the giant policeman to the toothless two-foot loner. So, with a little undetected smirk on my face, I was soon once more on the bus with my mother, this time headed home.

What a success story! Oh yes dear reader, a success story, for as I said earlier, success is the completion of any desired outcome, and you see, I neglected to tell the policeman, the store manager and especially my mother that my pockets were stuffed with plastic cows, sheep, and other livestock, and that indeed, "Old Macdonald had a farm, Ee i ee i oh!"

Being here to tell you this tale and to write about *THE ACTION SANDWICH* (a six-step recipe to success, by doing what you're already doing) is not only a success story, it is most likely the greatest story of my life, for I come from a place and from a time where success seemed like a stain, reviled, criticized, even feared. I come from a place where your friends were named anger, wits, fists and survival. Trying to attach a dollar figure to the success held between the pages of this book would be incalculable. This is a tale of how *THE ACTION SANDWICH* helped the boy to become a man, the fighter to become a healer, the storyteller to become a public speaker, and the singer to become a rock star.

The recipe for *THE ACTION SANDWICH* is simple and deliberate. Since embarking on this new pathway as an author and public speaker, I have talked to literally thousands of everyday people about life and the challenge of living it. We have also talked about books; the self-help, take-charge, be-godly, attract-wealth, release-the-lion-within motivational books, of which I have *inhaled* more than my fair share.

One thing that seems universal to our discussion is how absolutely overwhelming some of them make the adventure of living your best life seem. Just when you finally decide to reach out for help because you are feeling stressed, depressed, frustrated and at your wits' end, the instruction manual comes along and has you keeping journals, writing in diaries, sending out chain letters and so forth. And although I truly am not knocking this philosophy, I just know that for many people (including myself by the way) this just doesn't feel practical. I can NEVER stay on track when I attempt to keep journals or use mind-mapping techniques. I get frustrated and feel like I'm failing before I begin. So give me good old-fashioned, simple, practical directions, suggestions, affirmations and so forth, that I can read, digest and place into my mind and heart without having to stand on one foot while drinking a glass of water, hiding sticky-notes on bathroom mirrors or carrying painted rocks in my pockets, and I promise you I will get further. These techniques that do not work for me however, do work for many people, but for those of you who cannot make them work for you, I'm here to tell you that all is not lost. Abundance is for you as well.

I was at a seminar recently and I swear I couldn't tell where the motivation began and the infomercial ended. People high-fived and hugged their neighbours, "whooped and hollered," and got caught up in the frenzy of the moment. And, again, if this works for you then knock yourself out. But, personally, I do not want to be yelled at. I don't want to repeat little phrases like a parroting karaoke singer. I don't want to high-five and hug strangers while I am at a seminar. But that doesn't mean I don't want abundance or that my heart isn't open to teachings. It just means I like to think for myself.

For example, "The Bible" of so-called motivational books for me is *The Success Principles* by Jack Canfield. It is a simple, direct, honest, basic technique and Mr. Canfield by no coincidence also happens in my opinion to have the same simple, direct, honest, basic style to his speaking, which is why I am attracted to his teachings and why I look up to him as my mentor. It's a "take what you need and discard the rest" approach. It works for me and I know it can work for those of you who respond to this type of teaching.

I've made the principles of my book simple because IT *IS* SIMPLE and it is part of a lifestyle that anyone can adopt for everyday living. This book is not just for the enlightened business-savvy sector using information like this for reminders or top-ups for the success-plan that they have already implemented. This book is for everyday people, who work in all kinds of jobs. It's for bartenders and cab drivers, grocery clerks and waiters, nurses and bank tellers. This book is for people like my family, who still live within the clutches of the well-known acronym, "J.O.B." (Just Over Broke). This book is for those who struggle with the challenge of living, families who question philosophies, people who mess up, then move on. This is a book for you and for me, and just for good measure, I hope to make you laugh or perhaps shed a wee tear along the way. I have written this book to share some of the things I have learned in my journey thus far, and I have also peppered the pages with childhood and Rock 'n Roll stories that I hope will touch your heart or funny-bone. I hope you will read this book with an open mind and take from it whatever it gives you.

WHO ARE YOU? WHO, WHO, WHO, WHO?

Who are you?
What do you want?
No, what do you really, really, want?
Do you know? If so, do you know how to get it?
Do you need to change the direction that your life is heading?
If so, how will you change it?

It's all a bit frightening isn't it, the "who, what, where, why, and how" of your life? Have you ever had the courage to ask yourself questions like these, and then followed through with trying to find the answers? Some ask them and then leave it at that. Countless others never ask them at all. Successful people ask them all the time and they do not stop until they find the answers.

It's tough isn't it, dealing with this thing called life? The fun, the laughter, the sorrow and the pain, the anger, violence, love and hate, the "in sickness and in health 'til death do us part" of it all? We call it life's ups and downs, as though life were a roller coaster -- challenging, overwhelming and, yes, even terrifying.

Let me tell you how I have come to feel about it these days...I love it. That's right...I love it. The fear, frustration, pain, sorrow, as well as the love and the joy -- the PASSION of living. I love it, difficult as it can be. I'll take it all. This journey, this jigsaw puzzle we call life. I, for one, would not have it any other way.

First of all, what's the alternative to loving it? Choose anything else and you might as well dig a hole in the ground and get in. Why? Because you are here, and this is now, and that is a fact. You see, it does not matter if the divorce is pending or the cancer is spreading or the ship is sinking. All that matters is what you are going to do about it and how you react to it. So, what ARE you going to do about it? How much longer are you willing to stay this way? Is your life important enough to you, to do something about it? If your answers to these three questions are, "I'm going to do nothing", "I'll wait forever" and "no, my life is not that important", then pal here's the shovel, go dig. Hopefully as you read on you'll discover that my credentials are in order and you'll realize that I have the proper lineage to back up an understanding of what defeatism and bitterness can breed.

-Poverty? Check.
-Family history of alcoholism? Check.
-Violence? Check.
-Abuse, segregation, bigotry? Check.

This book is not rocket science. In fact, none of the so-called motivational books are. They are all based on fundamentals like common sense, right and wrong, good and bad, clever and stupid. Besides that, as you're about to find out, the amazing thing is that when it comes to the questions of life you already know most of the answers.

I really hope this book motivates you to live a better life, but be careful of the "motivational" label, for all too often we think that a book or a speaker is going to be a quick fix, our miracle pill. However, they are not. As I sit here, dear reader, alone in my writing room, I often glance at my bookcase where I see the names of past and future legends; Chopra, Hill, Dyer, Myss and Canfield, to name but a few. Such wonderful, visionary and inspirational teachers universally connected to a common source, the apex of light, and of spirit, INTENTION, goodness and wisdom. These books, however, do not live in the space between the slight of hand and the disappearing playing card; they are neither potions nor the stuff of magic. They are not written from visions or the remains of tealeaves in the bottom of a china cup. On the contrary, they represent the journey, the toil, the dedication, the hard work, the stuff of real life that lives between the question and the answer.

So the principle of this book is based on the concept that we are already using the recipe to make ourselves things that we do or do not wish to be. Your life to date is a culmination of using this recipe. If you are stressed, fat, unemployed, incarcerated, addicted, lazy, or _____ (fill in the blank), you are all of these things as a result of choice. So why not choose to use the recipe to make yourself empowered, fit, rich, charitable, energetic and passionate? Just as it takes as many if not more muscles in your face to frown as it does to smile, so it is with THE ACTION SANDWICH, for it takes just as much if not more effort to live a life of redundancy and stagnation as it does one of abundance and vitality.

Is this a "how-to" book? Perhaps, but I prefer to think of it as a "Do It Yourself" book because I don't know "how-to" get you to do anything, nor would I force you to try. Besides, I'm too busy trying to figure out "how-to" myself. To be successful and live the best life you possibly can, you're going to be asking and answering and "how-to-ing" until they put you in that hole that the other guy is digging. It never ends, but that's the beauty of it. That's the space between the question and the answer, that's the journey. So come on, grab your hat and let's get started. Don't be afraid, fear is not an enemy. Fear is a signpost and in many cases an ally. Or, dare I say, a friend? Is that possible? Can fear be your friend? I know this much, the only people who never fall are the ones who never stand up. Come on, get up and let's go.

DR ROBERT

Very early in my career, fear was my one true nemesis. Without a doubt the biggest challenge I faced each and every night was going out on stage in front of an audience. I was so terrified that I carried a little medical bag with me everywhere I went that I affectionately called Doctor Robert's Bag. It was filled with prescriptions and potions that I felt would help me combat fear and nervousness. Pills, sprays, tonics: you name it and I had it.

Back in the very beginning, a lifetime ago and then some, a few local musicians heard me singing at a party and offered me the chance to audition for the role of lead singer of their band. I was more than receptive to this notion but I was also young, naive and incredibly inexperienced when it came to being a musician. Though I was soon the band's singer, it didn't take long before I grew a little uncomfortable with the idea, and on more than one occasion when they would come to pick me up for rehearsal, I would have my mother go to the door and give the excuse of my impending death from some exotic twenty-four hour flu, or tell them of a problem I was having with constipation or the mange. So you see, right off the bat, my RECEPTIVITY, my DESIRE and my BELIEF were not balanced with living the truth about who I was or wanted to be. When it came to getting up in front of an audience I was a wreck, and within moments my gag reflex would kick in and I would go through this awful wrenching motion consistent with the feeling of needing to vomit. It truly was terrifying, so much so that in a world of readily accessible medications, I turned to my family doctor, who willingly handed out pills. I also remained aware of the fact that if they didn't quite do the trick, street drugs like pot, hash, uppers and downers were easier to get than money for a cup of coffee, and I would willingly try those if need be, for there was ALWAYS someone in the drug world that loved to hang out with musicians. To gain your favour, they would graciously offer to get you high if you so desired. So Mr. Bag of Nerves here set off into the world of Rock 'n Roll fully stocked.

Anyone who has known me through the years would understand that this was a strange dilemma, for I have always been a confident take-the-lead type of a guy. And even stranger was the fact that I truly love to entertain people and know with all of my heart that I am good at it. I had worked in an adult world since the age of fifteen in a variety of jobs. I'd been a shoe salesperson, a factory worker and a milkman. I'd recently started a job as a hospital orderly, which I enjoyed immensely. But entertaining, musically in particular, was my driving force. So being a guy that couldn't get up in front of an audience without showing them what I ate for supper that night was driving me crazy.

COMING TO TAKE YOU AWAY

We set off in 1977 on what truly was the quintessential Magical Mystery Tour -- so young, so green and oh so naïve. There I was, running back and forth to the wings of the stage (if there was a stage) or behind a guitar amplifier to periodically do an impersonation of a returning Emperor Penguin attempting to regurgitate the day's meal for the benefit of its offspring. Every few minutes I would dive behind the cover of the amp, then return with weepy eyes and some drool on my chin. They must have thought I was a lunatic. On one crazy occasion I was so fearful before the show that I allowed myself to smoke some hashish with one of the locals, which then led to what will go down in history as one of the shortest performances ever for a professional rock band. It went something like this...

Band takes the stage; crowd cheers; drummer starts a solid beat; crowd cheers louder; guitar riff to "All Right Now" kicks in; crowd goes wild; bass guitar joins in as if to say, "Let's get ready to rrruuumble!" The crowd is in a frenzy. Lead singer (yours truly) steps up to the microphone looking cocky, sexy and ready for some Rock 'n Roll ACTION; and the crowd goes wild again. But, wait a minute!

What the crowd does not know, dear reader, is that inside this young Rock-god's head he is fighting the paranoia between two questions. One, "What do they want from me?" and, two, "On whose head am I going to plunk this dollar-forty-all-you-can-eat-with-dessert-included-lunch." Let the show begin!

THE SINGER SINGS

"There she stood (gag) in the street (ga-gag), smiling from (gag, gag) her (gag) head...(gaaaaaag)...to her (gggaaaaagagag)."

THE SINGER SPEAKS

"Ladies and gentleman we're gonna take a short break and we'll be right back!" Length of show: thirty-four seconds.

THE SINGER RUNS

A mad dash for freedom ensues as the singer makes a break for it faster than Keith Richards can run up a bar tab. He is closely followed at near Olympic pace by a guitar player who is attempting to show why a guitar is nicknamed an axe, followed by a drummer whose wild attempts to "drop him" by firing drumsticks in his direction is beginning to look vaguely like a vintage episode of "Audubon's Wildlife Theatre," (you know, the one where the natives of Australia boomerang that unsuspecting Kanga to death), and finally a bass player who has also smoked the peace pipe with some locals, who is so stoned thinks the band is still on stage performing the show, while running.

"Get back here, you idiot, we're doing a show!"
"No!" (Gag)

Hyperventilating and sweating profusely, the singer makes it to his room, which is on the upper level of this not so high class BAR and OTEL (the letter H had fallen off back in '68) and locks himself in, only to be found in the fetal position some twenty to thirty minutes later when a furious bar owner grabs a screwdriver and removes the door from its hinges.

"Get back down there", they scream.
"I can't," plead I.
"Yes you can."
"No I can't, I can't remember the words and besides, I'm going to be sick all over the people in the front row."
"They're used to that!" cries the owner.
"Don't care, I can't do it!" (gag). "I can't do it!"
The night was explosive to say the least. No wait, I stand corrected. The night was a bomb.

Surprisingly the manager did not fire us. It took a long time for me to sufficiently recover and go gagging on again. However, this little story doesn't take the cake in my repertoire of facing fear. No my friends, sometimes it truly does have to get a lot worse before it can get better. Fear and I had another formidable showdown, but I will save that anecdote for a little later.

After telling you this, am I mad to say that today I believe fear can indeed be an ally or, better yet, a friend? It most certainly can. You see, you and fear have just got to come to a little arrangement. Read on dear reader, read on.

A DAY IN THE LIFE

In this book you are going to discover a simple strategy for success that I use each and every day and have been using all of my life, even when I was completely unaware that I was doing so. You see we're all using it, every day, constantly. You cannot escape it. It's like breathing. It's not something you have to be conscious of, but at times, like sticking your head under the water at the lake, or when climbing Everest, it suddenly becomes an incredibly conscious necessity. I mentioned earlier that we know the answers to the questions we ask ourselves like, why am I fat? why am I irritable? why don't I have a job? But knowing the question and the answer isn't the difficult part; it is the space between the two that is the challenge. It's the ACTION you take between the question and answer that counts. It's not that we don't know the answers. It's just that at times we simply won't face up to them. The truth, as they often say, can hurt. Why? Because it can be embarrassing, revealing, or perhaps hurtful. And in order to tackle it head-on, two key things that all of us dread are required -- fear and change. Or, more accurately, fear OF change. Fear of change always tilts our balance at first. For many of us, even when change clearly shows us that it will improve our lives, we opt to remain in a bad situation.

THE ACTION SANDWICH not only addresses the place where fear of change dwells, it's the place where it can be embraced and overcome. Understanding that change and fear may come as a package for this journey is the beginning step on the pathway to overcoming it. It's the hammer that lives between the hand and the nail. It's the paint between brush and canvas. It's the step between your foot and a walk in the park. Simple, humble, unassuming yet, when focused, practiced and built upon, leads to the Eiffel Tower, the Mona Lisa or the Boston Marathon. It's reorganizing the day-to-day practical things you're already doing in your life that allows you to accomplish amazing results. The true magic of this formula is that you are using it now. You cannot escape it and it will remain with you for the rest of your days. Hence the description, *a six-step recipe to unlimited success by doing exactly what you're already doing.*

You are using this blueprint in every success and yes, even in every failure that happens in your life. I have given it a name but I certainly cannot lay claim to its essence, for it has been with humankind for millennia. To use it effectively you must face up to and challenge head-on all of the unsettling questions that I asked you at the beginning of this book. Yet let me ask you this: how many wildly successful people do you know? Not many? Why is that? Because it is not easy. In fact it is extremely difficult, confusing and exhausting to face life-altering questions honestly, passionately and with determination and focus. And yet when you master this tool, you hold the key to an exhilarating, revolutionary and unlimited pathway to a successful life. I call it *THE ACTION SANDWICH*.

THIS BOY

I was recently booked to speak at an event that had a beautifully designed brochure resting at each of the invitees place-setting containing a welcome from the foundation's president, an itinerary of the evening's events and various silent and live auction items. Within the brochure was an Alan Frew Bio for folks to browse through to get a handle on who I am and on what the hell I was doing there. Let's face it, although I am a seasoned communicator, I am relatively new to the public speaking circuit and if I'm on the bill, I usually have a band behind me. As you read these words I thank you, for I am also extremely new at being an author.

Through the years I have had thousands of interviews with thousands of members of the media. I have had tens of thousands of words written about me in various magazines and newspapers and it is more than just a crap-shoot when it comes to whether or not they will get it right, and I DO mean even the simple stuff.

"Lead singer Alan Frey, sixty-two, said today that his '80s pop sensation Glass Eye is finally thinking of calling it quits, after it was discovered that Frey, a native Mexican, wishes to return to his homeland and settle down with his long term love interest, Frank."

Meanwhile, what you actually told them was that upon hitting fifty you wanted to settle for a quieter lifestyle and you were thinking about cutting back on the touring a bit, to enjoy some home life while taking some precious time to do some traveling with your family. I often think back to a time, more than just a few years ago, when I was sharing the spotlight with the phenomenal vocalist Steve Perry, when both of us were being interviewed at a radio station in San Francisco. Steve was asked what his opinion of concert reviewers was and he said, "Why do I need to wake up and read about what some newspaper thought of my concert the night before, when twenty-thousand ticket buyers gave me an instantaneous review?" My sentiments exactly, Steve. "Good on ya!"

I sat at dinner that night and opened up the brochure that was on my plate. This little Bio was written not by a paid professional but by a woman who was a volunteer for the foundation. And yet in all of my years I truly feel that who I am, where I come from, how I got here and where I am going has never quite been captured more simply and more honestly (except of course in this book) than in this woman's words. So I am going to pretend for a moment that I am awaiting the opportunity to come and speak to you and I will let her introduce me. Mrs. Volunteer, if you please:

"As with many success stories, Alan Frew took a rare and unlikely route to becoming an empowering, professional public speaker and author. Born in Coatbridge, Scotland, a town described by one author as, 'no worse place out of hell than that neighbourhood,' Alan's story of rising from a life of religious and social segregation, fueled with a sad abundance of anger and violence, to his becoming an award-winning, multi-platinum selling artist, is edgy, yet heartwarming and thought provoking. Alan had every reason to grow up angry, yet was an eternally optimistic boy, with only himself to truly rely on. He successfully learned to negotiate his way through an adult world of hardship, where a real man was a violent man, a woman belonged in the kitchen or, when needed, the bedroom, and as for children it was simple, they should be seen but never heard. He claims 'telling the tale of his life is easy but that surviving to be able to tell it was the hard part.'

Moving to Canada in 1972, he went on to become a registered nurse turned rock musician whose music reached millions. A natural leader and motivator, his first public speaking engagement happened purely by chance when he was hired to sing at a conference for a major pharmaceutical corporation, and was casually discussing his personal success formula with the management at a cocktail party. When the President of the company overheard his message he hired him on the spot to speak formally to his VPs the next morning. With nothing prepared, he used his wit, charm, business and street smarts, matched skillfully to his old country roots and entertaining past to captivate, motivate and enlighten a tour bus of high stakes business executives without missing a beat. It was an unrehearsed magical session, which without knowing it actually gave birth to *LESSONS FROM A TOUR BUS.*

He has entertained and been entertained by royalty. He has sung for and put his arms around the young people serving in the Armed Forces in places like Bosnia and the Middle East, and on more than a few occasions he has cared for and entertained the elderly, infirmed and the dying. Truly he has already lived ten life times and will surely live at least ten more before it's over. Milk boy, shoe salesman, factory worker, orderly, registered nurse, rock star, entrepreneur, actor, author, please meet the ever-inspiring Alan Frew."

There you have it, no Harvard degree, no doctorate in psychology, no Nobel Peace Prize (yet), but a lot of miles on the tour bus of life. I have to my credit adapted a combination of street-wise vision, common sense and tireless energy, and managed to turn it into my tour de force, my tale of a kid from a small town who does well, and I have been blessed to have experienced tremendous success along the way.

This book reflects who I am and what I know from living the life I have led. I know that truth lies within each bite of *THE ACTION SANDWICH* and I know that *THE ACTION SANDWICH* lives within the space between your questions and your answers. But this book is not a book of group hugs or high fives, nor will it win any awards from the Moral Majority any time soon. That's not where I came from. I came from the raw reality and hardcore nature of life on the streets, and I managed to parlay it into a successful and abundant life filled with everything my heart desires. I make no apologies for its rawness, for that would constitute apologizing for its honesty, which I cannot do. This story is living proof that abundance and success are truly for all, even, I might add, for a cheeky wee bastard from Coatbridge.

If you are truly committed to parting the waters of confusion, by understanding how to use the elements of *THE ACTION SANDWICH*, where RECEPTIVITY deciphers the signals the universe is sending to you and if you DESIRE the type of BELIEF system that you once had in yourself and if your true, unwavering INTENTION is to live the absolute best life that you can live, and you are committed to taking ACTION to make it all happen, then this book is indeed for you.

You may notice that although I have devoted a chapter to each of the six ingredients of *THE ACTION SANDWICH*, there remains at times an overlap, where perhaps I am speaking about INTENTION when suddenly you get a flavour of PASSION. Likewise I may be talking about DESIRE and before you know it, you get a little taste of ACTION. Why is this, one may wonder? Well, it's simple really. How can you possibly eat a sandwich and not taste all of the ingredients at one time? You can't pop it into your mouth and separate the chicken from the lettuce or the lettuce from the mustard. And besides, why would you want to? *THE ACTION SANDWICH* is no different. Each individual ingredient stands fresh and savory alone, yet when chewed, or lived if you will, the combining flavour comes alive in your mouth, invigorating and nourishing, giving you life and energy. Think of it as a bite of life, with your personally chosen combination of flavours giving you not only your originality but your individuality as well.

Success by doing exactly what you've always done? It sounds crazy doesn't it? I mean, if you are the first one to stand up and say that you are not successful, then how can I claim with certainty that you can indeed be successful by doing exactly what you are and always have been doing? Well, let's explore.

YOUR SONG

You've already read this book. In fact you have LIVED this book, getting to where you are today. You are living it …AND you would continue to live it even if didn't read another page. Think of your life as a song, think of the message in this book as the notes of that song. Think of me as no more than a fellow songwriter; a music coach if you prefer, here to communicate with you in a way that gets results, to inspire and empower your song to its fullest potential and together work to make a hit.

As any musician will attest, it is astounding and seemingly infinite, how no two songs are ever the same. Even when you think it's impossible that more songs can be written with only the eight notes of the scale, another comes along, and another and another, all unique. So it is with your *ACTION SANDWICH*, an exclusive version of your own priorities, passions and personality, written and executed with the precision of a master composer, through the discipline of positive thoughts, energy and INTENTION, all the while reflecting the humility, worthiness and wishes of your true self.

THE ACTION SANDWICH is being prepared and consumed by every single solitary soul on this planet today, no matter where they come from, what their social or economic status is, what religion they may follow, what sex they are or what their sexual orientation may be. It is with you ...ALWAYS. You are using it, so why not use it properly? Why not use it to be the very best that you can be? Why not use it for success instead of failure? Enjoy wins as opposed to losses, highs instead of lows and strengths instead of weaknesses. Why not use the same simple steps to bring about a fantastic result as you would for a mediocre one? You are expending the energy required to create the life you have, so why not redirect it and create the life you want?

The good guys use it and the bad, the skinny and the fat, the rich and the not-so-rich, yes even the downright poor, the motivated are pumped on it and the complacent, well, they just drag it along with them. In fact the only people not using it are the dead!

This book is here to help you not only discover and understand this recipe, but also to guide you in its use to a life of total abundance and unlimited success, whatever that means to you. It is of the utmost importance to understand that success can mean many different things to different people. This book can point you in the direction of fame, wealth, houses and cars if that is what success is to you. However, if success to you means getting a promotion at the grocery store, or coaching your son's baseball team to the playoffs, or figuring out how you can raise money for your local church, then that is also true success.

There are six mouthwatering, savory ingredients in *THE ACTION SANDWICH*, and the good news is that you already have all of these ingredients in your fridge. The problem is that so many out there never take the time, never have the inclination, never have the direction nor the energy to make a healthy sandwich. In this fast-paced, media-driven worldwide web of supply and demand, they are more attracted to Bob's Triple-Bacon, Double Cheese Burger and Heart-Attack combo (usually washed down with a diet-something-or-other). It just does not register, for is there anyone over the age of twenty-five that doesn't know how they feel ten minutes after eating junk food?

Success is NOT built upon the foundations of instant gratification. It is built upon RECEPTIVITY, DESIRE, BELIEF, INTENTION and the ACTION of living somewhere between where we are and where we want to be. We live in the world of MORE -- more people, more gadgets, more options, more possibilities, more opportunities than ever before. Why then is there more poverty, more anger, more hunger, more violence and LESS TOLERANCE, than at any other time in our history? Are we so catered to, that just opening our mouths and being fed garbage is acceptable? Has entitlement blinded us, so that we have lost sight of who we truly are and what our purpose really is? Here's an old-fashioned thought: are we lazy? Are we so obesely slow and unpurposefully driven, that we will follow the most extreme ideas and doctrines? Is it just me or do there seem to be more self-proclaimed leaders out there, for just about ANYTHING you can make up? Why does most of society seem so willing to let others decide it ALL for them? Here comes one of the simplest dictums for living the best life you can, filled with abundance and all you DESIRE. Are you ready? Decide for yourself. As Shakespeare said, "There's the rub." For by deciding for yourself, you are brought back to the issue of control and of how much say you have in your own life.

As children, we are taught that RECEPTIVITY equals education. BELIEF means "do what everyone else is doing and you'll be fine." DESIRE is reserved for money, the house and the car, and incidentally it is often associated with greed. INTENTION, being elusive and totally misunderstood, is not acknowledged at all, and ACTION means "get a job!" PASSION? Well you can forget about that, for it is only for the lucky, certainly not you. Often it is portrayed as an intensity to shy away from. After all, what do you have to be so passionate about anyway?

We limit ourselves then, because we have been taught since childhood to choose boundaries that make others feel comfortable with our pathway. But if you knew that you could tap into a life of unlimited abundance, why would you choose boundaries? There's only one thing stopping you and that's you. Just you. Your life can change right now. I know this as positively as I know that I love breathing, singing, writing or those plaid hipsters I've been hanging on to since 1976. Hey, go easy, they'll be back.

The doubters among you will already be trying to think of exceptions to this rule, even though you yourself are likely not an exception. Of course there are those who through absolutely no fault of their own find themselves at the mercy of their environment, specifically those in this world subjected to poverty, hunger or perhaps an oppressive society or government. However, no matter what your social, economic, mental or environmental situation is, you're using the formula. Even my little two year-old daughter knows how to use it, and as a matter of fact she is an expert at using it, for she puts no boundaries or limitations on anything that she desires.

You might be amazed to discover how those who seem to be in desperately hopeless situations can utilize the recipe for *THE ACTION SANDWICH*. Those who at one point in their lives felt like all hope was lost and that they were doomed to a life of despondency and failure, yet managed to reach inside and find their power, their source if you will and went on to rise from the ashes of pain and suffering, despair and hopelessness and proceeded to achieve successes beyond even their wildest imagination. People like Oprah Winfrey, Nelson Mandela and Terry Fox come to mind. It is from this source we all share that heroes come. If it can power a young man with only one leg and a body ravaged with cancer across the vastness of a country like Canada, then just think of what it can do for you and me.

TRUE COLORS

In its infancy *Glass Tiger* (then known as *Tokyo*) had a dual existence. The formation of the group happened when musicians from two separate bands became one, and it happened that the drummer of the newly formed *Tokyo* had also been the lead singer for his group, very similar to what Phil Collins, drummer for *Genesis*, started doing after Peter Gabriel quit that band. He drummed and sang, but eventually smartened up and became one and not so much the other. (Note to young musicians: Never form a band where the drummer is the lead singer, it looks goofy, and the band's timing suffers. It's a little like driving the car from the trunk. Got that? Good.)

So when the two bands merged, our drummer was rather reluctant to relinquish his duties as lead singer even though the band had a singer, namely me. The idea of change for him was too difficult to deal with and to accept, so our band would perform songs with me as the lead singer, then I would exit the stage for one or two numbers and he would take over. We continued this way for the longest time.

Our styles were different. I would be up there singing British pop and rock songs from *The Police*, *U2* and *Duran Duran*, then he would perform metal songs by *The Scorpions*, *Def Leppard* or *Ozzy Osbourne*.

If it sounds like a dog's dinner, it was. Not only was it disjointed and confusing, but it was extremely disconcerting to the audience as well as to any record company thinking about signing a new group. After months of this I was compelled to address the issue and tell them that I felt that our true color was one that had a lead singer who was also the front man. And I laid it on the line that I should be that guy. I told them that if they didn't agree, I would leave the group. They have all confided since then that it was the right move. Even the drummer went on to admit so, but it did not diminish the fact that he found the change painful and difficult.

A few years later it became apparent to him that the front man gets most of the attention. This made it even more unbearable for him, an even bigger change, and by all accounts he made an even bigger mistake when he quit the band and tried to go it alone.

News flash: None of this is easy. If an easy life with little effort is what you're looking for, this is not the journey for you. Making the choice to use *THE ACTION SANDWICH* correctly means that never again can you play small in this world. It means that you have finally acknowledged your place as being important. If you don't mind trading a few bumps in the road for a life full of PASSION and rich in abundance, then this recipe is for you. Are you ready? Let's get started on making that sandwich shall we?

HUNGRY LIKE THE WOLF

Everyone knows what hunger feels like. Your tummy rumbles, you have that empty feeling inside of it that sets off a trigger between your stomach and brain. You hear yourself say, "I'm hungry!" What you are really doing is showing RECEPTIVITY to the internal feeling of hunger. You think to yourself, "I want to eat something." Simply put, you DESIRE food. Certainly you know that you're entitled to eat, everyone is, so you have the BELIEF that you can and will take care of this hunger by eating. You get the bread, chicken and the lettuce and tell the world that it is your INTENTION to eat.

With knife in hand, you begin to make your sandwich. You've done it a thousand times, right? Now that you've taken ACTION, success is just around the corner and your hunger will soon be gone. It is the ACTION of putting it all together that is the key ingredient and the backbone to being successful, for indeed if you do not get up off of your backside and actually do the making of the sandwich you will continue to suffer hunger. You must DO to get DONE!

So there you are making the sandwich that will take away your hunger and make you a happy camper. However, even when you are really hungry it is highly unlikely that you will just take the chicken and slap it on two slices of bread and eat it. Dry bread and chicken would take away your hunger and sustain you, but it is the mustard, the mayo, the relish or even the good old ketchup that adds the taste that seems to make it all worthwhile. It is the vast array of condiments that bring the life and energy and taste to our sandwich.

THE ACTION SANDWICH is no different, and I invite you to experience a special condiment that I have added for you, which, like mayo, mustard or relish, not only enhances the flavour but also allows your success to taste even sweeter. The condiment I am referring to is PASSION, and here comes the best part. The beauty of this condiment is that while one person's ham might simply be just another person's ham, the condiments make the experience unique for each and every one of us. My mayo can be your mustard, which in turn is her relish, and so forth. And the good news is that the condiments are limitless. You can smother your *ACTION SANDWICH* in all of the joy and charisma that PASSION has to offer while maintaining your uniqueness and individuality. As a footnote you will discover that PASSION goes hand in hand with DESIRE and BELIEF. It is difficult not to be passionate about something you really DESIRE and believe in.

So pull up a chair, grab a stool, a bench or some lawn and join me as I present to you the recipe for *THE ACTION SANDWICH: A six-step recipe to unlimited success by doing exactly what you're already doing.* I hope you're hungry!

> *"A very receptive state of mind... not unlike a sheet of film itself -*
> *seemingly inert, yet so sensitive that a fraction of a second's*
> *exposure conceives a life in it."*
> MINOR WHITE

CHAPTER ONE: RECEPTIVITY

By definition, RECEPTIVITY is this: "Open to arguments, ideas, or change; ready or willing to receive favourably." I repeat, "ready or willing to receive favourably." I like that and I try to live by that standard every day of my life, yet it is not always easy. This is not a theory... it's real life. It's living, being, doing – and it's tough. Conversely, it does not necessarily have to be perpetually painful or stressful either, but the chances are good that you're going to experience some of both along the way. You must therefore unconditionally accept the fact that being receptive to a new wave of arguments, ideas and especially to change can indeed, and most likely will, bring with it a certain level of discomfort, stress and yes, even pain. It will however also bring a wealth of new perspectives and opportunities, so choose optimism whenever possible.

But don't beat yourself up like a crazy person if you find a little pessimism sneaking in from time to time, for I happen to believe folks that eternal optimism, though not a myth is certainly mythical in stature. I sure as hell have never been able to have my eternal optimism button in the "on" position 24/7, 365 days a year, and I don't remember knowing anyone who does. But I do know this: successful people focus their optimism on that which they

DESIRE and *never* stray from that focus. Even at the peak of my musical career, my mother constantly said that I should get a real job, and expressed this to anyone who would listen. I never listened.

THESE BOOTS ARE MADE FOR
a. WALKING
b. FOOTBALL
c. LOSING

Focusing optimism on that which I DESIRE has been part of my life-long journey. By the age of nine I was still only the size of a newt with its shoes off and I weighed in at a hefty sixty-five pounds if I had my school bag filled with books and if it was on my back at the time of the weigh-in. Now football (or soccer to the lesser mortals) is one of my greatest passions in life and as a boy I ate, slept and breathed it. I have always been decent at the game and looking back, with proper coaching, possibly could have done something as a player, one never knows, but at nine years of age my skills were certainly advanced and it was my DESIRE to play on my school team. I had two hurdles to overcome however, if I was to have any chance of doing that.

First, although it was not written in stone, it was taken for granted that boys generally didn't play on the team until the age of eleven or twelve. And second, it helped if you were bigger than the size of a sausage! Not to be deterred, I approached the coach and asked him for a tryout, which he denied me time and time again. I took to sitting on the hill down at the school football field and kept making eye contact with him as much as possible, the kind that said something like, "Come on, please will you give me a chance, come on I can do better than that guy, come on just gimme one chance and if you don't you know I'll break the windows in your classroom and let the air out of your car's tires! And...I'll pee on your..."

THANK YOU! And so I got my tryout. You see the three Ps, patience, perseverance and pee-pee are great motivators. Oops! That's four Ps!

With the fullest of INTENTION of making this team, I took to the field one day for my one big shot at it, and in short order managed to turn several defenders inside out and score a couple of goals, which led to the coach telling me that I could join the squad.

I went home ecstatic. "Dad! Dad!" I cried as I blasted through the front door, "I made the school team, THE school team, and I need a pair of football boots!"

Of course I would have been just as well off saying, "Dad! Dad! I'm opening my own safari park and I need money for a hippo!" For the end result would have been the same. "Are you kiddin'? Where the hell do you think I'm going to get money for football boots?" He then proceeded to tell me that a guy he knew at work had a son who didn't play the game anymore and that he had a pair of football boots that were going to waste and he was sure he could get them for me. Now at this point I wish I had been opening up a safari park for God knows I am sure he could never have gotten me a hand-me-down hippo no matter how hard he tried. The football boots that came into our home the very next day looked like something Moses brought down with him from Mount Sinai.

"God says he's not quite finished with the Ten Commandments yet," cries the weary leader of the Hebrews. "In the meantime he wants you to have...THESE!"
"You said you'd bring us the very words of God," cry the people.
"I know I did," says Moses. "But while we're waiting, let's have a game of football!"

Like many kids, I knew hand-me-downs all too well, so well in fact that they were a way of life for me. My sister laughs to this day over a certain pair of corduroy trousers that went from a lad several years my senior to his younger brother, then to me! When I wore them the hem was so big that my mother would gradually let it down in increments as I started to spurt. Those trousers went from a ten-inch to a two-inch hem with me in them the entire time.

I drew the line only once when I was forced to wear a pair of swimming trunks that had belonged to my older cousin Jim. They were made of wool!! Can you believe that? Wading out into the frozen North Sea in woolen swimming trunks? My God, even the Spanish Inquisition never thought up torture that cruel. I actually took them off while still in the water and pretended that the ocean had scooped them away. It was easier and more bearable to walk naked back to my towel than it was to wear a sheep over my balls in the freezing cold water. Having to wear a shirt, pants or a jacket however from a neighbour didn't bother me so much unless some other mother insisted on calling me for dinner thinking I was hers.

"No Mrs. Murphy, it's me, Alan. I'm only dressed like your Harry!"

The football boots were however a completely different matter. They were brutal.

The modern boot came into being in the sixties, when footwear looked sleek, and the cleats were replaceable screw-ins made of nylon, but this was not the case with these babies. Imagine if you will a steel-toed, ankle high work boot from 1945 worn by Ko-Ko The Clown in his circus routine, complete with nailed in cork cleats, and you might come close to getting the picture. By the way, my father had neglected to tell me that the son of his friend was nineteen and these boots were six sizes too large for my nine-year old feet.

"We'll stuff them with paper," said my rocket scientist father.
"Oh, no!" said I.

When I went to the first game my sweater drowned me, my socks went all the way up to my knees then folded and returned all the way back down to my ankles, then folded again and went all the way back up to my knees! Hold on though, for it gets better. My shorts, my soccer shorts, had to be held up with a belt! Already mortified, I brought out the boots. My goodness, times like these can seem so painful to the best of us but to a child it can be excruciatingly so. It is at such crossroads of life that character, willpower and soul can be constructed or perhaps destroyed. I knew that if I could just get past all of this peripheral junk and not internalize the mocking that was coming my way from some extremely amused older boys, that my skills could do the talking for me. I remained optimistic in the face of adversity and indeed went out and played what we call "a blinder", known more often as a great game. I remained on that team for the rest of my days at that school, eventually becoming the leader and captain.

After one match, I was traveling home as usual on a double-decker bus, when I decided to deliberately lose my boots by leaving them on the upper level. I must have looked like that little guy in the movie *The Omen* who was really Satan, as a wicked smirk formed on my pursed lips and I silently said goodbye to that cobbler's nightmare forever. When I arrived home my father asked me where my boots were.

"Oh no! I've left them on the bus Dad, sorry. Oh well they'll be long gone now," I emoted, hoping to make a believer of him.
He was already pulling his jacket on.
"Come on then," he said.
"Where we goin' Dad," I inquired.
"To the bus depot!"

Now, understand folks that this is Coatbridge, Scotland I am speaking of, known widely for its thugs, delinquents and thieves. Most have a demeanor that is one hinge away from the door falling off. Some of these people would not only steal the eye out of your head, but would have the nerve to come back to you and ask for a refund because when they got it home it was the wrong colour. Go back to the opening page of this book for a second. Do you see it? "There is no worse place out of hell than that neighbourhood." Never a truer sentence was ever written. It seemed therefore pointless to go trailing up to the bus depot for the boots would surely be on the feet of a well meaning thief by now. But go we did. On the way there my dad felt the need again to tell me how I should be more careful with my belongings.

"Football boots don't grow on trees you know!"
These ones did, an ancient, smelly, ugly football boot tree.
We approached the lost and found desk at the depot.

"Excuse me," my father said to the lady behind the counter. "My son was playing football earlier and..."
"Are you looking for these?" she asked, as she pulled out the boots.

My eyes were like saucers looking through a magnifying glass. Agog doesn't come close. Awestruck, maybe. Astounded, definitely. You see, when I left the precious cargo for all to see and hopefully take, I did so with the bus still having to complete another thirty stops! These free-to-a-good-home relics had traveled the entire length of the town and back again and not a soul had touched them! No sir, there they were in her hands right before my wide eyes and gaping mouth.

"Ah, lovely," said my father. "A wee bit o' luck eh son?"

NOWHERE MAN

Here's an interesting notion. At first when I was creating *THE ACTION SANDWICH*, I was inclined to use the word knowledge as opposed to the word RECEPTIVITY, my logic being that in order to set off on a formula for success the first thing one would require would be a great knowledge of the subject at hand. This seems more than reasonable, does it not? I do not, however, feel this way today and I will tell you why. Putting a demand on yourself that you must have knowledge about whatever it is you DESIRE can, if not approached cautiously, set you off on a pathway that I refer to as the pathway of "always getting ready to." Always getting ready to be, to try, to trust, to deliver, to see, to give and goodness knows how many other excuses. "I promise you," she says, "I'll start very soon just when I get a bit more money, a bit thinner, a bit better, a bit smarter, a bit more together." "Trust me", he says. "As soon as I get a bit stronger, wiser, faster, richer, leaner, funnier, you name it...and I'll be right there." I call this "Victim Speak" and victims are always easy to spot.

I'M JUST LOOKING FOR CLUES

Do you relate to these excuses? Do they sound familiar? Do you use them yourself? They are the voices of the "always getting ready to" talking. They are victims and they have two major qualities. First, they always live their lives as if life happens to them as opposed to them creating it for themselves. Second, they always have their fingers simultaneously on the blame and excuse buttons, ready to push them rather than owning up and taking responsibility for everything that has and will happen to them.

If you think of yourself as a victim, then you are one. How can you believe you will achieve great things if you don't believe you are full of greatness? It just won't happen. Don't look to your past for excuses to use for your future. What was may effect what is, but has nothing to do with what will be if you change your attitudes and actions now and move on.

RECEPTIVITY requires that you allow yourself to see the world through a variety of perspectives. When I stand on stage and look out at twenty thousand people, I have a different perspective than the audience does when looking at me. Sometimes before a show or while another act is on I will quietly wander out to the back of the venue and take in the view from the audience's perspective so I can be receptive to their vantage point. The venue remains the same regardless of where you observe it from, however the perspective of the viewer impacts the experience. Everything we do in life has different perspectives and the more open we are to various points of view, the more knowledge we will gain from the journey. RECEPTIVITY however doesn't necessarily require high levels of knowledge. In fact I would say that at times it doesn't require it at all. RECEPTIVITY is about watching for clues and living in the moment so you do not miss an opportunity that comes your way. It's about being fully awake, not wishing or hoping but rather being in tune with what is true and real in your life, from every perspective.

MATTED SPAM?

Let me share a couple of short stories with you. Look at the following image. What do you see – squiggles and dots on a page? Gobbledygook? Matted Spam? Well you're not alone because I cannot decipher it either. Yes, of course it's music, but what music? When you find out the answer could somebody please let this musician know? Thank you.

Of course I am being facetious, for I do indeed know that this is the music for a song that took the world by storm in 1986 when *Glass Tiger* made "Don't Forget Me (When I'm Gone)," a number one smash hit. But if you jumbled this musical score up with dozens of others and brought them all to me I would not be able to find it again because I cannot read music! This is where RECEPTIVITY lives, because as some of you may already know... I, along with Sam Reid and Jim Vallance, wrote this song, in fact I have written hundreds of songs. And yet to this day I still cannot read music.

So what would have happened if when I was approached to join my first band I had turned my back on the moment, been unreceptive to the opportunity I was being given, and asked them to wait for me until I received my degree in music? Would they have waited for me? I think not. Musicians are an excellent example of people who are receptive to the idea of *being and doing* while having limited or in some cases *no* knowledge prior to becoming. They just do it. They learn as they go. They know what an instrument is and that if you strum it, beat it, blow it or plunk it you'll get noise out of it, so they do have a certain amount of knowledge to begin with. The rest they refine as they go. John Lennon and Paul McCartney fell into this category while they created the greatest pop legacy in music's history... *The Beatles.* Even when they were writing "She Loves You," "I Want To Hold Your Hand," "Help," and so on, they too could not read music. So I ask you, knowledge or RECEPTIVITY?

TAKE ME TO THE PILOT

I was recently on a flight over the Rockies and I am not the best flier, but when I am in a small matchbox with wings attached and it has Bob's Airlines written in crayon on the side of it, I am even more of a wreck. Obviously, dear reader, since I'm here writing to you, we landed safely and I took it upon myself to speak with the captain after the flight. Our conversation went something like this. "Excuse me Captain, I have a question for you." "Yes Sir! Fire away."

"Well, since there are only six of us on a flight like this, in the case of a terrible emergency, why don't you give each of us a parachute?"

He looked at me as if I was pulling his leg.

"Are you serious, sir?"

"As a heart attack, Captain."

"Well sir, apart from the added cost let me ask you this, have you ever used a parachute? Have you ever jumped from a plane before?"

"Errrr... NO Captain I have never jumped from a plane and I have never used a parachute."

"Well, you see sir, you have no experience, no perspective, no *knowledge* of how to use a parachute."

"That may be true Captain," I said respectfully. "However I also have no experience, nor perspective nor indeed no knowledge of having my arse fly into a mountain at six-hundred mph either! Give me a parachute and I will take my chances and learn on the way down!!"

Isn't it the truth? Would you not take a chance with a parachute the moment you are told that the plane is going to crash? It is my BELIEF that knowledge, extremely important as it is, should be considered more of a journey, a life-long journey, than an immediate experience. I sincerely believe that if someone handed me a parachute screaming "Quick…put it on and pull this and if that doesn't work pull that!" I would jump and succeed in my very first sky diving lesson.

I am not making light of the power of knowledge. I happen to love it and the opportunities it can bring. I take every opportunity I can to learn new things. But in life you need to take the plunge sometimes and learn on the way down, or up, or even sideways if need be.

I'D LIKE TO TEACH THE WORLD TO SING

Being receptive is immediate. It lives in the here and now, and the beauty is that it contains knowledge but allows you to gather more as you go. It is important to note that being receptive does not mean letting everything under the sun that comes your way affect you. RECEPTIVITY with *selectivity* is what is most important. To enjoy a successful life you must raise the drawbridge and deny entry to the limitless negative influences that the information age wishes to feed you.

To be successful with your life, it is imperative that you control your own programming in order for you to control your own destiny. It is equally imperative that you spend at least the same amount of time culturing and nurturing your personal growth as you do on things like television and the Internet. We are bombarded by negativity everywhere we turn. Pick up a newspaper and see how difficult it is to find a story that is positive. I was appalled recently to read an article that a Toronto paper publishes each month titled, "One Month of Reasons Why The World Is Getting Worse." It lists an entire month's worth of disasters and disturbing things, like serial killing, famine, violence or just good old celebrity gossip garbage. Just what kind of message does this send out? Would an article called, "One Month of Reasons Why The World Is Getting Better" not sell enough newspapers?

Even if you choose to believe that the world is getting worse, does it not seem logical that if that is all we are prepared to focus our attention on, then we will simply create and receive more of it in return? People change the world and often one person taking a stand is all it takes to form a group of people who can make an incredible difference. People like Rosa Parks, who simply say "enough." People like Mahatma Gandhi or Nelson Mandela. These people are no different than you or me; they are not perfect and may not be highly educated, yet they believe as Gandhi said, "they must be the change they wish to see in others." Does it not follow that if you change something about yourself, no matter how small or seemingly insignificant, that you therefore change the world? Our planet as a whole is what it believes itself to be and if it believes it is a place of anger, war and bloodshed then it will follow that pathway. Conversely, if it believes it is a place of peace, kindness and abundance then that shall be our destiny.

MONEY, IT'S A HIT

In 1974, when Muhammad Yunus decided to loan $27.00 from his own pocket to poor women in Bangladesh who needed to buy bamboo to make and sell furniture, the spark of an idea was born. By 1976 he had formed the Grameen Bank (*Grameen* meaning rural area or village) and launched the beginning of micro banking, administering tiny loans, 97% of which were going to women. This was unheard of in a country where most women did not even borrow money from financial institutions, but Yunas believed not only that they were credible borrowers, but that in giving them this money he could stop the growth of poverty in Bangladesh.

The figures now speak for themselves. Borrowers own ninety-four percent of this bank, and the government of Bangladesh owns the other 6%. The bank has 6.61 million borrowers, 2,226 branches that cover 71,371 villages and employs 18,795 people. Yunus was correct in his assumption that these high-risk loans were actually not so high-risk at all, as the bank boasts a loan recovery rate of 98.85%, much higher than most North American financial institutions. Since inception, total loans distributed amount to $5.72 billion, of which $5.07 billion has been repaid. In 2006 the Nobel Peace Prize was divided into two equal parts, won by none other than Muhammad Yunus and the Grameen Bank for their efforts to create economic and social "development from below." Yunas knew that breaking the cycle of poverty by giving people needed funds to grow their businesses was the only way to improve his community while advancing the cause for democracy and human rights.

What a wonderfully fulfilling and inspiring story. Did you see that one on the front page of your daily newspaper?

The theory of the Butterfly Effect is that the flapping wings of a butterfly might cause tiny changes in the atmosphere that can eventually lead to a tornado on the other side of the world. The theory also states that the same flapping of the butterfly's wings might also prevent one from occurring. The

Butterfly Effect is a perfect analogy for the story of the Grameen Bank, for today similar banks are sprouting up in all corners of the world. Changing the world is about commitment to the positive creation process each and every day, in everything you think, say and do. We get frustrated because we cannot see how the world could possibly improve. We begin to point fingers at charities or celebrities, saying they are not doing enough or that they are self-serving. This is not the path to improving the planet. We do not know what is in someone else's heart. Albert Einstein said, "All meaningful and lasting change starts first in your imagination and then works its way out. Imagination is more important than knowledge." Change yourself, your words and actions and the world will change. Forty-two families with $27.00 each became almost $6,000,000,000...go figure!

LET IT BLEED

I grew up surrounded by hate in a religiously segregated world where Protestant and Catholic sectarianism and sometimes violence were the order of the day. I ran with some heavyweights who were always looking for a new notch to put on their rifles. Violence was like dinner to these guys and on many an occasion I even got caught up in the war with rival factions myself. In some cases it was simply survival. Fight or be beaten, literally. Soccer hooliganism and violence was at an all-time high in the late sixties. I witnessed horrors that today I can scarcely imagine. There is a saying that ignorance is bliss, and on rare occasions that may well be true. But ignorance is mostly a travesty. I recognized this, thank goodness, early on in my hooligan phase and even within that darkness as a twelve- to sixteen-year-old, RECEPTIVITY shone a tiny pinhead of light, showing me the way to go, eventually engulfing and eradicating the darkness that was my world.

I have chosen not to fill the pages of my book with descriptive commentaries of how I've witnessed people being seriously harmed, especially since in this day and age our television screens and computers are filled with it. It would be remiss of me however not to at least touch on the topic, because as you'll witness I could have been receptive to a very different pathway at that juncture of my life and only the heavens themselves know what would have become of me. But I didn't. At that tender and impressionable age I chose to use the power of *THE ACTION SANDWICH* for success, not failure, and for light, not darkness. I was already receptive to the idea that violence was a one-way ticket to more violence with the outcome being pain and most likely prison. I wanted a better life and I believed that I was different than those who by choice lived farther from the light. I chose to separate from those who enjoyed the violence even if they were still immature, perhaps even still children. I intended to get out of that pattern of violence no matter what others thought of me for doing so. Finally I took ACTION. I joined a group called "The Boys Brigade" (very similar to the Boy Scouts), where the focus was on self, community and helping others. I got a job in the clothing division of a large department store that kept me busy, off the streets and put money into my pockets. I used all of my communication skills and did more than a few song and dance routines to talk my way out of violent encounters rather than participate in them. On more than one occasion I convinced bigger and tougher guys that I was indeed the leader and they were the followers. If they must fight, the leader didn't have to. The generals always sat atop the hill and watched the battle, right?

This wasn't a perfect solution, and this new direction didn't happen overnight. I brought a lot of that street toughness, Scottish heritage and anger with me as a young adult when my family moved to Canada. It was not uncommon for me to lash out and violently beat a perpetrator for mocking me for being a foreigner or for being different, for it was the Coatbridge way. It was how we handled situations like that. Many of my co-workers in the early seventies were not shocked to see me limping at work since my foot was still sore from an altercation the previous weekend, or that I was sporting heavily bruised or cut knuckles from "that party" I was at the night before. I always knew though, deep in my being, that this was not the answer. Violence truly only begets more violence. You send it out, and you get more of it in return.

On one dark outing I entered a bar to meet my girlfriend when two seated men noticed I was wearing a toque with a Toronto Maple Leaf logo on it. I had just arrived after watching the Leafs win game seven of a playoff series on television with some buddies. (Remember those days?) My friends walked ahead of me but I stopped to listen to what the two had to say to me.

"Hey you! Where did you get that goof ball hat?"
"Sorry, come again?" I asked.
"Oh, RRRRight then laddie and the goofy accent too!"

They each had a beer bottle in front of them and as I focused deep eye contact with them, I gently brought one of their bottles closer to me.

"Look lads, I am in a good mood," I said. "My team won and I am here to have fun with friends, ok?"

Suddenly one of them put his hand up and flicked me under my chin pompously to dismiss me.

"AYE RRRRRight you are then why don't you just piss off, Scotty-boy back to the fields or wherever the hell you came from."

It was over in a matter of seconds. I need not give you gory details but in brief, number one got the beer bottle and number two got a "Glasgow Kiss" – a brutal head-butt to the face. Both were down and out but number one was doing some serious bleeding. As usual I tried to defuse things by pretending that I had no idea what had just happened. I saw my pal and my girlfriend look over with that, "Oh God, not again" look, as I made my way over to the bar and calmly ordered a drink. A girl screamed in the background and a waitress came over to me with finger pointed.

"You animal!" she yelled at me. "You animal, I saw that! I saw what you did!"
"What are you talking about?" I said with my innocent tone.
Just then the barman leaned over to me, "Alan, you better go...now!"

I took a deep breath and headed out at the very moment I saw number one being carried towards the washroom, blood pouring from his face. When I got home, I called the bar and asked for my girlfriend who came on the phone and started giving me regular reports on what was transpiring. She told me that "number two" was back on his feet, bleeding but standing. "Number one" was still in the washroom. She had taken a close look at him and it wasn't pretty. There was no police involvement as of yet, but she thought she overheard an ambulance being called. I felt sick deep within the pit of my stomach, as I had done many times before when these things happened and I admit that they had happened all too often. The feeling of wondering if you had harmed someone to the point that they might have lost an eye, or far worse, was awful, and the waiting for the doorbell to ring and the police to arrive to arrest you for assault causing bodily harm was equally debilitating and nauseating. I detested it. What became of the incident? Nothing. No charges were ever laid and I never saw those lads again.

I can only surmise that like many I had grown up with, they were accustomed to playing rough and that this incident had just been a losing battle on their part and they moved on. Difficult as it may seem, for you dear reader to understand, it was "how things were done" where I came from. Sadly it must have been that way for them as well.

Retaliation is such a natural human instinct. In sport, interestingly enough, especially soccer, it is usually the retaliator rather than the perpetrator who catches the referee's eye and inevitably gets reprimanded. The 2006 World Cup Final quickly comes to mind, and Zinedine Zidane's now infamous head-butt on Italy's Materazzi, which led to his ejection. It is now his cross to bear forever as he retired following that game from the sport to which he has given so much. If given the chance would he take it back? Only he knows for certain, but for my money I'm sure he would be receptive to a much different outcome.

I believe that we are obligated by everything that nature truly stands for to try and make this a better world to live in. Try harder than ever before, to catch yourself when you bask in the negativity of things like anger, revenge and obsession that the world feeds you – and turn it off!

"Are you joking?" you ask me. "I get up in the morning and watch the news, get in my car and listen to talk radio all the way to work, read the paper at my 10:00 a.m. break, put CNN on at lunch to get any breaking news I've missed and just for good measure, you can find me at six and eleven, staying up-to-date on what's going on in the world."

Well, what would happen if you didn't? What if you didn't know about an earthquake or train derailment? What if you didn't know about the disgruntled office worker who has just killed ten of his colleagues before turning the gun on himself? What if you didn't listen to Washington's spin-doctors for a little while? Has your knowledge of this in the past ever helped you? Have you ever personally saved anyone of these victims because you happened to be watching at the time? Have you EVER felt better watching one of these horrendous reports, fed to us ad nauseam, than you did before turning it on?

I want you to try a little experiment. I know it's not easy but I guarantee you, you will feel just a bit more liberated, refreshed and replenished if you can accomplish it. I'm asking you to try not watching the news or reading the newspaper for one week. Just seven days without letting the media and the news influence your life. It's an experiment to see how it affects your outlook. In place of the media I want you to notice every good thing that crosses your path no matter how small, because that's the news no one tells you about. I'm telling you it will change your perspective and your life. As Dr. Wayne Dyer said, "When you change the way you look at things, the things you look at change."

If you find that you must get your fix of the *News according to...* then so be it. However if after the fact you find yourself focusing on the negative of what's wrong with the world or your life, ask yourself a positive question about all that is right with it and all that your life has to offer you and those around you. Perhaps even hundreds of times a day you will need to bring your attention back to the positive things that enrich your journey to combat the negativity that came with your news fix.

If you adapt to this practice of switching negativity to positive thinking, eventually it will become second nature, eradicating your defeatist attitude and filling your life with the kinds of things that you really want by matching your new experiences to the thoughts you are projecting.

I'M ASKING YOU SUGAR, WOULD I LIE TO YOU?

This is not a book of exercises. However, here is a simple little choice you can make when you awake in the morning and just before closing your eyes at night. Focus on something positive, no matter how small or insignificant it may seem. Be receptive to what made it a great day. It could be that you woke up early and worked out, went for a walk or perhaps helped your little one solve a problem with his or her homework. Perhaps it is how you felt coming home tired from a hard day at the office to your wife's pot roast or maybe even the success you had in making one for her. *THE ACTION SANDWICH* will work to improve your golf swing, your marriage or our planet. Your RECEPTIVITY to troubling issues and their possible solutions, your DESIRE to make things better, your BELIEF that we can have a greater world, your INTENTION to do all you can to accomplish that, your ACTION to give of your time, encouragement or indeed your money, whatever you have to give, and being passionate about helping others, will effect change.

Focus on the life you want. Be the change you want to see in others. When your positive thoughts include being grateful for the life you have or tapping into a PASSION you have for helping others, you will reach your goals even faster.

Did Lance Armstrong have the legs for winning the Tour De France seven times before riding a racing bike? Why did Warren Buffet tell his middle-class wife way back in the early sixties that they were indeed going to be wealthy beyond imagination in such a matter-of-fact manner, as if they were indeed already rich?

The late great actor Jimmy Stewart was a stage hand on the movie set when he was asked by a director to be an extra in a scene, which led to more extra work and then to some solid acting roles. Upon meeting Spencer Tracy on the set one day, he said he was going to leave the movie lot for a while and use some of the money he had made to take acting lessons and become a full-time actor because he loved it so much. Spencer Tracy said, "Are you nuts? You already are an actor. You're working aren't you? Act as you go." He was receptive to the advice and became the legendary actor we all know and love.

If you cannot swim I don't advise that you dive in at the deep end, but get in the water! Start at the shallow end. Splash, feel what it is like to put your head under, get comfortable with water, find someone who can teach you to swim, be receptive. Watch for the signposts and knowledge will follow. Pay attention. Try this simple exercise. Listen more. Speak less. Listening is a tool for success. Many times the words of others contain the clues you are looking for. Allow the perspectives of those you respect to give you a wider view on each decision in your life. Ultimately, trust your heart, your instincts, your intuition and your gut, and NEVER let fear be the beacon that lights your stage.

Remember I promised you the tale of when fear and I had our final showdown? Well, if you liked the story of the shortest show in the history of Rock 'n Roll just wait until you read this!

CAUTION: MAY CAUSE NERVOUSNESS

Kingston, Ontario, Canada circa 1977, at Queen's University. They had a very happening pub there that offered bands a six-night stint Monday through Saturday, which was very common in those days. The bar scene back in the seventies and eighties was extremely vibrant and most offered live entertainment.

As a fan myself, I used to see great bands like *Rush*, *Triumph* and *April Wine* all play the local scene before hitting the big-time, and I loved it. We were far from the big-time and usually when you got a six-night gig you used the first three nights or so to win people over and hopefully after word of mouth had spread you would get a happening Thursday, Friday and Saturday night. That is exactly how this particular gig began. Monday night we entertained four people, three of whom were staff (the other was the University outcast), but we rocked. If there is one thing I have learned through the years, it is that you give your best show to everyone. Four, forty, four thousand or forty thousand, I have played them all. One thing remains a constant: concentrate on the performance, not the applause. Go on stage, give everything you have to give and leave nothing behind. So on this Monday evening the outcast and the staff got the best show in town, so much so that the next night, Tuesday, saw at least the outcast, the staff and ten others in the pub for our show. We were winning them over. Wednesday saw at least fifty for what turned out to be a great evening, setting Thursday up for more of the same. Word was flying around the campus and we were told to "get ready for Friday, it's gonna be a zoo!"

Ah…"a zoo": music to a musician's ears right. But what about Gag-man? Remember him? Doctor Robert's bag was still with me but I knew I daren't try to street medicate to get through the evening, not after the debacle in Quebec weeks earlier. This event called for something the doctor ordered.

I truly was a bag of nerves, pacing up and down, stopping to stare at myself in the mirror and say, "You can do this, you can do this, you can do this." But wait! There was an echo. "No you can't, no you can't, no you can't," said that other voice, sounding so familiarly like mine. What was a boy to do? I was an absolute wreck. Fear had become so painful for me, so controlling, that I just could not seem to cope. It was a battle that I was now losing before even taking to the battlefield. I couldn't stand it.

"Okay let's see," I said to myself as I slowly opened my little black bag. Inside I had an array of goodies to help me combat my fear. I decided to take a few things. There were some little blue pills that promised to settle my nerves and I think a red one that was specifically for the nerves in my stomach. Are they not all just nerves? I popped them and for good measure I decided to clear my sinuses by inhaling some menthol vapour nasal spray, of course failing to notice that written along the side of the container were the following words: "Caution: may cause nervousness."

That's just what I needed. It seems this stuff can cause nervousness all on its own, and here I am prescription medicated to the hilt and without knowing it have a healthy dose of nervousness racing me to the stage. Here we go again, it's show time!

The drug combination was beginning to have a serious affect on my system. I felt a warm tingling sensation in my ears, nostrils, and eyeballs. My tongue was forked and my hair suddenly wanted to stand up all on its own. My heart raced and, just to add insult to injury every minute or so, our one and only roadie would come up to me to say, "This is gonna be grrrreat!"

The pub was jammed, with as many lined up outside the building as had been inside the previous four nights. The other lads in the band were pumped.

Faster and faster my chest pounded and I thought to myself that if I slipped out now, before the gig started, I could run the three hundred and fifty kilometers home to Toronto and be tucked warm and cozy in my bed before anyone even knew I was missing, but I bailed on that idea when I took a moment to look down and realize that my feet were missing. I had to be hallucinating. I mean my feet were still there, right? I decided against running, just in case. Suddenly the moment of truth arrived.

The band takes the stage; crowd cheers; drummer starts a solid beat; crowd cheers louder; guitar riff to "Alright Now" kicks in; crowd goes... Oh never mind, by now you get the picture.

What followed was so far into fear that really no words can do it justice. However this is a book and words are necessary, so here goes. I swear I couldn't be more scared sunbathing on the Iran-Iraq border. I had just entered hell and found that it is full of Queen's students with 1970's hairdos.

I was sweating profusely, yet had been on stage all of thirty-one seconds. The band was rocking but I had yet to sing a note. I leaned into the bass player.

"Wayne", I yelled over the blasting music.
"Yeah man?" he yelled back.
"Wayne, they're all staring at me."
"Who?" He enquired without missing a note.
"THEY ARE!" I said in disbelief.
"They're supposed to man," said Wayne. "They're the audience!"
He urged me to relax and to get up to the microphone as the band could only keep this intro going for so long before it melted. I slowly, painfully approached my spot. Girls were smiling and winking, guys were cheering and howling. The world was ready, willing and very able to rock!
I clenched my fists and low and behold out came my first words.
"We're gonna take a short break and we'll be right back!!!!"
And the Lord said, "When in doubt...Runnnnn!!"

I was off again like a U.S. border guard as they continued to play the intro. When I reached the dressing room I began to board it up by grabbing anything that was not bolted down. Benches, tables, waste bins, anything would do. Suddenly I heard the voice of our roadie on the other side of the door begging me to come back to the stage. I could hear in the distance that the band had begun to play "Rocky Mountain Way" by Joe Walsh, which was the one and only song that the guitar player could do without me, so it was a race to see if they could get me back up there before the well ran dry.

"Hey man, come on! Please come back to the stage, they're going to riot and we'll get our asses fired." By this time I was boarding up all the air vents just in case they tried to come in that way. I had completely lost it. On stage the lads heard the following message coming through their vocal monitors.

"Alan is not coming back."

Meanwhile, back in the dressing room...I passed out. Fear, it seemed, had its final victory.

When I came around it felt like *War Of The Worlds* and I was the alien. My body drenched in sweat was under a bench in the far corner of the room. The lads were getting the last of the gear together and were obviously shuttling things to our little van outside. The silence was deafening.

"What happened?" I asked the bass player.
"Oh, we played "Rocky Mountain Way" for about forty minutes until they booed us off the stage."

He continued taking his stuff out to the van. Upon his return he looked down at me again.

"Oh yeah, by the way we also got fired. We're in the van. You comin'?"

The journey home was a nightmare for me, as I was still tripping. Our van consisted of a driver in the driver's seat, someone in the passenger seat and someone in the middle seated on a milk crate. The rest of us were huddled together under jackets and blankets in the back as the Canadian winter howled up at us through the large hole in the van's floor. On this occasion, I huddled alone.

Thinking my music career was surely over, I laid low for days. Not only was I convinced that the guys would certainly not want me anymore, I was equally convinced that something was severely wrong with me and that perhaps I just was not cut out for this business of being in the public eye. Yet, amazingly enough, I still knew that I was good at it and that somehow it was what I was meant to be doing. A week or so later I got a call that we had an offer to do a gig way up north in a tiny town called Temagami.

"Is there any point in taking it?" I was asked.

I felt it was better for everyone to give them relief and say the right thing and turn it down. I should say no.

"YES! Yes, let's do it!" I said almost immediately.

Where the hell had that come from? Why did I say that? I was supposed to say no. They wanted no, and I wanted no!

OH NO NOT I, I WILL SURVIVE

As I write this book I have performed live for over twenty-five years and for literally millions of people. As part of *Glass Tiger*, I have looked out over audiences at festivals numbering in the tens, twenties and thirties of thousands. We have performed on national holidays for one hundred thousand and more. I have toured and performed with Rod Stewart, Tina Turner, *Journey*, *The Moody Blues* and dozens more who consistently have hundreds of thousands of people come out to see them. I was the first ever voice to sing live at Toronto's huge domed stadium, the Skydome, now known as the Roger's Centre, when *Glass Tiger* was part of the opening ceremony. If you take into consideration home viewing audiences who have seen *Glass Tiger* from the comfort of their living rooms on the wide array of shows we have done, then I have indeed sung live for hundreds of millions through the years. How then did I do it? How did I win the battle against fear? How did I get the courage to tell the director of the Skydome opening ceremonies that we would do it only if I could sing live (knowing that this would make me the first to do so) or the courage to do the same with the director of an enormous Latino show filmed out of Miami that had a viewing audience of some seven hundred million world wide?

How did Gag-man beat fear? Well, the answer is simple. He didn't, for you don't beat fear. Ask any soldier on the front lines and I am sure he or she will tell you that he is scared each and every time he goes into battle. Ask any firefighter, police officer or search and rescue team, and I am positive they will tell you that they have fear when faced with life-and-death situations. Fear is not a sin. Fear is human. You do not beat it, you accept it, acknowledge it, and understand that it is present. It is what tells you that you are alive and in the moment and that what you are doing is not mundane, or stagnant and certainly not common. It's part of the "if it were easy, everyone would be doing it" category. Successful people know that fear is not the beacon that lights their way, but rather a caution sign that says, "Stop!" but stop doesn't necessarily mean retreat, go back, or give in. Stop means evaluate, question and *think*. Fear is a powerful tool that we have all used even if we don't recognize it as such. Remember your first day of kindergarten. Better still, if you are a parent, think of your child's first day, for that is fresher in your mind. Was he or she afraid? Of course. Most recently, my little one entered a kindergarten class clinging to her mother's leg, but by day's end she was telling us to "go back, not finished yet, Mummy."

Was fear a sign that we should not start school? Of course it wasn't. What about elementary school or, God forbid, that first day of high school? I remember it all too well, being an alien, a foreigner, someone from another land, that thinks, looks and speaks differently from everyone else. What a living nightmare that was! Fear was present in all of these scenarios, yet you overcame it; you worked through it and grew from it.

So that's what happened to me some twenty-five years ago or so back in that little dive in Temagami. I gave myself permission to feel the fear that accompanied going onstage and performing before the public. I looked in the mirror again only this time I said, "If you are going to be sick, then be sick." Moving to the back of the stage for a few seconds to be sick could not possibly be worse than running for the hills and destroying the gig. And what do you think happened? Correct, nothing happened. After coming to terms with the fact that doing something extraordinary carries with it a sense of fear and that this fear is normal, human and acceptable, I never gagged again. I never was sick again. I never popped another pill to get me on stage ever again. Today do I have fear before going on stage? You're darn right I do. Does it prevent me from performing? Never.

What will separate you from the crowd is seeing fear and pain for the guidance it brings you instead of using it as an excuse to be negative, or to quit. Any negative thought, or any chosen suffering will hold you back from the growth you are seeking and the goals you have set for yourself. Peace Pilgrim in her amazingly simple way described following the right path as, "If you should be doing something, start it. If you shouldn't be, stop it." How is it that the simplest things to understand are often the most difficult to implement? The fact is that once you start using *THE ACTION SANDWICH*, when you see things you should be doing, you will get to the point where you must do them. Your new headspace will not allow you to do things you are not meant to do, just those things that enrich your path.

Stop waiting to live! The show is *always* on and it is performed in front of a live audience every moment of every day.

TALKING HEADS

What must it have been like for Jackie Gleason, Art Carney, Milton Berle and all the other pioneers of early television, when everything was live in front of thousands and eventually millions of viewers. I will bet that if you asked them, they would tell you that they NEVER felt more alive than at that moment when the red light went on and the cameras started rolling. I implore you to ask yourself what change you can make no matter how small or insignificant it may seem. Do it right now, at this very second. Try following the little "think it, do it" rule. This is where you implement something immediately upon thinking of it and not give procrastination a chance. The speed that you move from "thinking" to "doing" is equivalent to the speed in which you will fulfill that which you DESIRE and in turn determines the speed at which your dreams are fulfilled. RECEPTIVITY to the need, not only to "think" but also to "do" is like discovering the gas pedal in a running car. "Thinking it" expedites the process of not having to find the keys, open the door and start the car but it still remains up to you to push down on the pedal determining how fast you go and how much road you will cover each day of your life.

Not too long ago I wrote a line in one of my songs: "Years are only days holding the seconds of each passing hour, history is now for all I know." Simply put, the clock is ticking and as we get older it ticks at what seems like an alarmingly faster rate. What is important to you and worth doing in the time you have left? Are you important enough to yourself to make the change?

Stop the blaming. Kill the excuses. Be receptive. As the eloquent Maya Angelou puts it, "This experience, this life, is our one time to be ourselves." The one time not the dry run or the practice or the dress rehearsal. You do not have to know everything that is going on under the hood in order to be able to drive the car. Let's go! The journey begins now. See, you are hungry aren't you?

TEN STEPS TO RECEPTIVITY

1. MIND YOUR OWN BUSINESS - RECEPTIVITY should be for things over which you have true control or influence. Understanding, and being sensitive to global issues is important, however, worry and negativity over things that you have absolutely no control, is useless, draining and unproductive. Dude, the dinosaurs are dead. Let it go.

2. I HEARD IT THROUGH THE GRAPEVINE - Your ears remain two of the greatest tools you will ever carry in your toolbox. There is a vast difference between hearing and listening. Many times, more clues lie within what you are being told than what you are saying. Listen.

3. SIGNS, SIGNS EVERYWHERE A SIGN - The universe responds to what you send out in the form of thoughts, ideas, dreams and wishes. Don't ally with luck, coincidence or things that you can't measure. Your RECEPTIVITY should match with who you know yourself to be and who you are becoming. Look for signs that not only uncover what is on the surface of your mind but also dig deeper into what is hidden or dormant. Sometimes our greatest talents live there and only need to be awakened. Wake up.

4. THE GREAT PRETENDER - Acting as if you are already where you need to be or that you already have all that you DESIRE, raises the bar on how your subconscious mind perceives your place in this world and improves your ability to send out higher quality messages to the universe, thus raising the level of your RECEPTIVITY. Don't have it? Act as if you do.

5. DARE TO TRUST - Innocent until proven guilty. Give the world around you the benefit of the doubt by entering into negotiations and new relationships from a point of trust in yourself and in others. You cannot be receptive from inside a bubble. Inevitably at some point you may be hurt, let down or disappointed, but that is called life. By its incredibly positive nature, trust will always bring you more riches than rags, more light than darkness and more success than failure. Trust yourself.

6. SMELL THE ROSES - RECEPTIVITY is your gut's sense of smell. When the situation feels skunky trust your gut instinct and walk away. Toxic people and situations will drain you dry. Lose them.

7. C'EST WHAT? - "Well Mr. Smith, I'm afraid you're dying"
"Can I get a second opinion, Doctor?"
"Ok, you're ugly too!"
Being receptive means not succumbing to or taking for granted that the first answer is the ONLY answer. Question yourself, others, and the universe as much and as often as it takes to find the only true answer, regardless of how the truth makes you feel. Speak up.

8. FEELINGS, WOO-O-O FEELINGS - As someone who was raised in a world where, "Big Boys Don't Cry", I can attest to the fact that it is essential to be receptive to your own feelings as well

as the feelings of those around you. On this road to a life of abundance and success there is no room for blocking out your sensitivities and ignoring those of others. If you do, you will damage your natural relationship with the universe and limit the level of experience that this world can offer you. Feel it.

9. TAKE THE TASTE TEST - Savour every moment and everything in between that is wonderful in your life no matter how small or insignificant it may seem. If you cannot enjoy, love, cherish and appreciate your life then WHAT'S THE POINT? No one's last words are, "I wish I'd spent more time with my nose to the grindstone!" Be receptive to meager treasures, for it's on their shoulders that true fortunes rest. Taste it.

10. GIVE A LITTLE BIT - So you want to get? Then give. It is an indisputable fact that the only way to receive anything of worth in your life, is by giving. Want more love in your life? Give love. Short on cash? Give something to charity. Want more happiness? Easy, make someone happy. Whatever it is that you want on your journey is exactly what you need to send out to the universe through thoughts, ideas, dreams, goals and passions. Give.

MY SONG
Opus 1

1976 - 1979

Here's a question for you. What would you have to be given in order for you to be receptive to living above a bar that fills each and every night with a crowd of biking enthusiasts whose taste for illicit activities such as prostitution, illegal pornography, extortion, drug trafficking, and good

old fashioned retribution in the form of murder and mayhem while
filling their human engines with the fuels of their creed, such as, alcohol,
marijuana, cocaine and heroin as they anxiously await your arrival in
order that you might entertain them? What would you want in return, if
asked, to live in a place where the bed is a battlefield for bugs and fleas
that decide to call a truce during your stay, in order that they might
share the spoils of your torso? What about a place where the exotic
dancers keep you awake at night as they begin the toils of their second
trade as exotic hostesses for many of the clientele from downstairs. What
would it take to get you to live in a situation in which eating something
like uncooked macaroni from a box held under some hot running water
because there is no oven, is still considered a luxury? In this place, on
any given night you might find a rat or even the occasional mole in bed
with you trying to stay warm. Would you consider yourself lucky if your
room sat above the filthy kitchen, where the heat from the deep fryer
leaked through the floor boards, giving much needed warmth? Of
course smelling like a giant french-fry is a cheap price to pay in order
that you don't freeze your butt off, so what would it take to get you to
do it, a million dollars, ten million, fifty million plus a lifetime
membership to the "Looney Of The Week Club?" Let me ask you this.
Could you love something enough to be willing to live there for fifty
dollars a week? What about twenty? What about NOTHING?

In some eastern traditions the word for PASSION has two symbols, the
symbol for love and the symbol for suffering. To say that I find that
poignant would be an understatement. LOVE AND SUFFERING, is that
truly what lies between the question, "Are you passionate about what you
want from this life" and its answer? Is it necessary to suffer in the name of
PASSION? Perhaps not, but would you, if you had to? What road lies
between indifference or apathy and the magic of PASSION? I want to
take you on a journey with me. It is a journey of two symbols, LOVE and
SUFFERING. It is a journey of PASSION, which in turn means it is a
journey of true purpose for when all is said and done, true purpose is the
real meaning of this thing we call life. This will be the story within my
story. I call it my Opus and it is readable as one continuous story or as I

prefer, it can be "staggered" which I hope will cause you to anxiously await what comes next. Here we go, follow me.

I'VE GOT THE MUSIC IN ME

Hearing The BEATLES for the very first time and being given my first guitar as a boy had a profound effect on my psyche, although it took years for it to manifest itself into the form of true purpose. From the stories I tell in this book, I'm sure you will soon get the impression that even as a child, music played a leading role in my existence. The performing for friends and classmates, my father putting on living room shows for family, friends and stragglers alike, the transistor radio being our early morning inspiration as we gathered around a single paraffin heater to dress in the unbearable cold and damp conditions of good old number 16 Kirkshaws Avenue. And of course there were the television shows like *Top Of The Pops* or *Sunday Night At The London Palladium* that were such mainstays in our lives, allowing us to forget the times and places we were living in, and to live vicariously through the PASSION of such a wonderful array of entertainers who had the ability to elevate our spirits and our souls. They made us smile, sing, dance and laugh in the face of adversity and the challenge of living hand to mouth day in and day out. Entertainment made living in hard times, in this hard-man's world, just a little bit easier. Looking back it still amazes me how we were riddled with debt and constantly facing the challenges of poverty yet STILL we managed to have an old telly functioning, around which we gathered to be transported away from our worries and woes.

Music however, between the ages of twelve and seventeen was nothing more than a pleasant distraction but I certainly would not rank it higher than my love for football (soccer). I enjoyed it, was good at it but that's where it ended. So what happened?

What suddenly made me receptive to living my life through art and music? What was the epiphany that sent me on the pathway that I remain on to this very day some thirty years later?

1973

Within a year of landing in Canada, I met a chap named Martin Ridgely who was a fine entertainer in the tradition of the classic folk singer/songwriters of the late '60s and early '70s. Martin and I took to each other very quickly and soon struck up a friendship. We would get together several times a week and share our love of music by Elton John, *The Beatles*, David Bowie and new up-and-comers *Queen* and *Supertramp*. He taught me several new chords and pretty soon we were taking our guitars to parties and playing for anyone who cared to sit around and listen to us. It was however, still very Karaoke-like in as much as we were merely performing our own interpretations of songs written by others. Then, it happened one night while sitting around plunking on my guitar. I hit a chord (it was an E chord, not that it matters) and I sang a little melody. There's nothing unusual about that, but this melody wasn't just any old melody, in fact this melody wasn't anyone else's melody. This one was mine. I continued with these original lah, lah, lahs, until words started flowing from my mouth that I was not familiar with. They weren't McCartney's or Taupin's, Jagger's or Taylor's, they were Frew's.

"Holy shit! I'm writing a song! My first original song! What do you make of that, world?"

"Hey Mum, Dad, guess what? I've written a song!"

"That's great, hey nip out to the liquor store for me and get a 'wee' forty-ouncer would ye? And hurry back!"

I played it for Martin.

"That's cool," he said enthusiastically. "Let's write more."

And so, we did. That was the moment, a little magnificent magical, unadulterated original moment, when my lah, lah, lahs, became my very first song called, *You're The One*. That's it, without question, the moment where my DESIRE in music and entertaining was ignited and it all went from being a pleasant distraction for me to becoming my true purpose, my PASSION and it has remained so ever since. For any of you out there that care, I finally recorded *You're The One* in 1994 for a solo CD I did called, *HOLD ON*.

Martin and I continued writing our little ditties and continued entertaining and even got our first paying gig at a wedding for a friend of ours, although if memory serves I am not sure if money or beer was the remuneration.

CHAPTER TWO

2

*"DESIRE is the starting point of all achievement,
not a hope, not a wish, but a keen pulsating DESIRE
which transcends everything."*

NAPOLEON HILL

CHAPTER TWO: DESIRE

The next step to achieving success in anything you put your life force behind is DESIRE. Now this part always sounds and looks simple on the surface. I say, "What do you want?" and you say, "I want a million dollars...cash, and a yacht and a summer home in Tuscany. Oh yes, and a Rolls Royce and a large dog called Fetchmyslippers." Well, let me tell you something. It is perfectly reasonable for you to DESIRE all of these things. However, if I ask you what your next move is on your journey to obtaining all of these things and your answer contains the words *casino*, *lottery*, or *race track*, or if it has anything to do with a nylon stocking over your head the next time you visit the bank, then I will say that we need to talk. Step into my office.

The late great George Bernard Shaw once said, "Hope is DESIRE with an expectation of accomplishment." Now although I am not a big advocate of hoping as a means of achieving, I love this quotation, for it contains the beautiful and profound notion of having to have an "expectation of accomplishment." In other words, your desires must have some connection to that which we call *common sense* in order that you can give them the type of structure needed for success. "Sense and Sensibility" are just as important today as they were in the time of Jane Austin. It is still more than reasonable for me to learn to skate at my present age, but to DESIRE, believe and intend on securing an NHL contract would be pushing it. It does not border on ridiculous; it IS ridiculous, and therefore has zero expectation of accomplishment. For a teenager it is possible, but for me to exert my power and life force behind a notion of skating anywhere other than the frozen pond near my home is a total waste of time and energy. So the fast cars, the luxury yachts, the home in Italy, or whatever your desires may be are very possible, however don't forget that an expectation of accomplishment must come with it. DESIRE anything you want but it is better to DESIRE those things that remain within the realms of common sense. You must be able to believe that you can have the things that you tell the universe you want.

Desires can and should be established incrementally. What you want today may be different than what you'll want once you're a millionaire, because how can you know what you will want as a millionaire when you've never been one? Work towards your attainable desires in the moment and you cannot go wrong. Desires with expectations of accomplishment based on common sense will lead to achieved goals as you negotiate and conquer each rung of the ladder on the way to a successful life. Today you want to prepare the most important proposal you have ever written so that tomorrow you will close your largest business deal, which in turn will secure that raise, which someday will help pay off the mortgage. Remember the thousand-mile journey? One step at a time, my friend. A journey to success is no different. DESIRE, BELIEF PASSION all are just steps on the stairs of life and it's perfectly okay if it is three steps up and one back, because that's also part of the journey. Life isn't one staircase negotiated at breakneck speed from bottom to top all in one go.

The crime being committed day in and day out by literally millions of adults all over this planet is that so many have no DESIRE at all because they have no idea what they want out of their lives and they have no INTENTION of finding out why this is. Give me an eighty-five-year-old dude who has his *ACTION SANDWICH* knob turned to "ten" desiring to be a male model in Milan and I say, "Good on ya mate!" While most of us might chuckle at the idea, I would also admire his courage, his tenacity and perhaps even his suit. However, show me an eighty-five-year-old who lived an entire life of "always getting ready to" and who never ever knew what he wanted from this world, and I will show you a human tragedy. I'm striving to be at it like Andy Rooney, who at eighty-seven still has a voice, or Charlotte Hamlin the seventy-five-year-old long distance cyclist who is telling the world that fitness is essential for everyone.

Once ignited, DESIRE is an ageless and renewable resource. It grows within you and when satisfied becomes restless again with the need to achieve more. Successful people are in tune with this concept and use it to build empires. Bill Gates doesn't stop at twenty, thirty, or forty billion dollars. He continues the journey that he loves and is so very passionate about.

Promise yourself right now that you will not fall prey to society's definition of success. You must define it for yourself in order to be happy. For Bill Gates that means billions, but for others it's a two-bedroom cozy cottage.

Don't try to fix your dissatisfaction in one part of your life by distracting yourself in another. If your DESIRE is to have a great marriage, a bigger house and faster car will not fix it, if things are not all right at home. If your DESIRE is to have a healthy relationship with your children and you're failing, all the money in the world will not make it better. Align your desires and actions, and do not assume that the answer to everything is monetary. Your ultimate goal must be to live YOUR life to YOUR standards, whatever they may be, and your gut is your best gauge.

EVERY STORY TELLS A PICTURE

Being in a vocal booth at a recording studio was nothing new to me. In fact you could say it was old hat. I never lose sight of the fact that I am blessed to be able to make music that so many people listen to and enjoy. Having sold so many CDs, and hearing my songs on the radio still thrills me, so being in THAT vocal booth on THAT particular day felt like I was doing what I was meant to be doing. On that day though, I was sharing the space with another singer, for my vocal part on the track was already in the can, as they say in the industry – completed, secured, and I didn't have to re-sing any of it. So what was I doing in THAT vocal booth you might ask? Well, THAT singer was going to put his part down for me and turn my song into a duet, and he had asked me to come in and sing as he warmed up to the track and learned his part. When he was ready to go I would leave the booth and come out to the front and just listen, but for now I was there to guide him through my lyrics. There was one particular moment, however, that I will never forget as long as I live.

The vocal booth was dark except for one small light shining down on the lyrics of my song sitting on a music stand. I could have been anywhere, in any number of studios, in any city in the world. But I wasn't. I was in THAT city, in THAT studio, with THAT singer, and for a moment the silence was broken as he decided to do a little warming up of his precious vocal chords by performing some bluesy and R&B type scats; that is to say, some off-the-cuff non-lyrical lah, lah, lah's and oohs and ahhs, which he did so effortlessly, ahead of singing the song for the first time. I closed my eyes. A soft chill went down my spine and the small hairs on the nape of my neck tingled as I listened to THAT voice in my headphones.

My heart raced. Suddenly, as the singer continued his warm-up, in the darkness of my mind a bright light began to shine way off in the distance and an image became bright and crystal-clear. I remembered the scene so vividly at that moment, as it had been back in 1969 when it all took place for the very first time.

Ah, there's my dear old dad sleeping on the chair after having a well-deserved supper. He had pork chops tonight. I on the other hand had soup with lots of bread in it to fill my hungry twelve-year-old tummy. But after all, he is my dad and he deserves the pork chops and besides, I know I will get to chow down on whatever he leaves.

There's my mum at the sink. Boy, she looks young. Funny I've never thought of my mum as ever having been young before but that's silly isn't it? She just got home from work not long ago, as both of them have to work to make ends meet. In fact my dad holds down a second job at a betting office on Saturdays, where men come to gamble on horse racing and greyhounds. That job causes such arguments here because my mum swears that "That tart who works with your dad on Saturdays is after him." He says it's a load of "bollocks" but it sure does cause grief around here. Sometimes they fight so ferociously that I am terrified and it usually ends with my mother asking me to "decide" whom I want to be with. "Him or me," she'll say. It's a loaded question because even if I say him, she'll grab me by the hand and say, "No you're coming with me," and then we'll walk the length of the town to my grandmother's.

Still the singer continues his warm-up.

There I am, over there, on the floor in front of the television. Boy, I look so tiny! It must be Thursday, because I am glued to something other than football so it has to be, yes I see it, it's *Top Of The Pops*, a weekly show featuring the music world's biggest stars and new up-and-comers. I love this show and I couldn't be any more receptive to its PASSION and power than I already am. Look at my young face and my eyes. They are literally dancing to the music. It would be fun to do THAT someday. There is no doubt in my mind that I DESIRE attention, for I love to entertain people so much that when the teacher at school asks who will come up and entertain the class I am always the first to put my hand up. Then, taking charge, I bring Willie, Davy and Ian up to be *The Beatles*, to the delight of the entire class. Of course, we have only air guitars but that's okay as the class doesn't even notice or care. By the way, I am always Paul.

Man, this guy beside me can really sing.

I have been waiting for this great new artist who has been number one for the last few months. I love him. Some day I want to be just like him, having hit songs, making music, entertaining people, and one day I will even sing with him. Now that would be success. I don't care what it takes; I just want to do it. What an entertainer this guy is on our old black and white telly as he struts his stuff up and down the stage in his tight leopard pants and sings with THAT voice, that one-of-a-kind, bluesy, raspy, R&B voice that could only belong to...

"Alan, hey Alan! I'm ready man, let's start the track and go for it."

Suddenly, back in the moment, I jumped and shook my head a little like you do when returning from a deep sleep.

"Where am I?" I wondered. Ahh, yes, I am here, here where I belong, doing what I was born to do, and I am working with him, THAT singer. "Okay, Rod, let's do it," I said confidently, masking the fact that I cannot believe for one second that I am doing a duet with none other than my friend Rod Stewart.
"I was just watching you on the telly," I said.
"Where, when, what the hell are you talking about?" says Rod confused.
"Never mind" I say sheepishly. "Who'd believe it?"

The *ACTION SANDWICH* would.

AM I HEARING VOICES?

What separates DESIRE from the realm of wishes and hopes is the concrete foundation it builds as it burns within your heart and mind and the core of your body, as opposed to existing only within your passing thoughts. It is fuel for the fire that is yet to come. It is a very delicate piece of the puzzle and it is easily driven in a downward spiral by self-sabotage or a negative voice within. Have you ever driven through a beautiful neighbourhood or walked by a car showroom and as soon as you hear that little voice in your head say, "Wow I'd like to have that," there's another one that says "Yeah right, that'll be the day?" Well, that's the daydreamer talking to the self-saboteur. As easily as one hopes for it, it is sabotaged by a sense of unworthiness, disbelief or failure. This can be one of two things. It can be your own insecurities at play trying to sabotage your goals or just a lack of true DESIRE. You must decide which it is. It would be like me in a Ferrari showroom. I don't really care about Ferraris. I can appreciate the beauty of the car and the momentary ego-boost it provides, but for me when that little voice says, "Right, that'll be the day," it is correct. Because I should be focused on another model of vehicle. I do, however, have a tremendous DESIRE to be a working actor; therefore *THE ACTION SANDWICH* formula has kicked in full steam ahead and when it comes to acting there are no negative self-sabotaging voices of any kind in my head...period!!

I cannot stress enough the importance of that voice within your head. It is fair and reasonable if it is saying *NO* to you for the right reasons i.e. "No, Alan, you don't want a Ferrari." However, a voice such as, "No, Alan, you don't deserve a Ferrari" is simply not acceptable and would never stand a chance inside of my head. You must not let it exist inside of yours. Chat with it, wrestle with it if you must, look at where it comes from but at all cost you must take the time to acknowledge, dominate, defeat and rid your mind of it.

We all experience this but it is the focused, motivated and well-intentioned who take the time to understand and rid themselves of their self sabotaging thoughts and then go on to succeed. I'm telling you that if you don't let yourself DESIRE all of the great things you could have in your life you won't get them. Success is dependent upon DESIRE. DESIRE is dependent upon an expectation of accomplishment. Things must make sense. Whether it is to make a lot of money from a particular idea that you have, or to make beautiful music, if you are receptive to it and DESIRE it then you are on the road to success.

Let's see, you are now receptive to a particular outcome that you wish to achieve and you have the fire of DESIRE burning in your belly. You now know what you really DESIRE. Is this enough? No, DESIRE alone is incapable of moving you to a state of INTENTION. What must come next is BELIEF: true, unwavering, undeniable BELIEF. You must truly believe that you are capable, worthy, entitled, and deserving of success and of the life you DESIRE. So let's meet BELIEF. Where's my sandwich?

TEN STEPS TO DISCOVERING YOUR DESIRE

1. I'M STARTING WITH THE MAN IN THE MIRROR - Knowing what it is that you truly DESIRE is essential. Desires should not be fleeting thoughts but rather penetrating experiences built on solid foundations, infused with deep emotion. Reinforce this message and image of the happiness you seek as you go about your day. Be aware.

2. FLY ME TO THE... TOWER? - It's perfectly fine to DESIRE the moon but I ask you this, "Will it fit in your living room?" Having a sensible expectation of accomplishment is essential on the journey to success. DESIRE must be attainable. If need be, increment your desires as you would your steps on a journey. Grab the Eiffel Tower, then the moon.

3. DECISIONS, DECISIONS, DECISIONS - What does success look like to you? That's really the secret to a prosperous life. Never come from a place of wishing and hoping but rather from believing and knowing exactly what it is that you need in your life to feel successful. Deciding is the first step to achieving. Decide.

4. MY POGO STICK, PET ROCK, BELLBOTTOMS, LAVA LAMP AND OH YES, MY LAWRENCE WELK COLLECTION - If you could only have five things, what would they be? Decide today and plan to go and get those five things. Have you signed up for the class, called the travel agent, bought the cookbook or joined the club? Go get five things you want and when you succeed, pick five more and go get them. Go.

5. IT'S MY LIFE - Every thought starts with you, and you alone. Don't wait for someone else or some profound circumstance to bring you what you want. Remember self-responsibility doesn't necessarily mean going it alone. Soliciting help or partnership may be the difference between success and failure. Be open.

6. BIT BY BIT - Accomplishing small goals allows you to feel successful immediately. Skyscrapers are created one brick at a time. If necessary walk success before running it. Create.

7. MY PLACE OR YOURS? - What constitutes success? You do. To some being in the pit is a lifelong dream while others can only be satisfied behind the wheel of the roaring Formula One engine. But in order to win the world championship all of us must be the best at what we do. Excel.

8. I KNOW I KNOW I KNOW - Don't let THEM, IT or THAT get to you. Do what you know you should be doing regardless of what the chatter around you is saying. Stay aimed at your target, focus, persevere and smile because you are doing what you love and that my friend is success. Love it.

9. DON'T SURROUND YOURSELF WITH YOURSELF - Never stop helping others in the achievement of their dreams. When assisting others you are focused on manifesting a positive outcome not only for them, but also for you and indeed, the universe. "Butterfly Effect" my friend, "Butterfly Effect."

10. FRIENDS IN LOW PLACES - Critics, back-biters, fault-finders, skeptics and toxics have no place in the life of someone who is committed to success, abundance and living the best life they can. These detractors are dedicated to helping you stand still or lose ground. Dump 'em.

MY SONG
Opus 2

COME TOGETHER

By 1976 I was approached by some musicians who asked me to join a band, not as a guitar player I might add, but as their singer. They arranged a band rehearsal, yet neglected to tell their regular singer that it was happening, making this all very clandestine indeed. I sang one song with them, "Get Back" by none other than *The Beatles* and they became putty in my hands. The deal was done. The original singer, who I swear to you, had the last name of Singer, was doomed. They took a vote. To this day, *Glass Tiger's* bass player claims he didn't vote as it was already unanimous by the time it came around to him, for you see dear reader, Mr. Singer, the now ex-singer, was at the time his closest friend. Et tu, Brute?

Such is the way of bands as they weave the web that the world becomes entangled in. By the time I recorded my first CD some twenty years after getting into the business, I had only been in two bands, yet within the makings of what finally became *Glass Tiger,* I have probably worked with fifteen or twenty guys.

As I mentioned earlier, I didn't take to being in a band immediately and on many occasion I would dodge rehearsal preferring to sit by the fire and watch *Hockey Night In Canada* or a good movie instead. Finally though it was the emergence of our first original song as a band that sent me back on the pathway to becoming successful. It didn't hurt I might add, that I had just seen what the world was calling a video of a concert filmed live in the famous Budokan, in Japan. The band was called *Cheap Trick* and the concert is now legendary. They were adored and worshipped by thousands of screaming girls and when you watch the footage of them performing you just know they are working at their true purpose. I looked at the screen and said without any hesitation, "Oh yeah! I want that job!" My epiphany was about to become a pilgrimage.

You see, once true PASSION takes over, you are helpless in an attempt to fight it. No question. You will suffer until you fulfill your DESIRE. You obsess with the need to do something, love someone, try something, and be something. Your stomach knots, your heart aches, you lose sleep, you're in a fever, driven uncontrollably to follow the path that love puts you on.

PASSION made Shakespeare the Bard of Avon, put Armstrong on the moon and caused Martin Luther King to change a generation. It drove a deaf Beethoven to write symphonies and a Gandhi to his demise at the hands of his assassin. Yes LOVE AND SUFFERING absolutely are the two symbols of PASSION.

I sit here today, fifty years of age, somewhat matured, very reflective yet deeply content and I feel equally as empowered by my true purpose today as I did as a scrawny twenty-year-old, back what seems like a million years ago, yet only yesterday. When I ask myself the question, "Am I doing what I love?" the voice that asks the question is indeed a fifty year old one, but yet the echo that returns a resounding "YES!" is that of the Believer, the Desirer and the Intender, and it is ageless. It has no number attached to its being. It is constant. It is immortal.

They say be careful what you wish for, for you might just get it. I know what they mean. Wanting that job and working at that job, were two entirely different things.

We decided right from the get-go, that we wanted to look and sound like a 'real' band, a big-time band, which meant having to rent a bona fide sound system, a great lighting rig and a small crew to run them. The cost usually ate up whatever we were being paid that week, sometimes even exceeding the amount of our payment, forcing us to dip into our own pockets to make up the difference. On infrequent occasions, we might manage to bring it in under the wire, leaving ourselves a small wage. No wait, a "wee" wage, no that's not it, a tiny, miniscule, minute wage of ten to twenty dollars, which of course was to feed, intoxicate or numb you, depending on your preference, for the entire week. Remember now we were not at home and this scenario would be taking place far away, perhaps in the frozen tundra's of northern Ontario or Quebec. I always threw caution to the wind when I was handed that ten or twenty dollar bill, and I would immediately order a steak dinner and a few beers and use it all up in one sitting, then the game was how I was going to eat for the rest of the week.

Now this isn't the story of a choirboy, nor is it a tale of the boy most likely to be high school president. This is a tale of a guy in 1977, singing in a band, doing his thing, working the room, holding up his end of the bargain and living under a huge billboard sign that reads, "Sex, Drugs and Rock 'n Roll, Right This Way" with a big arrow pointing right at him. All this boy wants to do is stay alive. Stay alive and live to tell the tale someday.

MONA LISAS AND MADHATTERS

"God bless groupies!"
"What did you just say?"
"You heard me, I said God bless groupies. Oh yes and strippers too!"

Think what you want folks but if it was not for so-called groupies and the girls of the dance-pole, I am certain beyond any doubt that I and many like me in the music industry, would have been nothing more than a group of performing skeletons. The dancers simply made tons and tons of money. Yes I know some of them had an extra job on the side, a job that many do not approve of, the oldest known profession on the face of this earth but what the heck, who are we to judge? So they were loaded, and they had mercy, which they lovingly bestowed upon the starving musicians along the hallway. A pizza, a sandwich or a cup of tea was always most welcomed by the lads in the band. These young women were generous, sweet and kind. They knew we were broke, it wasn't hard to figure that out and so they helped us. Due to their numerous costumes that they wore on stage, they were all quite proficient seamstresses and they would gladly help sew a hem, stitch a button or put in a patch, as your clothes slowly fell apart around you. Ironically, I can't recall any instances where sex took place between any member of the band and these girls, even though sex was their trade. We all truly bonded as entertainers, road warriors, just trying to make a living, just trying to get a foot on the bottom rung of the ladder of success. They were our peers and I always think back on them fondly.

Now groupies, they are an entirely different breed. I am certainly a man of the world, not prudish in any way and I definitely don't believe in censorship except on behalf of our children and I most certainly cannot deny that my promiscuity in those times, reveled in the sheer number of women that came out to see us play. The groupie thing goes far beyond the mere concept of two people finding each other attractive enough to have instantaneous, intimate relations together, for the groupie syndrome goes deeper, much deeper than sex. These girls begin to behave as surrogate girlfriends or even mothers uncaring of the fact that there may be a significant other or even a spouse at the home of the musician. I have and never will understand the mentality of anyone who feels compelled to somehow lay claim to a guy in a band by sleeping with him and in doing so then believes somehow that they two, are now one, a couple, at least until he leaves town on Sunday!

I am not about to dedicate page upon page to the distorted mindset of the groupie, however it is relevant to my story to note that they wanted something and of course I wanted something, so the playing field and the rules of the game would be set pretty darned quickly. Within minutes you were new best friends, like you had known each other since childhood as opposed to only the last seven minutes. Her desires usually had something to do with you, your jeans and her bedroom, while on the other hand, your DESIRE usually had something to do with her kitchen, her pantry, her washer and dryer and God bless her, yes her bubble bath! Oh yes, there was sex, lots of sex, but even sex isn't as great a motivator as hunger. Borderline starvation will bring out the 'tramp' in you pretty fast and so it was that I would carefully place myself in a group of females knowing all too well that one, two or perhaps all of them would be fishing for one of the boys in the band and as they chatted eagerly divulging who they were, where they came from and where they lived, I would listen for keywords.

"Cooking." (There's one.)
"Roast beef." (Lovely.)
"Mashed Potatoes and gravy!" (Music to my ears.)
"Bubble bath!" (THAT'S IT! I'm going home with her.)

And so without fail, I would end up staying at "Sally's house" and we'd live like the couple next door, playing the role of 'your neighbours,' doing everything except inviting the in-laws over for tea. My clothes were clean and my belly was full and I was ready to face whatever 'crack house' we had decided to go to next. Sad really, yet at the time, it was as normal as my life is today.

During this period of my life I decided out of the blue that if my career as rock star was going to evade me that I should "become" something else and so I decided that the something else I should become was a doctor.

By this time I could have said male stripper because God knows, I had all the moves down pat, from watching the dancers, but I didn't, I said doctor instead. And so I applied to medical schools and colleges around the province of Ontario and very soon thereafter letters of rejection came flooding in. I swear some were like, "Dear Mr. Frew, We are sorry to BWA! BWAH! BWAHAHAHAHAHAH!!"

It was at that moment I wished I had taken things just a little more seriously back in my high school days, for it was now apparent that although smart, my school marks did not speak of intelligence and to boot I had basically no credits in the fields of science and biology. Every one of them told me to forget it but I think you know by now that I am not very good at that and so I had to draw up fresh battle plans.

WHO'S CHEATING WHO?

"Ladies and gentlemen, I give you employee of the month, Alan Frew!"

My dad looked at me rather skeptically out of the corner of his eye, for he knew I detested this place and had only taken this job out of necessity and that I had always attempted to do as little as possible here, so how then, was it remotely feasible that his son, yours truly, had been selected as employee of the month for turning in the highest quota of freshly cut tubing? Simple really, however before I tell you the answer, let me tell you where I am.

It's a large tubing factory where my job is to take twenty-foot long rods of steel tubing and cut them into pieces six inches long. It was the worst job I had taken since working in a plastics factory a few years earlier where I had twelve-hour shifts watching plastic form into rolls similar to what a toilet roll looks like only these were huge. I got so delusional there one time I deliberately cut my hand only to be taken to the hospital, stitched up, and relieved of duty for two whole weeks.

This steel tube cutting job wasn't much better and indeed I even went as far as to do a smaller hand cutting job on myself to get out of it for a few days. Insane as this sounds, this job was a family affair, for my father, mother, brother and brother-in-law all worked in this hell hole at the same time, the only difference being that they worked the day shift while I on the other hand worked nights. My God I hated it and so I started a campaign of phoning the local hospital to ask if there was an opening for an orderly or porter position, my logic being that if I could just get into a hospital I may be able to plan my next move as to how to become a doctor! I was relentless, calling sometimes two or three times per day. It got to the point that as soon as they answered the phone in the office and I said a word, they knew who it was.

"Hello!"
"No Alan. As I told you two hours ago, there are still no openings," she would say, referring to me on a first name basis.

I began purchasing medical and science magazines that I would read during my spare moments and while on my breaks. Of course as always, I found lots of humour in this factory and had lots of laughs within its walls. Still I never lost sight of where I wanted to go next and so every day I would call, while every night I would cut, well I would kind of cut. On night shift, which I disliked immensely, I would sneak off to the toilet for forty winks or read my magazine. Upon my return I would look at the quota of the two shifts prior to mine and then I would add a whole lot of their work into mine, basically fabricating my count.

Now I am not advocating cheating and of course it was inevitable that if this process were to continue over a period of time, that my misconduct would be discovered and my backside would be shown the door, but these were desperate times for me and I did not care, for I was getting a job in the hospital and I was going to be a doctor and that was that!

Looking back on it, I would have handled it differently, by actually cutting above and beyond my quota of tubes and in doing so, becoming the employee of the day, the month and even the year if need be. By doing this I would have left an indelible mark of positivity behind that would have allowed me to know that I had honestly done my best in a place that I detested and under painful circumstances I would still have shown integrity. They in turn would have lost a good worker, who they would have spoken highly of, sending out the right message to the universe on his behalf, instead of the negative one they would surely send upon discovering a cheater who had wronged them by fixing the numbers.

"Sorry Alan, still nada!" the lady in the hospital employment office would say regularly.
"Okay let's see then, how many did I cut tonight?" Said the tube cutter.
"Six hundred and sixty seven. Okay time to log that into the records."
He writes 9, 9, 7....
Hey! What's a six but an upside down nine, right?

My father looked at me out of the corner of his eye, for he knew me all too well.

"Alan, with an astounding tally," said the foreman, "Has cut more tubes this past month than anyone else in the entire workforce. Why it's as if he's cutting for all three shifts!"

(The employees all smile as the tube-cutter clears the back of his throat).

The days past and the nights were long. I had cut back on gigs due to the fact that I was working steady nights but I did continue to rehearse and rehearse and rehearse with the lads as much as possible. Then one night not long after being caught sleeping in the toilet, (again), for which I received yet another warning, I was told to go to the office.

"Shit, they're on to me!" I said under my breath on the long walk to the head office. I entered cautiously and addressed the staff.

"Someone sent for me?"
"Hey Mr. Employee of the month," said one of the girls from behind her desk. "You have a phone call."

I was a little worried for it was still only 6:30 a.m. and so I was afraid that something was wrong at home.

"Hello?"
"Alan?"
"Yes."
"This is York County Hospital...Do you want a job?"

THE FIRST CUT IS THE DEEPEST

"What are you doing son?"
"Easy, I am aligning my actions with my dreams."
"What are you thinking?"
"Simple, I am thinking about what it will be like when I am one."

"And what exactly is it that you are going to be?"
"Why, a doctor of course."

As a youngster I had a curious fascination with the human body. No not that. That came later. I am talking about biology, the ins and outs of how we are "put together." Interestingly enough, I remember as a child a lady came to our door and told my mother that for the fair sum of sixpence and a cup of tea, she would "read" the tea leaves in the bottom of my mother's empty cup, telling her, her future and what lay in store not only for herself but for her family. Tasseography as it is called, has been around for centuries, originating in Asia, Ancient Greece and the Middle East and it was not uncommon for a woman to earn her living, going door to door, offering her psychic services to others who were in dire need of good fortune and my mum of course, was one of them.

Now I admit that I have always been a bit of a skeptic around those purporting to have such powers and since the Seer basically looks at the pattern of tea leaves in the cup before allowing her imagination to play around with the shapes suggested by them, I haven't changed my position and to this day I remain skeptical. However, something was said that day to my mother that I will never forget and it's one of those things, those eerie things, the kind that can leave even the most skeptical among us, wondering if perhaps, it just may be real after all. She looked in the cup and said as she nodded in my direction,

"That one's going to be a doctor."
"Alan? Are you sure?" said my mother.
"Oh, yes dearie, I sees it all here, a doctor he'll be."
"Oh, I don't think so," said my mum confidently.

What the hell did she see in the bottom of the cup exactly, Dennis The Menace with a rubber glove on one hand? Who's to know, of course at that time she would have made as much sense saying that I was going to be the Prime Minister, but a doctor? I hated doctors and I was terrified of her too, so I scampered off as fast as I could leaving her and my mother pouring 'seconds' and getting ready to find out if my dad really was having a fling with that blonde tart in the off track betting shop he worked on Saturdays.

"Me, a doctor?" I thought to myself. "That'll be the day."

3

*"You can have anything you want
if you will give up the BELIEF that you can't have it."*
ROBERT ANTHONY

CHAPTER THREE: BELIEF

Sadly, this quote from Robert Anthony fits all too well with the day-to-day lives of so many of the multitudes of people that I meet in my travels. "Victim-speak" oozing from their pores, telling me why they are stuck, why they are broke, why they live with abuse, why they will never get ahead, why they will never own a business, why, why, why, why and almost always at some point they bring up the topic of BELIEF and worthiness even if they are not aware of it. Interestingly enough, when I was formulating *THE ACTION SANDWICH* I once again was tempted to insert knowledge here as opposed to BELIEF, and yet once again I resisted, held firm and did not. There are those who say that BELIEF is knowledge with an option, meaning you will believe as long as things seem to be going forward as planned, but as soon as life throws out a knuckle-ball you drop the bat, walk off the playing field and quit. I whole-heartedly disagree with this assumption and say that BELIEF is knowledge with certainty.

You cannot fake ideology. You cannot half-believe. You either do or you don't believe. There's no out-clause. You can force yourself to suppress, you can cover up true INTENTION, you can delude yourself all you want, but you cannot hide from that which is true. Now don't think for a second that it becomes automatic that if indeed you believe in something with total certainty that you will necessarily succeed, for BELIEF is not enough in and of itself. Remember, there are many parts to *THE ACTION SANDWICH* and it's all about the performance in all of these areas not just the applause at the end of the day. But BELIEF isn't interchangeable. BELIEF is concrete; again, you either do or you do not believe. You must know with conviction that you are on your right path every single day, and believe that your choice is taking you to your perfect outcome.

In fact, I'm going to tell you that the truly successful people in this world don't give personal gain much of a thought. They are passionately absorbed in the journey that they are on each day of their life. Each morning these rare souls can't wait to get out of bed and get working on what they left waiting from the day before. They love their work and their lives and the financial gain and the accolades are simply a bonus and byproduct of their efforts. Frank Sinatra sang because that was his gift to honour, not because he wanted to make a million dollars. Anthony Hopkins is an actor who happens to be a millionaire as an outcome of his PASSION. Stephen King writes, because an author is who he is. And you, too, have a gift, a reason for being that will fulfill your heart's DESIRE each day as well as pay life-dividends along the way.

> *"Life is like a box of chocolates,*
> *you never know what you're gonna get."*
> FORREST GUMP

The ACTUAL outcome in life is never completely one hundred percent within your control, no matter how much you may believe. I do not care who you are, what you do or how rich you may be, you cannot with certainty predict the outcome of everything and get it totally right.

Everything changes, so learn to love it and once you get good at implementing the formula of *THE ACTION SANDWICH*, you need to also be one step ahead of yourself, knowing what you want next, because there is no end. Bill Gates is indeed super-rich, yet is he finished being rich or is he going to be even richer? And if so, just how much richer is he going to be? Even he cannot know with certainty. However, what he can say is that he believes he is on the right pathway to becoming even richer than he is at the present time. When he was a teenager dabbling in that which was to become Microsoft, do you really think for a second that he knew with certainty that it was going to lead to his amassing some fifty BILLION dollars? There are an infinite number of outcomes to the same opening in any game of chess. So focus on the matter at hand. RECEPTIVITY is just one part of the journey; DESIRE another, as is BELIEF and knowledge and PASSION. Honesty, integrity and yes, anger, violence, pain and suffering all have their place and must be handled appropriately. Remember *THE ACTION SANDWICH* is working regardless of who you are and what your intentions may be.

Do you get my point? Life is not just black and white or hot and cold. Answer me this, how good is good? How rich is rich, how talented is talented? And by the way, how do you know when you've arrived? You would drive yourself crazy trying to figure it all out, would you not? Outcomes lead to more outcomes and change – that is the one thing you can count on. Successful people don't get their lives set up and then follow a particular pattern from then on. The successful ones look to attain "control." That is to say, they decide to have as much "say" as possible in how their lives are going to play out, but sometimes the universe has plans for them that even they cannot predict.

MAMA WEER All CRAZEE NOW

Here's a question for you. What do Mother Teresa and Osama Bin Laden have in common? No, I am not crazy. Just answer the question. What if I told you that I believe that they have a lot in common – would you agree with me? Probably not, yet I truly believe that they have a common denominator not only with one another but with countless other highly motivated and exceptionally successful people. In fact, with you. Well, what exactly? Let's see, RECEPTIVITY to purpose, unwavering DESIRE to succeed, BELIEF with certainty that the pathways chosen are the true ones, and INTENTION that enough force, focus and willpower fueled by great ACTION leads to the highest levels of achievement in their respective fields. And as for PASSION, need I say more? So the only major difference between the two of them on a strictly superficial level: outcome. One endeavored to spread human kindness, love and peace at the highest level of energy, while the other is the antithesis wreaking havoc, causing mayhem and inflicting death on those he calls infidels. As a matter of fact, his strategy is so powerful that he can convince many, many others that his RECEPTIVITY, DESIRE, BELIEF and INTENTION is also theirs and so they apply their actions to doing his bidding for him and of course history has shown us all too well how deadly and dangerous that can be.

Yet I say to you, they both have shown the highest level of commitment to what is or was important to them. Does my comparison of these two energies shock you? Good. It's meant to. Now I wonder if those searching for Bin Laden are as receptive, desirous, believing, intended and passionately "actioned" as he is, about catching him?

Everything depends on how the formula applies to you and only you. What do you believe your purpose is? What journey do you believe is the right one for you? The only way you will accomplish great things in your life will be to believe, to KNOW without doubt that what you DESIRE will happen for you.

Take the time to make yourself answer the difficult questions of life such as those I posed to you at the beginning of this book. Give yourself the gift of a turning point in your life. Find your purpose and be clear with yourself about who you are right now, and who you want to be as you grow. You are either rich or you are not. You are in shape or not in shape. You are either focused or you are not. Face up to what is, so that you can make good decisions about what can and will be. Then let "what is" go. *THE ACTION SANDWICH*, as I mentioned, is already working for you regardless of whether you are aware of it or not. It works for the good guys and it works for the bad guys and it also works for the indifferent. The only difference is the outcome. The pathway you choose to take towards the outcome is what is important. Did I know with certainty that when I chose to be a musician I would write one, three, seven or ten hit songs? Would I earn $100 or $100,000 or even $10,000,000? Of course I did not know. Did Wayne Gretzky know for certain that he was going to be known as the greatest to ever play the game of hockey? I say no. However, what I am certain of was that both he and I and all other successful people are on the right pathway to our successes and that everything else like the money, the fame and the accolades are all just by-products of that BELIEF in our choices and in ourselves.

> *"Sometimes I've believed as many as six*
> *impossible things before breakfast."*
> LEWIS CARROLL

Please remember that money is a natural outcome but it is not a life force and deserves only the attention that is required to use it for its intended purpose. Don't focus on it, fret over it or pine for it. (Try not to steal it either!) It is inanimate. Your real currency is your thoughts, because they attract more in kind and inspire you to make the moves in your life that bring inanimate objects like money, cars and houses to you. If your thoughts are constantly on the next achievable step, and they are moving you towards your ultimate goal, then each expectation of accomplishment will ultimately take you there.

Here is something I find truly fascinating. Have you ever heard anyone talking negatively about something they truly believe in, even if the outcome is something negative? Sound confusing? It isn't really. Let's say the topic is a negative one like "I believe I am too fat and I believe that I will never be thin." It is usually said with such positive conviction that the person saying it succeeds in their BELIEF, thus staying fat. You see they are using the rules of the game and are mapping out their destiny. *THE ACTION SANDWICH* is working just as hard for them in keeping them exactly where they have decided they belong as it does for overweight people who truly believe that their purpose is to lose weight and will take the necessary steps to accomplish that. You must eliminate the power of any thought, ACTION or person in your life that does not inspire you to believe in yourself and your goals. "Whether you believe you can or you can't, you're right!" said Henry Ford. Truer words were never spoken.

I want to go back briefly to what I call "victim-speak" and share with you a true story and a classic case of someone whose BELIEF system is so far out of whack that she abandoned her journey and her purpose long ago.

I recently chatted with a room full of prospective business owners in a small town in Ontario, Canada. During my break I chatted with a woman who was sitting in a chair that was no more than fifty feet from the room where the conference was taking place. Within two minutes of saying hello to me she was telling me how dull her life was pouring coffee and waiting tables in a diner. She lived alone with three dogs and said she wasn't pretty enough to meet someone. She believed that everyone else had it good while she did not. Then she said something very interesting – to me it was like a siren going off. She said that nothing ever happened around these parts, and the only thing worth doing was saving her money because there wasn't much out there to spend it on. I told her there were a whole bunch of people just like her in the other room finding out about the possibility of taking their capital and applying it to owning their own businesses. I mentioned that perhaps she could look into that idea for herself.

I was getting excited for her. Here she was just a short walk from an opportunity, or at least on the edge of what she could turn into a life-changing thought process. But then she did what so many often do. She discounted the idea that she could have a better life. Even though I thought she could improve her life, she didn't want to hear me or believe me. "Are you kidding?" she said. "Me, own my own business? Get real, I'm not smart enough to do that!" As she put on her coat and prepared to leave I got bold enough to ask her a question that was burning in my brain. "If you don't mind me asking, just how much have you managed to save over the years as a waitress?" With her back to me, and already well on her way to the sliding doors she answered back, "About seventy-five thousand dollars," and toddled off.

Seventy-five thousand dollars?! Empires have been built on less. My father, in all of his eighty-six years, never saw that much money in one lump, and he probably earned the better part of a million dollars in weekly wages, maybe even more if we took the time to try and add them all up. No, this woman was smart enough, frugal enough, disciplined enough and dedicated enough to save seventy-five thousand dollars, yet could not conceive remotely of the notion of taking control of the helm of her own life. What a tragedy. She couldn't walk the twenty steps to hear about an opportunity or even spend the thirty minutes to explore it or the positive ideas that may have come from it. This woman did not recognize the most fundamental truth. Everything she needed to be successful, she already had within her. If her choice is to believe in herself, then the sky truly is the limit. If not, then it merely is limited.

It takes as much energy to believe you CAN'T as it does to believe you CAN. As you learn to be positive, it will become even clearer to you just how exhausting it is to be around negative people. Their flaccid personalities will have you wanting to shout, "Make it stop!" You can feel the life force draining out of you as they speak with jaundiced enthusiasm about the gloominess and "doominess" of life.

YOU'LL FIND THAT LIFE IS STILL WORTHWHILE, IF YOU JUST SMILE

"Te audire no possum,
musa sapienum fixa est in aura."

To this day I am fascinated by people who can find the ability to laugh at themselves or are able to find humour in some kind of drastic situation or disaster. Brits and those from the Republic of Ireland seem to be particularly adept at this. Give them long enough and they'll find the funny side of virtually anything. I like to think of it as part of the therapy that we call healing. It bonds us with those sharing our pain and also with those that we may have lost. Most recently, my father's passing on Aug 11, 2006, exemplified this notion when after his funeral people were coming up to me and saying, "Alan, please don't take this the wrong way, but I had a great time! This is the best funeral I have ever been to!" My father would have loved that, and of course is probably a bit pissed off that he wasn't there. Humour in the face of tragedy has been a part not only of legendary careers but also part of the everyday lives of countless folk just like, well, these three for starters.

Murphy and Fagan are standing outside Patrick O'Reilly's little hobbit-sized home in the middle of nowhere, Ireland. O'Reilly is on his deathbed and the lads are here for a visit to cheer him up.

"Now whatever you do Fagan," says Murphy, "don't mention the words death or dying now, ye hear, 'cuz Paddy doesn't know that he's dying see, and we don't want to give him any terrible thoughts or ideas."
"Aye of course I won't," says Fagan. "You won't hear them from me lips."
And so they head on into the tiny cottage, ducking as they go because their height causes them great difficulty to move with any ease. As they sit by the bedside, O'Reilly is a mere skeleton of a man, weak, feeble but quiet and content to hear from his two old pals.
"Sure yer lookin' good, man," says Murphy
"Aye, grand," says Fagan. "Why, I'll bet you'll make the bingo this Friday night coming, don't you think so Murph?"
"Why sure 'n' all, I declare he will."

This goes on for quite some time and indeed O'Reilly seems to be almost picking up his spirits from all of the positive feedback he's been receiving. But soon it is time to leave and the boys prepare to say farewell.

"Well, Patrick, we must be off, but we will see you at bingo Friday, never fear. And remember to wear your tie boy'o for we're off to the pub and the dancing afterwards with all of our winnings."
"Right, we're off then, Patrick."

The two men stand quickly and Fagan completely forgets about the need to duck and so when his head buries itself into the ceiling above with a mighty thud, he blurts out...........mhm"Jaayzus boy, how in the name of God are we ever going to get a coffin oot o' here?"

Laughing in the face of adversity is precisely how I handled having to look constantly into the face of anger as a child growing up. I laughed at it. I sang to it. I played and I believed.

But what was there to possibly believe in, in a place filled with such bitterness? I guarantee you that if you go to Iraq right this minute that somewhere, some way and somehow good and decent people are finding a way to still laugh and to smile and cheer each other up all in the face of such unbelievable horror. May their God love them, for they certainly deserve it.

So I refused as a boy to believe that everything had to be dark and frightening and angry and violent. I NEVER conformed, ever. It is not within my nature to stay connected to indifference and anger and pain. Of course, as a youngster I listened to those around me and said that I believed what THEY believed, and so as the songs were sung and the battles were fought we children too had our heels dug in and lines drawn in the sand.

"Proddy dogs eat the frogs," they would say with all the venom they could muster.
"Catholic cats eat the rats!" was always the reply.

And so when elders teach children that dying for a cause such as for "God and for Ulster!" or for "God and for Ireland" is worthwhile, they believe it. Funny how poor God always seems to get roped into all of this mayhem isn't it? But throughout all of this bigotry I still had pals who were Catholic and the extent of my mayhem was usually no worse than a wrestling match or a bloody nose. Best of all, I would befriend my enemies, make them my BEST pals and then teach them songs, Protestant songs. THEN I would tell them to go in and sing for their mums and dads as I watched through the window. It never failed.

"Alan Frew, I will kick your arse. Get back here!"

And so the chase would ensue, with me running like the hammers of hell with somebody's mammy chasing me with some object that would "brain" me if ever they caught me... they NEVER caught me. That doesn't mean however I was never caught. Word would spread to my house and inevitably my mother or father would be waiting for me.

My mother did most of the spanking. I liked that. Why in the world would I say that I liked my mother doing the spanking? Well, it meant that my dad wasn't doing it, for when my father spanked it was always memorable. When he was after me I would stand out front near our little gate by the street, while he stood in our front doorway. Usually I had done something *trivial* like hitting a lamppost with a hammer. The kind of lamppost that hums when you put your ear to it and contains all those meaningless electrical wires and stuff that short circuits the entire neighbourhood when hit by a hammer, leaving every bugger in the dark part of town even darker. *That* lamppost. The kind that can get your parents prosecuted for damages to government property.

"Get in here," he would command.
"Nope."
"Alan, get in here now!"
"You'll hit me!" I would reply.
"I won't hit you." He would say unconvincingly.
"Aye, you will!!"

This seesaw of words would continue until he would vanish back inside. From my vantage point, I could see the open door of our little washroom beckoning me to safety. I would run like a bugger, similar to one of those poor bloody wildebeests, trying to make it across the flooded plains of the Serengeti, all the while trying desperately to not become an afternoon snack for some famished predator. Nine times out of ten I would be way too fast and much too slippery for "the hand" that would emerge just as I was passing by the living room door. But he had to nab me only once and this little "wildebeest" would find it very difficult to sit on his "Serengeti" for quite some time.

My mother on the other hand "cuffed" my ear almost daily. Doctor Goldie our family physician, examining me:
"Mrs. Frew, do you ever hit your son?"

My mother: "Just with my hands, doctor."

She never ever hurt me. Come to think of it, she couldn't stop talking long enough to give you a good one because she always liked to tell you why you were getting hit as you were getting hit.

"See (hit) you (slap, slap) ya wee (hit, slap) shite, (hit) that was (hit, hit, hit) my favourite hat (slap, hit, slap) you gave away (hit) to those Gypsies (hit, hit, hit, hit, hit)."
Time out.
Puff cigarette.
Continue: "It's ruined (hit, slap) because they cut holes in it (slap) to fit it over the ears (hit, slap, hit) of their donkey!!"

My granny on the other hand was a combination of my mother and my father. Standing all of four foot six inches, she was a human dynamo. She had the talk-as-you-slap-ACTION down to an art, but always ended with her secret weapon, a crescendo of arse-numbing whacks, bumps and thumps, ranging from kicking you with her woolly-slippered toe, to hacking at you with whatever was within her diminutive reach. A book, a boot, a rolling pin, a chair or a dog, it didn't matter because if she could pick it up, you were getting hit with it. Fending her off took an entirely different strategy, and I came up with some sheer artistry.

The best one ever, came after watching one of my favourite movies, like *Bataan* or *The Sands of Iwo Jima*. I went out into the back yard to dig a hole, not just any old hole mind you, this one was like the Japanese soldiers dug during jungle warfare, (minus, of course, the spikes in the bottom that would normally be used to capture and kill elephants, tigers or American soldiers). They would cover them with twigs, leaves and dirt and await the enemy or victim. Yes this was a special kind of hole; this was a J.J.G.T, A Japanese Jungle Granny Trap.

When I was an infant, my father cared about his garden. When I was a toddler, he cared somewhat less. Later, when I was a boy, he just didn't care at all, and thus provided me with my very own private jungle just outside my kitchen window, which was probably an aesthetic nightmare for our neighbours. But for a boy it was nothing short of marvelous!

So take one smart remark bestowed upon one axe-murdering granny, then run like hell. She usually gave chase, but not for long. On one particular occasion however she was relentless for not only did she chase me down our garden path and out the gate, she followed me all the way across the street and into Mrs. McDougall's front garden.

"Hello Mrs. McDougall," said I to the wee head sticking out her kitchen window.
"You'll never make it!" she calls to me with mirth. Then to my granny she calls out, "Do you want me to set Kim on him Chrissie?"
Kim was her big black slobbering mongrel killer-dog that bullied and terrified our entire neighbourhood. The animal however was afraid of only one person, and *SHE* was chasing me!
"No, it's okay Iza," says my granny. "I'll get 'im."

I ran back through the front gate but she was still on my tail. I headed for my jungle and the large bush beside the shed, yes *that* shed, the one I will set on fire a bit later in my life. Is she gone? Nope. Okay, drastic measures. A little "deke" to the left, a quick head fake to the right. That's it, let her almost grab you. Closer, closer...RECEPTIVITY to the fact she'll kill you if she gets you, DESIRE not to get caught, BELIEF in your skills at hiding holes, INTENTION meet ACTION...and...
"There she goes ladies and gentlemen, right down the old Japanese Jungle Granny Trap!" *THE ACTION SANDWICH* strikes again!

Like an old vinyl record with its needle stuck, I repeat. Do what you do because you're meant to do it. Do it because you can and because you love it. By following the path in front of you and focusing on where you're going rather than where you have been, you are sowing seeds for the future, for there is ALWAYS a future.

WITH OR WITHOUT YOU

God bless you Mrs. Biggart, you old bastard! For if it wasn't for you and that bloody umbrella I would never have been in Rock 'n Roll.

It's 1965 and I am told, not asked, that it is time for me to join the youth division of The Orange Order, a Protestant fraternal organization founded in Loughgall, County Armagh, Ireland in 1795, the same year Coronation Street first aired. The "Juveniles," as they are called, took part in many of the marches, the major one taking place each year on the twelfth of July to commemorate the outcome of the famous Battle of Boyne, which occurred in 1690 when protestant King William III defeated Catholic King James II. Coincidentally, 1690 is the same year that Scotland last qualified for the World Cup. Look it up if you don't believe me.

Interesting how most of the crap that the world is still entrenched in today almost always seems to stem from the antiquated wounds and principles from those of centuries and indeed millennia ago.

Anyway, there I am all dressed up in my best duds and I am told that I am going to be one of four kids having the honour of carrying one of four cords attached to a huge decorative banner identifying the branch of the fraternity which in turn is to be carried by two strong men from the Lodge. If you were to ask me what the images on the banner were symbolic of, I would not be able to tell you because it all comes from the hidden world of secret societies and secret hand shakes. God knows I still get a kick out of chatting with the funny handshake club members like the Freemasons and Lodge guys. I have family and friends to this day who are members and in fact two of my best pals in the whole world, *Brother Bryce* and *Brother Kenny*, are members.

Me: "So what does that symbol mean?"
Them: "Join and find out."
Me: "C'mon, I won't tell on you, it's a riddle right? What's the big secret?"
Them: "Well for starters, it's *not* a secret, because the truth is that the answers

to the symbol, in fact to *all* of our symbols are right in the Bible!"

They make it sound so simple. Just match the symbol to the significant clue in the Bible – easy, peasy. Now let's see, the banner's symbol is a painting of a young virginal woman, with one eye in the middle of her forehead and she is dressed in a long, flowing robe, one breast exposed, and she is standing on one of the heads of a six-headed ram. In her left hand she's carrying a sword, while in her right she is holding a book with the word "Freedom" on its cover, only it's upside down – the word that is, not the book. Behind her is a dragon standing on one foot and in the talons of the other foot is a serpent that has an upside-down pyramid on its head and blood pouring from its mouth. Two eagles are flying above them, one has fire coming from its ears while the other has just dropped twin baby boys from the sky and, miraculously, they appear to be landing safely on the branch of an apple tree that has one apple hanging on it. All the other apples have fallen to the ground and are being devoured by a one-eyed white tiger, which appears to be smiling right at you.

So you open up the Bible and immediately say, "right, there it is, that's smashing, okie-dokie, I've got it then, thanks. I'll just get going now." I mean get a grip lads, I can't even find Waldo. Give me a break.

Right then, so we have the banner, the men, the cords and the kids and with the responsibility of carrying the cord comes "Your best behaviour!"

"Right you are, Mrs. Biggart. My best behaviour."
"The single most frowned-upon crime that a boy can commit," she says in a flurry of spit, "is dancing and swinging that cord to the sound of the band. Do you understand me, ALAN FREW?"
Why is she singling me out? It's not like I'll do anything wrong. Hold on! We're off. And a left, left, left right, left.

The parade consisted of a large flute band followed by a lot of people in bow ties and bowler hats followed by big heavy banners carried by large sweaty men. They were surrounded by children being chaperoned by Helga the S.S. Queen, formally known as Mrs. Biggart, followed by hundreds more bow ties, bowler hats, kids with cords, and chaperones who are all being followed by thousands of the general public. Of course, there was the occasional detractor popping his or her head out the window to shout abuse at you or empty out the potty filled with the morning's constitutional. All very civilized, wouldn't you say?

"What's that sound? It's drums and flutes. That's magical and I like it, yes, I do. I like that very much. It makes me want to, waggle my bum a wee bit. Look at me, for I've got a skip in my step. This is great. Let's see what I can do with this corrrr..."

"BANG!"
"What the hell was *that*? Good God, I'm blind and deaf and if I'm not mistaken I think I've also pissed myself!"
Helga's umbrella had entered my ear with a crushing thud, sending it on its way to somewhere other than Coatbridge. And as if that's not bad enough, here comes the craziest part. No one cared. Not one single solitary soul gave a monkey's damn about me, my ear, or the fact that I was nine years of age lying on the ground with a bleeding ear drum and the perpetrator of the crime was this old drill sergeant five times my age and twenty times my size!

"What did he do then?" says the bowler hat.
"He swung the cord Alec! THAT is what he did. So I just had to put him down!" says Helga.
"Right you are then," says the hat. "Keep moving!"
"You heard the Grand Master then, young Frew. Keep moving!"

And move I did, off like the clappers as fast as my wee legs would carry me, much to the consternation of Helga and the bowler hat. But do you know what? I remember it now as if it was yesterday. The second the umbrella attempted to introduce itself to the grey matter of my brain via my ear canal, and I felt like someone just stuck my head into a pan of frying chips, two thoughts came to mind instantaneously. One was, "Oooooooooohhhhhhhhya baaaaastaaaaard!" And the other?
"Piss on this. I am joining the band!"

And so I did. I decided right there and then that if I could not beat them, they could follow me. And so it was that I took up the flute immediately and never went back to the lodge, ever. And so was born my musical career, thanks to a cord, a maniac and an umbrella.

If you don't love it, then don't do it. If you don't believe it, then it cannot happen. Never did it occur to me that I was destined to stay in that place, with those people. I always knew that one day I was going to leave it behind. And do you know why? The answer is simple. I believed.

"You Can't Always Get What You Want"
MICK JAGGER

"Yes You Can"
ALAN FREW

One of the fundamental yet most often misunderstood and unaccepted laws of the universe is this: "What I think about, I get." Well, I have news for you – IT'S TRUE. What you DO indeed think about you WILL indeed get. Now this doesn't mean that if you think about a cool million in cold hard cash, you'll wake up to find it lying beside the bed in the morning. What it means is that if your focus and your energy are applied positively toward the BELIEF and worthiness of wanting something (yes, even a cool million) as opposed to being applied to all of the reasons why you cannot or should not have it, it stands to reason that you at least have a fighting chance of figuring out the ACTION required to get a million dollars. Some people, when asked why they play the lotteries against such seemingly insurmountable odds reply, "If you don't buy a ticket, you cannot win." Well, you know what folks? In that, they are 100% correct. So I ask you this, if you don't believe that you can ever have a million dollars or if you don't believe you are worthy enough for a million dollars (or, for that matter, a dollar) then how can you ever possibly get it? Surely if I focus all of my energy on never having something then I will succeed and never have it. It is the focusing on and the sending out of energy from within me that says, "I want, I deserve, I am worthy of and I believe that I can and will have," that sets me up for answers that will direct me to the

ACTION I need to take in order to set off on the required pathway to my DESIRE of anything at all, never mind a million bucks. Think of it like sending a telegram, making a phone call, or like hitting the send button on your email. Of course this may require a leap of faith on your part, but ask any successful person about leaps of faith and I am positive you'll get a mountain of answers regarding when they took theirs.

Have you ever noticed how you feel when things just seem to be going your way all the time? Funny isn't it? You start wondering and questioning why this is so. "What did I do to deserve this?" you ask. But I ask you: can it possibly be just coincidence and luck and just plain old good fortune every single time something great happens to you? Conversely, is it simply coincidence and bad luck when things go wrong all of the time? No it is not. You ARE creating it, all of it, the good, the bad, the ugly and the indifferent.

Look, it's easy. If the mailman came to your front door with a smile on his face, and gave you a pleasant, "Good morning," and you said "Bug off! Leave me alone!", he probably would and you would get what you want. If you did the same to every single colleague at work, you would get the same result. If you went on a local radio station and told all the listeners the same thing, you would again get the same response. National television? Ditto.

Energy. It's ALL energy. The energy of communication, which includes what you are thinking, what energy you are "giving off" or "sending out" to the universe, received by the energy of others, the human listener, in fact the universal listener, which is simply the gateway to telling the world to give you what you're asking for.

We all, at one time or another, have had the feeling that someone was giving off a bad vibe without even really knowing them or perhaps without them having even spoken to us. Have you ever returned from an event or perhaps a meeting to be asked, "So how was it?" and found yourself replying, "Hmm there was a weird vibe in the room. It felt hostile yet nothing bad actually happened?" What is that? Coincidence? Bad luck? Of course not; it's energy. You can't deny it, can you? So why believe it of others and not of yourself?

Focus your thoughts and your energy with the same care you would give your bank account and if you don't have a bank account worth talking about, then focus on fixing that. Just concentrate on what you want. If you are thinking about some "thing" that you DESIRE, then you are going to get *something* back in return. However, if you're thinking about nothing, or the lack of something, then guess what you're going to get? Hmmm, where the hell's that lottery ticket? I know I put it here somewhere.

Once you declare your BELIEF in something, you WILL be challenged. You can count on it. People will challenge you, and so will life. There is a phenomenon that happens as soon as you say, "I believe" – something or someone will come along to challenge the depth of your commitment. This challenge is there to help you. Defending your beliefs and having to stay the course through thick and thin reinforces your resolve, which benefits all areas of your journey. A little leap of faith perhaps?

Believe that you can have it, do it, deserve it, and are entitled to it and it shall be. Surround yourself with people who have strength and their strength will be yours to draw on. Avoid the toxic nature of others, as their weakness will become a part of you and will drain your strength. People like Nelson Mandela, Deepak Chopra, Richard Branson, Angelina Jolie and Mother Theresa are role models of tremendous strength. What do highly successful people possess that attracts more success? I believe they channel the same force that was powerful enough to take a pinpoint single bang and turn it into a sprawling universe some twenty billion light years across. To some, it is God and I respect that with all of my conviction. I believe it is the same force that brings a man and woman together and creates a beautiful newborn child, or that transforms the caterpillar into a butterfly. Sound heavy? It is. Welcome to the world of INTENTION.

TEN STEPS TO BELIEF

1. YOU GOTTA HAVE FAITH - Go on, dare to believe in something wonderful. What's stopping you? You may get disappointed? You may believe in something that doesn't happen? So what, change your tactics and try again and again if need be. BELIEF in nothing is nothing. So believe.

2. PLAY BALL! - Hit the ball three times out of ten and you're a Hall Of Famer. I have had about 10 hit songs in my life yet I have written a thousand! Missing the mark and rejection are a part of success. How many strikeouts did Babe Ruth have, or game winning shots did Michael Jordan miss? How many light bulbs never lit up for Edison and yet they rank as three of the world's greatest believers. Never quit.

3. I AM, YOU AM, HECK! WE ALL AM - Don't wander aimlessly without questioning who you are and what it is you truly believe about this world and your place in it. Take an inventory of what you have to offer, your gifts, your skills and your talents. Believe in and nurture each thing on that list no matter how small it may seem. Honour your BELIEF.

4. IMAGINE - Visualize the outcome you DESIRE in your mind before it arrives. Create the picture and set an anchor to it. Make it strong, passionate, healthy, and the most beautiful thing you have ever seen. Taste, smell, hear and feel it all for this is what it will be like when you get there. Put yourself in the picture. Click.

5. HEY JUDE, DON'T MAKE IT BAD - Take a sad song and make it better. Does your inside voice tell you that you are too old, too fat, too broke or too late? If so then you must fight it,

argue with it and tell it to get lost. This is non-negotiable. Lose this voice, or lose.

6. I'M JAKE THE PEG - If you have a deep conviction about something then nourish it with the highest regard. Step outside the circle and find your own truth. If society says you are trying to fit a square peg into a round hole then so be it. It's your peg.

7. 10, JACK, QUEEN, KING...? - Don't be wishy-washy. Take a leap of faith, even if that leap is small. Get used to experiencing what that leap feels like because one day the stakes are going to be much higher and in order to turn over the ace you'll need faith in spades. Ready, jump!

8. KEEP YOUR EYES ON THE ROAD - Money and the things it can bring are by-products of being on the right pathway. Do you want lots of money and things? I do. Focus on the highway not the destination and let the means by which you arrive be the universe's job. Life really *is* a highway.

9. THIRTY-DAYS HATH SEPTEMBER - Life and death, fear and calm, happiness and sadness, are all just extreme ends of the same energy. All required, all necessary, all normal. Stay on your path and focus on living your life each day. In 30 days you will have had the best month of your life. In twelve of those months…you know the rest. Being alive and living each day are two different things. Know the difference.

10. BUT TOMORROW MAY RAIN SO… - Change is frightening but completely reliable. You may not realize it at the time through the anger, tears or sense of loss, but change can be a gift. Look deeper and turn it into an opportunity. Embrace it.

MY SONG
Opus 3

THERE'S A WHAT IN MY BUCKET?

On my first day at the hospital, I was notified that we were short three orderlies, due to two quitting and one being fired. They were so understaffed that I was asked to start immediately in on-floor training, as opposed to the two or three weeks of orientation and classroom studies normally afforded a new employee. In my case, Jake, the head orderly trained me as I just stood by his side watching. Now this may not seem like a big deal to you but can you non-medical folk out there imagine that you are told to leave your office, or department store, or perfumery or whatever line of work you are in and go immediately to the city hospital, whereupon you are then told to go into a patient's room and shave and prep his groin for a hernia operation? Oh, and just for good measure, you are to also give him an enema! Still think it's no big deal? One minute you're a grocery clerk or a bank teller (or a tube cutter) and instantaneously without any classroom instruction you are actually doing these kinds of things! It seemed madly surreal, yet it was my baptism. So there I was, fresh from factory work, dressed in whites, doing things so unbelievably foreign to me that I was dazed and confused by the whole thing. Here's a doozey. Near the end of my first shift, Jake's pager went off so he called to receive instructions from the switchboard.

"Right, okay, will do," says Jake and he hangs up the phone.

"What is it?" says the ex-tube-cutter.

"They want an orderly to go to the operating room and pick up a specimen to be taken down to the morgue for disposal."

Now dear reader, although this activity was to become second nature to me, on this day, this my very first day, I was petrified that he might say, something crazy like he wanted me to do it.

"I want you to do it."

"What?" I replied shakily.

"I want you to go pick up the specimen, take it downstairs to the morgue and place it inside the freezer. It's your job," said Jake very matter-of-fact.

"ME?"

"Yes...you... now get going!"

That wasn't a question, so off I went to the operating room sweating profusely as I cursed myself for being so diligent with my calls to this place. This antiseptic filled, clinical, medicinal place, where they give ex-tube-cutters "things" in buckets to take down to a place where they keep dead people!

"Oh no! What in the name of the wee man have you gotten yourself into?" asked the voice inside my head.

"The hospital," I replied.

Suddenly the voice inside that cranium of mine burst into guffaws of laughter.

The bucket I held in my hand was of average size. It was white. It was opaque. It made a sound, a squishy, slop-slop sound that intensified as I walked. It sounded positively icky.

"What in hell's bells is in this bucket? What is this thing?"

SLOP-SLOP-SLOP.

I entered the elevator on the fourth floor. There was one person on board.

"Hello," she said.

SLOP-SLOP-SLOP

"Hello," I replied, quietly.

"And just what do you have there?"
"I don't know, they didn't tell me."

The door to the elevator opened on the third floor and as she exited she said,

"Hmmm, curiosity would kill me. If I were you I would just have to look inside. Bye now!"

The doors closed and the elevator resumed its journey to take me to the basement.

"No, I can't, I said to myself. I can't just open it... can I? That would be wrong, wouldn't it?"

SLOP, SLOP, SLOP, I couldn't stand it. It was killing me. I just had to peek.

Slowly, ever so slowly I pried the lid up. I closed my eyes until they were little slits, as if squinting would help me.

SLOP-SLOP-SLOP.

"Okay", I told myself. "On the count of three, open your eyes and look. Are you ready? I'm ready. Here we go. ONE...TWO...THREE...Oh dear God, it's a... "

FATHER AND SON

"Zeppelin!!"

"C'mon man, do some Zeppelin will ya?"

The battle cry of the masses roared, the bar-crowd the audience.

What of course they were really saying was, "I don't give a shit about you and your original songs, play me something I know!"

The bar owners didn't help matters either, for they loathed original material even more than the patrons did. The idea of a band trying out original material only meant fewer patrons, which of course equals less beer and liquor sales. The bottom line was if you want to work here, play music by bands that already have hits on the radio. By now I was a fully-fledged orderly in a hospital working days instead of the graveyard shift, so I was also back taking gigs and playing for the 70s generation, the one that made John Travolta, and *Pet Rocks* famous. Now you younger readers probably think I am speaking of a band by that name, however I am in fact referring to the 1970s fad conceived by a California advertising executive who sold ordinary gray pebbles bought at a builder's supply store as pets.

Each "creature" came accompanied by a training manual, with instructions on how to properly raise and care for one's newfound pet. The people who purchased them usually gave them names, talked openly to them, petted them, and then said that they were teaching them to perform simple tricks. Mercifully, the fad lasted only about six months, but it held in long enough to make the creator a millionaire.

We had left the swinging '60s and entered the super '70s and unless you played *Zeppelin*, *Hendrix*, *Fleetwood Mac* or *Foreigner* bar owners simply did not care. I had also married my childhood sweetheart at the ripe old age of 19 without anyone of maturity stepping forward to try and bring me to my senses by telling me that I was still a kid, growing, developing and hopefully maturing. We tried to be man and wife at 19 and 17 respectively, I holding down a full time job as an orderly while singing and performing in bars. It was a very stressful time for a young couple of such tender years. We struggled. We struggled hard and just when it seemed like it couldn't get any tougher...it did.

"Push, c'mon, you can do it...P-U-S-H! That's it, that's it, there we go!"

"Congratulations! You have a son!"

It was 1979 and I had been slogging it out now as the Rock Star orderly for going on four years becoming depleted, worn out and broke. The music scene wasn't paying me but costing me, as the bills and the debt were mounting. To emphasize just how bad it was, on the very evening that my son came into the world, the bass player was waiting for me in the maternity ward because we had to drive to a town in Quebec obligated by contract to perform in some flea bag pub, leaving my wife and not yet two hour old son at home.

Meanwhile back at the hospital something interesting was brewing. Upon my return I was asked if I would like to go on down to the morgue and witness an autopsy, something that not only fascinated me but also gave me a leg up (pardon the pun) on the biology needed for my quest to become a doctor. I readily agreed. I had seen numerous autopsies by this time and had witnessed death first hand throughout my four years on staff, so off I went to the place where I had taken that little bucket on my very first day. You know, the one containing that...oh never mind. So when I got there I was asked to gown-up and within minutes I was receiving requests from the pathologist.

"Hold this please."
"Grab that, would you?"
"Can you hand that to me? Thanks."

Shortly thereafter the doctor asked me if I felt I was cut out (again with the puns) to do the job of assisting him and his colleague due to the retirement of their regular assistant. I told him of my goal to one day attend medical school and he assured me that he would always leave the most interesting autopsies to last so that he could take the time to teach me as much as possible.

"You have a deal," I said shaking his hand.

So now the plastic molding, tube cutting, orderly, Rock Star... was "Cadaver Man!"

This was a turning point for me in more ways than one, because it was at this point I threw in the towel, waved the white flag in the face of Rock 'n Roll and said, "I surrender!" Or so I thought.

I called it quits. Enough already, although things were dodgy at home and my wife and I were really just like acquaintances. I adored my son and wanted him to have his daddy around full time. I told my wife that I was quitting music for good, told her that I was going to apply to nursing college as a mature student and that along with my orderly experience and autopsy experience I felt I was a shoo-in to get accepted. She, on the other hand told me she was moving out.

It was of no real surprise to me that the break up had come, for we were living separate existences, with separate friends and interests. I was however a little bruised in the macho department, due to her being the one to say, "I'm outta here!" My ego got the better of me and talked me into saying something ridiculous like, "Well I'm telling you, if you go out that door, then there's no coming back!" (I cringe, even now just writing this).

And so off she went to her new life and off I went to nursing college, never the twain to meet, but alas, she had my son with her and that was a dagger in my heart. True love has no boundaries, walls cannot contain it nor keep it from penetrating, and the love I had for that baby boy was all of that and more. I made up my mind right there and then, that not only was I going to be a doctor but that I would not lose him in the process. I knew in my heart I would undoubtedly be the better parent for my son. I decided in my mind that he was coming to live with me. I was of course told by many that I had no chance of fighting a system, which in 1979 could not comprehend giving custody of a child to a father when the mother was available to give care, but nevertheless in my mind, he was going to live with me. My RECEPTIVITY, DESIRE, BELIEF, INTENTION and of course my ACTIONS were of a man who had his son living with him as a single parent and so that is what I told the universe. It was non-negotiable.

So let's see, I'm broke due to the fact that my student loans are garnisheed to cover debts that my band has incurred. I'm a full time student again at age 23 in a school with 300 females (that's another book entirely). I'm holding down a full-time job as an orderly and a part-time job as a pathologist's assistant. I see my son only by popping into his mother's home every day on my way home from school and on my way to work to then begin an eight-hour shift until midnight. I've moved back in with my parents. What the hell else could possibly happen?

"Alan?"
"Yeah."
"It's Wayne."
"Yeah."
"Sittin' down?"
"No."
"Could you?"
"Yeah."
"Are you?"
"No."
"Will you?"
"Yeah."

"Ready?"

"No."

"Wanna join a band..."

Was he insane? He had to be. I had just given that all up. It had drained me dry, physically, emotionally, mentally and financially. I had popped pills, smoked pot, drank like a fish, not to mention lived with people I didn't even know and taken bubble baths all in the name of Rock 'n Roll.

"Just come and meet them," said Wayne. "That's all I'm asking. Just a meeting."

How could I not say no?

I was supposed to say no. You must say no.

Go on, say no.

"Yeah, Okay, I'll meet them."

PASSION. Pain and suffering. How prophetic. Needless to say I met with them and I sang for them.

The singer, "Okay, I'll join your band, but on one condition."
The band, "What's that?"
The singer, "That it's just a hobby for I am never going back on the road!"
The band, "Okay, great!"

So now the nursing student, autopsy assisting, single dad is also a rock 'n' roll singer in a band....again.

I'M SO TIRED

I graduated from nursing college in 1982 and was given a full-time job on day shift as Alan Frew R.N. I was and still am very proud of those letters.

In the meantime I had faithfully visited with my son on every possible occasion, so much so that my soon to be ex-wife was now very comfortable with me having him stay at my place every available chance. My work was certainly cut out for me now. I was working dayshifts that included rotations of seven straight shifts in a row at times. My band was working full time at night, Monday through Saturday. I was also being called in on Saturday and Sunday mornings to assist in autopsies. It was a frantic pace. Death on two legs actually and something had to give. A typical week had me going into work for 6:30 a.m. and working in an already overworked, under staffed environment and finishing at a frantic pace somewhere around 4:30 p.m.

I would then pop in my car and drive over to see my son for one hour before hopping back in the car and driving up to wherever we happened to be gigging that particular evening. Sometimes the gig might be as far away as a two-hour drive. Typically we would go on around 9 p.m. and finish around 1:30 a.m., at which time I would get in my car, drive back home, get in around 4 a.m. only to sleep "upright" on a comfy chair until my alarm went off at 6:00 a.m., at which time I would splash water on my face throw on some clean clothes and head back to the hospital to begin it all over again. Tell me, can you see the train wreck coming?

I had met my wife as a fifteen year old when I myself was only seventeen. We dated, we married and we split. We had a beautiful boy who by now was spending more and more time at the home of my parents and myself. After our separation, she was finding more and more joy in going out on weekends and partying, content in the knowledge that our son was at my home as opposed to being in the hands of a babysitter. The periods that he would be with us, would stretch longer and longer until one day I suggested that he stay with me and that she could come by anytime she chose to see him or pick him up. She agreed, and the living arrangements changed which made me extremely happy on the inside even though by now I was killing myself with work.

It seemed like I was always awake, either while nursing, singing or dissecting some poor soul who had met his demise the night before. It was relentless. On one occasion I was with a patient and the last thing I remember was leaving the room to grab a face cloth.

"Can I help you Alan?" said the voice.
"Suddenly I stirred from what seemed like a deep sleep."
"Are you ok? Can I help you with something?" she said again.
I found myself behind a curtain of a patient's bed area. There was a nurse from a completely different floor attending to an elderly woman. I did not recognize this patient as anyone from my floor.
"What did I do?" I asked the nurse. "What are you doing on my floor?"
"You did nothing," said the nurse. "You simply walked in here and stood there, staring and I am not on your floor, you are on mine!"

Good God, I had actually walked from my patient's room on the fifth floor, taken the elevator or the stairs and made my way to the fourth floor, entered this room all while asleep. Shaking I immediately went to my supervisor and told her I felt ill and must go home. It was a terrifying experience and I can only thank the heavens that I did nothing that led to discomfort, injury or indeed something worse for any of my patients.

On the other side of the coin the band was making great headway and I on a personal basis now had credentials that a medical school would take a look at without laughing. I had my son living with me as I had intended but what else, oh yes! Now I remember, I was coming apart.

LOOK INTO MY FATHER'S EYES

Gary Lyman Pring was a man who entered my life as a then unknown manager of decent, hardworking bands and yet by the time he left my life he was my father, or at the very least, that part of a father that I never had.

The band was officially called *Tokyo*, from a little southern Ontario town called, Newmarket, and I was never going on the road, not ever, as it was just my hobby, my side-line, for I my friends, was going to become a doctor.

This was the beginning of a new decade, the '80s, and styles were changing rapidly from the rocking '70s. Techno was happening and at a rapid pace. There was a bit of a Japanese thing going on in clothing with headbands and oriental symbols and I believe this is where our inspiration for the name *Tokyo* came from, although we loved to tell people that it was because we had heard that there was a band from Tokyo called.... "Newmarket."

We were good. We were very good. And after we worked out who the final lineup should be and who the lead singer was, and what our style would look and sound like, we started to come into our own.

Gary had asked on a handshake if he could become our manager and he told us that he would deliver us a record deal within six months or the handshake was null and void. We agreed and he went tirelessly to work on the Record Labels in Toronto. Soon *Tokyo* was packing them into the bars on the local scene and was being wooed by several major recording companies with Island Records leading the way, founded and headed by the legendary Chris Blackwell who went on to start the careers of Bob Marley, *U2*, Steve Winwood, Melissa Etheridge and *The Cranberries*.

Capitol Records who had played the wooing game, even going as far as to dedicate our own label representative to us while funding our demo's had all but resigned to the fact that Island Records had us in the bag, but they never refused an opportunity to come out and see us perform in the hopes that they might still persuade us differently. I admit I always enjoyed Capitol's company and loved sitting down at their table, partaking in their hospitality, which knew no bounds. It was decided that Blackwell himself was going to fly in from Jamaica to hear the band, just prior to putting pen to paper, a formality really, and one which the head of the Canadian label looked forward to, for he felt that after meeting the "Legend" himself, we would have no reservations signing the contract.

And so the stage was set. A small club in Bradford, Ontario would serve as our stage, for we were certainly local heroes there and the place was jammed to the rafters every time we played. Capitol Records came along that night, just in case.

Crummy little flea-ridden rooms were our dressing area, all very normal though and still a sign of our times. We hit the stage around 9pm and did a blistering set that left us invigorated, drenched in sweat, deeply satisfied and most certainly "Masters of our Domain." As the lads basked in a bit of adoration from the crowd I was quickly whisked away to meet the man himself. It was short, sweet and to the point.

He extended his hand and we shook. This was the exact moment however, that I knew that he had no INTENTION of ever putting his ACTION into signing our band to any contract.

He finished up with a few pleasantries and went on to meet the rest of the guys, before heading back in his limo to the airport and straight back to the Caribbean. I was sitting with the Capitol team having a beer, before his arse had settled into his limo seat, but how could I possibly have come to the conclusion that his words and handshake were saying two different things? Well the truth is, I don't know. Was it what I call a clammy handshake, one that seems, weak, damp and somehow deceitful? Perhaps. Or was it the sound of his voice? Did it waver or seem to stumble as he searched for what he was going to say to me? Who knows? But whatever it was he was sending out thoughts and desires and INTENTION that this meeting between us was to be the first and last and my RECEPTIVITY was picking up on all of it. My gut therefore knew full well that this was the last time that I would ever see him again at least on any professional level.

I was correct, for soon after that fateful meeting he claimed that *Tokyo* was a bit too similar to the approach they were taking with a relatively new band he was grooming from Ireland called, *U2*. A huge step at the time for a man known for his love and development of the eclectic sounds of the islands.

At the time it was a devastating blow, but I do not look back with blame or ill will regarding his decision. *U2* became the biggest band in the world and all was good for Chris Blackwell, but one of his employees, the head of Island Records Canada, never fully recovered from losing us and will tell you so to this very day. My resolve to keep going was strengthened by this affair so back to the drawing board we went while Gary made what was to become a key move. It was never about the money for Gary. It was always about the journey. As a manager he could have had us exclusively but from the beginning he had brought his day-to-day partner Joe in, and in so doing split his commissions. He was now prepared to do it again.

Gary contacted a manager in America, an Englishman, called Derek Sutton, and told him if he knew what was good for him, he would make the trip to Canada to check out this new band that he was shopping around. Derek made the trip, saw the talent and almost immediately a deal was cut between himself and Gary making Derek our International manager. It didn't take long before Capitol made a move offering us a deal but it was a somewhat like a martini for indeed it had a little twist.

Gary and his partner Joe held a conference call telling me we were to go to the boardroom of Capitol Records that day, so off I went to meet the other lads to finally put to rest where *Tokyo* was going to belong.

Walking into that building still gives me a little buzz even to this day, but back when it was still Capitol Records it felt like the home of *The Beatles*. The foyer displayed *Beatles* awards and the whole atmosphere gave me goose bumps. I was quickly ushered into the boardroom to find Gary, Joe, Tim Trombley, our record rep, and…no band. Was I just early? The atmosphere in the room told me no. Something was afoot but I did not know what. We all made small talk with comments on the weather, the hockey game and world news when Deane, who was the head of A&R (Artist and Repertoire) at the time, entered the room.

"Well did you tell him?" asked Deane matter-of-factly.
"No we were waiting for you," someone spoke up.
"Tell me what?" I asked.
"Well here it is in a nutshell Alan. We are offering you a deal. Perhaps one of the guys, I'd say perhaps the guitar player, can hang with you, maybe, but I want to send you to England to join a great musician that we have over there and we're going to build a band around you."

My mind was racing, Deane's mouth was moving but I wasn't getting it all. I knew the musician he was referring to but I also knew Deane (being an ex-drummer) had a reputation for being hard on rhythm sections and splitting bands up because he felt insecure about many of them when it came time to sign contracts.

"So you see the rhythm section just can't cut it and they gotta go. So what do you say, is it a deal?" He again sounded so calm and to the point, and yet my head was spinning.

"I uh, I am not sure what to do."
Gary looked at me and shrugged his shoulders a little.
"Your call," he said, "but I'm backing you regardless."

Deane went on to offer me a signing bonus that at the time was more money than I could make in a couple of years as a nurse. He was however expecting an answer on the spot but I just couldn't do it.

"Can I have a little time to think about it?" I asked sheepishly.
"Sure", said Deane, "But soon, okay?"
I headed from the building in silence. Instead of going with Gary and Joe for a celebratory beer, I simply told them I would catch them later.

I tried talking it over with my parents but they were too detached to be able to give me sound advice. My mother was all for me taking it because I mentioned it was good money. She never understood the music industry and always thought that being an orderly was like being a doctor and constituted a real job. Her mind just could not comprehend what was going on. My dad on the other hand, simply said, "It's up to you and you'll know what to do." Of course at the time, I didn't think I did.

I knew this band had something. I knew we were good. I cared about these guys for they had become my friends. I didn't know what game the gods were playing but I decided not to call Deane back. Gary could if he wished to but I was staying with the band. The LOVE AND SUFFERING was beginning to feel much more like suffering and suffering.

Meanwhile back at the hospital, the staff was beginning to notice changes in my behaviour. It was obvious something was up, as I had dark patches under both eyes, which were sitting just above my upper lip, a dead give away of exhaustion. I also weighed around 130lbs, if I was carrying a golf bag full of clubs to work. It was hard to decide what I wanted most at this time for I truly did love being in medicine. My patients were my family and I enjoyed giving everything I could to help them heal. To many it would be difficult to understand but I loved that clinical smell of the hospital. I loved dealing with doctors and with crisis and with the drama of life and death. I loved being with my patients, one on one on a surgical floor or a medical floor, but I shocked my fellow staff members when I told them that my next move was to take the O.R. course and become part of the Operating Room Team, still seeing myself as a surgeon somewhere down the road.

"Who does that little Scottish prick think he is? Does he not realize what I am offering him? Isn't this what he always wanted?"

Gary told me Deane was furious and ended his rant by saying that all bets were off and that Gary could take us wherever the hell he wanted. Meanwhile Derek was calling in one very big favour to one of his peers in management, a favour that would finally change the course of my life forever.

There were however just a few more twists and turns still to go on this road to LOVE AND SUFFERING.

We continued to fill every bar we played and the owners could care less if we were original or not for their beer and liquor sales were going through the roof. The occasional record company guy would pop in now and then but the ACTION had cooled off quite a bit. My son, now living with my family and I full time, had seen his mother drift off into the sunset as I had always known would be the case. On any given night the bar where we were playing would be well stocked with hospital staff who still came out in great numbers to support me, which of course pleased the rest of the lads greatly because it meant a room filled with pretty nurses. On the surface, all seemed to be going well...then I hit the wall.

It all began when Gary called to tell us some exciting news. First of all we had a gig in a club that we loved to play in a town called Oakville just west of Toronto. The gig would run Monday to Saturday as it had in the past but we all wondered what was so exciting about that. "You can use it as a rehearsal for Maple Leaf Gardens," he said enthusiastically. "Derek has us two nights opening up for *Culture Club*!"

At the time, *Culture Club* with their more than flamboyant front man
Boy George was one of the top bands in the world. They were selling
out venues everywhere and Toronto was to be no different. A complete
sellout for both nights and *Tokyo* would be there along with every major
recording label in the country. My mind shot back to the first ever
concert I attended at The Gardens, which was a double bill showcasing
Johnny Winters and the madmen from England, *Slade*. I vividly
remembered telling myself at that concert that one day I would hit that
stage and knock 'em all dead. Seems that you do have to be careful what
you tell that old universe you want because you just might get it!

Several years prior to all of this, back in my "Dr Robert's bag days" I had
tried "speed", an amphetamine (stimulant) that is now used primarily in
the treatment of narcolepsy and attention-deficit hyperactivity disorder.
"Beans" or "Bennies" as we commonly called them, turned your brain's
dial to ten. You were stimulated to the point of declaring yourself, the
best or untouchable and you went out and gave the performance of your
life. I went on stage one evening in a small town called Newcastle in
Ontario and performed like Mick Jagger's wee brother "Flash." From the
second I hit the stage I was like a jackhammer. I danced on tables and on
chairs. I grooved like the grooviest. I was on fire and nothing could stop
me. At the end of each song the crowd roared. Well I am sure the crowd
would have roared if there had been one, for you see the only two people
in the audience that evening, were the "Two Billy's," both my mates but
you see folks, beans don't care what size an audience is.

"You on beans," said Billy number one.
"Yeah! Yes! Yeah! Uh huh! That's right I am, I am, I am, Oh yeah. By
the way, how can you tell, how can you tell, can you tell?"
"Wild guess," said Billy number two.

This gig that Gary had for us had fallen on the exact same schedule as
my seven day straight hospital shift, so my schedule consisted of me
going from 6:00am to 4:00am non-stop. Working, driving, working,
driving, it was horrendous. On the Friday evening I had several friends

with me in my vehicle, including one who was visiting from Scotland so I needed to be "on." Rumour had it that several record labels were popping in, perhaps even Capitol, which I found hard to believe. The crowd was lined up for a block around the corner and the buzz in the room that night was electric. I popped a pill and then just for good measure...I popped another.

We were brilliant. Gary Pring was ecstatic about how good we were. He felt a record deal was just a matter of time. I wasn't so convinced of that when we set off in my car to return home, my nervous system on fire as I tried desperately to keep it all together, a far cry from the nervous systems of all who were crammed in beside me, for they dropped like flies almost immediately upon my starting up the engine of the car, each one falling into an alcohol induced sleep leaving me, my brain, my exhaustion and my "Beans" alone at the wheel with no one to assist in trying to keep me calm or awake.

I am sure that many of you out there have had the horrible experience of nodding off while at the wheel of a car. It leaves you palpating, shaking and discombobulated to say the least. Your eyes open and you immediately say to yourself, "Oh God, I'm driving!" You feel that you have just had some sort of "out of body" experience. Your eyes focus on the road ahead and even if not religious by nature you begin thanking heavens that at least you didn't hit a...
"WALL!"
"ALAN!"... A WALL!" someone screamed in my ear.

My eyes opened some twenty feet or so from the brick walled siding of a bridge we were going under and it was coming in fast! Normally, one would simply negotiate the curve in the road as the wall ran along side your vehicle. But we were not negotiating any curve. We were heading straight for disaster. Instantaneously I turned the wheel slamming the driver's side of the car into the immovable object. We scraped along for some twenty or thirty feet before I managed to steady things and get us back on the road again. I had flirted not only with my own death, but also inexcusably with the lives of others. I slammed on the brakes and stopped at the roadside to try and compose myself. A female friend beside me didn't say a word, she just held out her hand to take mine. I was shaking noticeably.

"Oh good, are we home?" said a voice from the back.

After dropping everyone off and returning home I went to my son's crib and just stared at him, imagining what in the world would happen to him if I had killed myself on this night. I drifted off to sleep in the fetal position on the floor beside his crib, thinking about how I had to make a decision about whether or not I should continue my medical career, not knowing that I would sleep in missing my work and that my boss would make that decision for me.

"Alan we love you here," she said reassuringly. "And firing you is not something I care to do. You are a fine nurse and will make a great doctor, but you are killing yourself and we are watching it happen right before our eyes. You have to choose I'm afraid. Doctor or entertainer, choose."

She told me to take a couple of days off to rest then upon my return she wanted me to give her my decision. Would I quit the music industry and continue on my quest of becoming a doctor, or would I do one final shift as an R.N., take an extended leave of absence, and pursue my LOVE AND SUFFERING?

I told her of the upcoming gig at Toronto's famous Maple Leaf Gardens and I asked her if I could make my decision after that performance. She agreed but in one of the greatest ironies of all time, the two super-shows fell on my schedule when I had to work midnights. This would mean being on stage at the Gardens in front of a huge crowd and then hauling my ass into the hospital at night. I couldn't help but laugh at the absurdity of it all.

Rumour had it that no unsigned band had ever taken that famous stage before *Tokyo* did. I cannot tell you if this is true but I can tell you that going on in front of 20,000 people at a venue worshipped by musicians (including myself) was as nerve-wracking as it comes. In that building I had seen *The Who, Queen, Bowie* and even comedian Steve Martin back in his, "Wild and crazy guy!" days. It was a shrine to say the least.

I remember standing in the shower of our dressing room not fearing going out to sing for them but rather being petrified of what I was going to say to them between songs. I had made one special request to the band for this gig. By today's standards it seems trivial but on that evening it was to prove a major player in our destiny.

"If we can only afford one thing for this gig," I said pleadingly. "Please make it a cordless microphone!"

Seems a silly request today doesn't it? I knew however that if I was not constrained by a mic cord, I could utilize the stage to its maximum. I could be Rod Stewart... I could be *Cheap Trick*... I could be... Alan Frew.

CHAPTER FOUR

*"There is an immeasurable, indescribable force
which Shamans called "intent" and absolutely everything that exists
in the entire cosmos is connected to it."*
CARLOS CASTENADA

CHAPTER FOUR: INTENTION

As the brilliant Dr. Wayne Dyer reminds us, "You can call it spirit or soul or consciousness or universal mind or source. It is the invincible force that intends everything into the universe. It's everywhere. This source is always creating. It is kind. It is loving. It is peaceful. It is non-judgmental, and it excludes no one."

Those of us who read books such as this one will know by now that the word INTENTION seems to be over-used and rather hip and chic at the moment. And here I am using it once again. To not use it in a strategy for living a successful life would be like not using the word love when connecting to your children, your mother, best friend or even man's best friend, which in my case is a funny little Lab-Poodle cross named Harry (who, by the way, just finished a movie with Freddie Prinze Junior, so even he's using *THE ACTION SANDWICH*).

INTENTION is the single most unassumingly humble, yet incredibly powerful source in the universe, regardless of whether you use it in a religious context or a spiritual one. My grandfather used it in the latter fashion. "Jimmy the Exorcist", they called him, because whenever he came over to your house, all your spirits disappeared. For me it has nothing to do with religion, yet for another it may be spoken of as God, Allah, Mohammed, Buddha or the likes.

By now you have probably deduced that I am not a religious man. Why not? Mainly because organized religion has never been a logical explanation for me. I do, though, understand why, when I discuss my thoughts and feelings on the topics of energy, higher power and INTENTION, those of you who do take comfort in and require an organized religion in your lives may feel that I am just using different words to describe a similar thing, namely God. So be it. I call it the Source, the Centre, INTENTION, and perhaps we are all talking about the same thing.

Dr. Stephen Hawking, probably the most famous living scientist in the world, has sold in excess of ten million copies of the tenth anniversary edition of his book, *A Brief History of Time*. For a book to sell so many copies is essentially unheard-of in the field of science literature. Those who have not read *A Brief History of Time* may be surprised to find that the book's central figure is God. Doctor Hawking tells us a perfectly sound explanation is possible for The Big Bang some trillionths of a second after it happened, yet none was possible prior to the actual moment. I wonder how many times this has been debated, at dinner tables, water coolers or over a cup of coffee. Even Albert Einstein relented and said that the necessity for a beginning must have required the presence of a superior power. One asks then, if everything that begins to exist must have a cause and if the universe began to exist, then does it not follow that the universe must have a cause?

Dr. Hawking, whom I respect immensely, is quoted as saying:

"It is difficult to discuss the beginning of the universe without mentioning the concept of God. My work on the origin of the universe is on the borderline between science and religion, but I try to stay on the scientific side of the border. It is quite possible that God acts in ways that cannot be described by scientific laws."

God, Allah, Buddha, the force that connects us…only you can decide which energy is for you. However, I guarantee that all explanations given for the existence of the universe will convey the message that any or all gods had great INTENT, so regardless of what doctrine you march to ladies and gentlemen, the meaning of life always comes full circle back to the power of INTENTION.

When you are raised within a divided community based solely on misinterpreted doctrines that are called religion, it makes for a very interesting childhood to say the least, for it almost inevitably leads to pain, suffering and heartache of some sort for some poor bugger. You only pray it's not you.

I know I am certainly not the first one to ask the question of how many people have suffered terrible fates in the name of religious intolerance. It's mind-boggling to those of us on the periphery, agape at the ridiculousness of it all. In the end, you just have to stay true to yourself and to your purpose and live the best life you can.

This reminds me of a little story about Sister Mary Margaret, who worked for the local Home Care Agency in her town and who was on her way to deliver a bedpan to one of the agency's bedridden patients. On the way there she ran out of gas, which brought to light the fact that she had forgotten to replace a small gas can that she kept in the trunk. But Sister Mary Margaret was an ever so resourceful type, so without hesitation she decided to take the bedpan with her to the nearby gas station. She returned promptly to her car and began pouring the gasoline from the bedpan into the gas tank. Just at that moment two Presbyterian ministers were walking by and saw her, which prompted one to say to the other, "I'm telling you, if it starts, I'm turning Catholic!"

FATHER FIGURE

My first major introduction to religious differences took place when I discovered that my pal "Wee Peter Gallagher" had to regularly attend a thing called confession, while I on the other hand did not. This was something neither of us could seem to figure out. I mean for me it was a case of, "Why break it, steal it, eat it, or do whatever to it, if you then must tell someone that it was you that did it?" This wasn't an Einstein theory as far as I could tell, and confession made absolutely no sense to me and would probably have meant that, had I been born a Catholic, I would have had to spend every day at the chapel in order to keep pace with my mischief.

Wee Peter, although jealous, did not entirely believe me, so upon rounding up several other Catholic boys, which is never difficult in Coatbridge, we decided to put it to the test.

Every day, Father D'Arcy would ride his bicycle down my street either on his way to or from the chapel and so it was decided by the Catholics that the wee Proddy (that is, Protestant...namely, me) would jump out of the bushes, flash him my, "Dickie-Bird" (Hey, we were seven years old and that is what we called it), call him a bad name and then beat it to the safety of wherever the hell the nearest safety happened to be.

We toyed with vile and outrageous bad words to prove beyond a shadow of a doubt that the Catholic Church could not harm me. We thought long and hard. Bugger? No, not dangerous enough. Cross-eyed? Good, only he wasn't. Arsie? No, that won't do, 'cuz that's his name really, isn't it? Father D'Arcy.

Dickie-Bird, that's it! Perfect. After all, you're going to flash him with it, so why not call him it. We tittered and laughed at the very thought of it. Who would ever dare call a priest, their priest...a penis! After having done this, if I was not forced by my mother to go and "confess", then indeed I was not a Catholic and they would believe that confession played no role in my life.

We all agreed, so the game and this clever plan were afoot. As usual, my entrepreneurial skills kicked in and I decided that it should also cost them each a penny if I was going to do this, for it had to be worth something, right?

And so we hunkered down behind Mrs. McDougall's big hedge and waited. And we were not disappointed, for very soon along he came.

I neglected to tell you that I had my "bogey" with me. What, you may well ask, is a bogey? Well, it's what we in Scotland called a homemade go-cart. Basically a large plank of wood used lengthwise for the body of the vehicle, with two smaller pieces at each end creating the cross beams, each with an axle and two wheels. A wooden apple box served as the seat or the cockpit, and a piece of rope ran from the front axle into the hands of the driver, making it possible to steer. Since it had no engine and worked solely off of gravity, you just found a large hill, got in and held on for dear life. I still carry bogey marks to this very day from some legendary rides and crashes.

There I was behind the bushes, my "Dickie-bird" in one hand, my bogey's rope in the other, when Father D'Arcy came, cycling and whistling along on his merry way completely oblivious to the ambush that was awaiting him.

What did I think he would do? Nothing, I guess. Oh wait, hang on, as a matter of fact, I DID NOT THINK THAT PART OUT AT ALL! Out I leapt, almost giving the poor bugger a heart attack.

"Hello Father DICKIE-BIRD!" (Waggle, waggle, waggle). Could he see it? Was it big enough? The young priest stopped on a dime and I swear to this day he pulled a wheelie that made him look like he was riding a fine stallion as opposed to a woman's bike of the 1930s.

Envision if you will the following: It's today, and you look out onto your street from your kitchen or living room window, to see a young lad of seven years of age and he's running fast. In one hand he is holding on to a thick piece of rope that is attached to a soap-box cart bigger than he is, and he's clumsily dragging it behind him. Looking rather frantic, he repeatedly takes quick glances over his shoulder while trying to stay on his feet. In his other hand is his penis. Okay, have you got that image? Good.

Picture if you will again this young lad, rope, cart, glances, penis – and there is a young priest chasing him down the street! What goes through your mind?

Pedophile? Police? Fire Department? Marines?

But this is not today. This is 1961 and this is Coatbridge and this is as normal an occurrence for people to witness as seeing a dog with a blonde wig on, as it saunters down the street, stops, lifts its leg and pees on a drunk sleeping on the roadside. It's as routine as a baker, who as you are standing watching him, puts the holes in the top of his apple pies with his pipe, or perhaps the man at the bar whose stomach is a little queasy politely excusing himself, stepping out the front door onto the street, throwing up, taking a deep relaxing breath, and walking back into the bar to pick up where he left off.

So forget it kid, just because you're running down the street with your dick in your hand while being chased by a man of the cloth, don't think you're getting any help here.

Two ladies stand yakking at the garden fence.

"Hello Mrs. Anderson, hello Mrs. Gallagher!" I shout as the kid, the go-cart and the penis go whizzing by.
"Hello yourself, Alan Frew!"
"Did you see that Mary, he's got his willy out again?"
"Aye Betty, shocking!"
Now it's the priest's turn to cross their path.
"Good Morning Father," say the ladies.
"Good morning ladies," he pants, robes pulled up around his knees. "See you at mass later, Mrs. Gallagher?"
"Aye Father, that you will."
"Oh, he's lovely Mary, isn't he?"
"Aye, he's a real charmer, Betty."

The ladies resume their chat and the priest seems to be gaining on me. Drastic measures must be taken, for if this guy catches me he'll tie me up, put me in a sack, carry me back to the dungeon in his chapel and keep me there with all the other kidnapped Protestant boys. How do I know this? My dad told me. That's how!

I deliberately slowed my pace to allow the holy man to get to within about six feet of me when suddenly I deked to the left, letting go of the rope and leaving the bogey directly in his path. He didn't stand a chance. His immediate reaction was to jump on it like a surfboard, as opposed to breaking his neck by tripping over it. And for a brief shining moment he was doing well. In his panic he then attempted to take the controls, but as the cart was in full flight now and just about to head down the hill at the bottom of my street, he ended up in a kind of luge position, you know the position those maniacs in the Winter Olympics take when they lie on that skid and propel themselves down the ice at the speed of light? Ok, well he was like that, only BACKWARDS!

Now it's not every day, dear reader, that you see a priest facing backwards, laying flat on his back on a speeding go-cart, flying down the street toward the bus stop, and I must admit I was howling as I stood in front of our garden gate outside the little house that I called home.

Suddenly I heard a voice, my father's,
"And what are you howling about then?"

I turned to face him just as poor Father Dickie-Bird vanished over the horizon of the hill, denying me the chance to witness his landing.
"Nothing," I said rather sheepishly.
"For a boy that's laughing at nothing, you seem to be very happy."
"Ahh, it's nothin' Dad, really."
"All right then, get in here, yer dinner's ready."
"Ok, Dad."
I walked behind him in what seemed like those giant footsteps of his.
"And Alan?"
"Yes, Dad?"
"Put your dickie-bird away before anyone sees it, okay?"
"Right, Dad."

If you are part of an organized religion that brings you joy, I truly think that is a wonderful thing. I couldn't do it myself but make no mistake, I am a spiritual man and I know that there is a greater power, a greater INTENTION connecting me to everything and everyone in the universe, even to Father Dickie-Bird.

NO DOUBT

INTENTION, when called upon through RECEPTIVITY, DESIRE and BELIEF, is a powerful force of natural energy that transports determination from the image in your mind to your desired outcome in the physical world. INTENTION carries everything you need from your "source" and brings it to the doorstep of ACTION, which produces your ultimate goal. INTENTION, however, will attach itself to whatever you are focused on. If you attach it to fear or a limiting BELIEF you carry from the past, it will take you to a destination that you do not want. This is why it is absolutely imperative that you know exactly what you want and do not allow doubt to erode your commitment to your goals.

I know of no one that doesn't believe in energy of some kind. Even the most die-hard of skeptics and pessimists will agree that energy surrounds us, passes through us and strengthens us. It's a scientifically proven fact. Why then would our thoughts be any less? They are not, and in many instances they are even more powerful than the energy required for physical accomplishments. If you send out thoughts like "I am no good at what I do; I have tried and keep failing", and you're in the coffee and donuts business, you are basically telling the world that your coffee and donuts suck and that we should not buy them. If I go to auditions in this the infancy of my acting career, with thoughts in my head that I cannot act, I am basically telling the director not to even consider hiring me. Does any of this seem remotely familiar to you?

Those of you who appear to fail at virtually everything you try should be interested in this because we stand at an important juncture in *THE ACTION*

SANDWICH. This is the moment where people destined for success send out positive thoughts and positive energy and emotion into the world. This is where achievers act and behave as if they have already achieved the outcome, and by doing so they add the intense power of INTENTION to their already positive thoughts and energy.

All right, so now you are receptive to what it is you want. You DESIRE it in your heart and you believe that you deserve it, that you are entitled to it...is that enough? I know that I am receptive to my tummy rumbling, and I really can DESIRE to have a sandwich and of course I believe that I deserve to eat. However, my plate remains empty. This is where the power of INTENTION must kick in and leave no doubt in my mind that the object of my DESIRE is attainable, for it is INTENTION that says, "There is no stopping me from having that which I DESIRE." At the moment when failure is no longer an option, INTENTION becomes the fuel for your dreams. Let me give you an example of this.

FOOTBALL IS THE ONLY REASON, GOD GAVE US FEET

During the last World Cup I was the spokesperson for a sports network in a between-game segment called *Frew and Fans*. This happened purely because I intended it to. Rather cocky of me, one might think. But it had nothing to do with the network, at least not in the beginning.

I decided that I wanted to be part of what in my opinion is the most beautiful game. And so for over a year I would drop this idea into conversations at dinner parties, special events or with various business contacts, therefore intending it into being. I had my manager completely convinced it was happening long before we had our first meeting. I was receptive to the idea of being on a sports program. I truly desired this to happen. I believed that I would be an asset to any show covering soccer. I put all of the aforementioned criteria behind my INTENTION for this to come to fruition, and then I took

ACTION. I dropped the hint one day with a high-ranking contact who in turn fired my idea off the head of programming for the sports network. Shortly thereafter, I got the call. We set up a meeting, to which I brought all of the PASSION that I have not only for soccer, but also for communicating, promoting and performing. It was a cinch! I knew what the World Cup was, I love football; I wanted to be part of the World Cup and I believed that I was the guy for the job. When I included the power of INTENTION, it was like a door opening and lo and behold my goal stood before me. By the time the position was offered to me, three networks had joined forces to show the World Cup and all decided to use me.

I now bring this same recipe with me for my fledgling career as an actor. I bring it into the realm of public speaking, and it is how this very book came into being. You see *THE ACTION SANDWICH* was required in order for me to write a book about *THE ACTION SANDWICH*. Go figure!

As for the acting career, well, it brings every aspect of what this book is all about into play. In all of my life I have never felt emotions careening through my body as they do when having to perform an audition for a professional acting job. Man, it's nerve-wracking! Walking into a room with several people sitting behind a desk staring at you, a camera rolling, and you have to transform yourself into what the director desires.

"Okay, let's see, Alan. You're an Irish-Tibetan monk, totally addicted to Guinness, who secretly desires to be Donald Trump's personal massage therapist and......ACTION!"

Transformation is a word that I love. I'm not exactly sure why, but I do know that I love the way it feels in my mouth as I say it, and I notice that I feel a certain way after using it. It becomes like a little dose of positivism for me. Transformation means a change in form, appearance, or character, yet you know that it is grander than that, beyond the idea of mere change. When someone says, "he's changed," it just doesn't seem to reach the level of something like, "My God, what a transformation she has undergone!" Transformation Glasgow Style:

"Awwright, Willie?"

"Aye, Frankie. I'm doin' just fine, how's yourself?"

"Doin' great, Willie. Did ye' hear about Jimmy though?"

"Naw, I did not. What about 'im?"

"Well he's...goin' through one o' them transformations."

"Transformation? How so?"

"Well, it seems he's gone from being a prick, to being an absolute prick!"

OH WHAT A LUCKY MAN, HE WAS

INTENTION is the purity of that moment when life itself came into being and joined the universal family. As a footnote remember this: from the perspective of the universe you were never intended to fail. The true INTENTION of so great a power is too positive for such a stance. Think of INTENTION and FAILURE for a moment. Now change that thought to INTENTION and NEGATIVITY. Or, for the purpose of this little experiment, change it to NEGATIVE INTENTION, which in my opinion now constitutes an oxymoron. All right, scholars out there don't get your knickers in a twist – hear me out. I say oxymoron because INTENTION is not about negativity. Saying someone intends to harm a child, kill another human being, rob a bank or rip off old people of their pensions, these are human frailties and weaknesses that bastardize the very nature of the word INTENTION, which in its purest form would be incapable of such dark acts.

INTENTION is the cancer's remission. It is the unexpected windfall you have just as you prepare to painfully borrow money from a friend. It is the great job offer that comes on the same day you take the stand and say goodbye to the job you know you should have never taken in the first place. It is the guardian angels that show up when you need them, and then slip away before you can even thank them. We call it luck, coincidence, six degrees of separation, chance, and a host of other names that make us feel comfortably disconnected from what is truly our spirit or, as I prefer to call it, our source at work. But make no mistake about it, INTENTION surrounds all living things and is most easily activated when you immerse yourself in and fill your mind full of positive thoughts about the outcome you DESIRE.

I was on a winter road trip last year with *Glass Tiger* and as part of promoting the show I had to visit several radio stations during the morning and afternoon, yet still sing in the evening. It was wearing me down. On one extremely cold evening in Edmonton, Alberta, I was asked, much to my consternation, to sing "live" on the drive-home show at 5:00 p.m. I reluctantly agreed. I was accompanied by a record company representative who was getting an earful from me on the way out telling him I was fed up of jumping through hoops. It was forty below outside; I was tired, freezing and hoarse.

You name it, I complained about it. As we exited through the main doors a van was blocking our pathway. I saw the driver slide back out of view and I wondered what this was all about. Suddenly two side doors on the van slid open and I saw this chap in a wheel chair. A few seconds later, an electronic-lift brought him to the ground and he approached me in his chair. He had only one arm and was a double amputee just below each knee.

"Mr. Frew," he said, "I have driven almost an hour to get here. Would you be kind enough to sign my CDs and photographs please?"
"Of course," I replied.
"I am one of your biggest fans, I love your music," he said with enthusiasm.
"Thank you," I almost whispered. Then I thought to ask him something, "Tell me, are you coming to the show tonight?" My idea was that if he was not I would offer him free tickets.
"Oh, I would love to," he said "But I gotta be gettin' back to town. I have to coach kid's hockey tonight, sorry though. Well, thanks kindly. Bye now."

He backed up his chair onto the lift, and within a few seconds he was gone. With no legs and one arm, there he was, heading back to town to coach kid's hockey, missing the concert of one of his favourite bands and doing it with PASSION and enthusiasm. He had driven over an hour just to come and say hello and get me to sign a few items. I stood silently for a moment watching intently as he pulled away in his van.

"He was meant to be here," I said trance-like.

"I beg your pardon?" said the record rep.

"That guy was meant to be here tonight. That was no coincidence. It was intended that he would meet me here at this precise moment."

"I don't understand," said the rep.

"That's okay, let's go." And so I headed back to the hotel deep in thought. Here I was complaining about being tired, having a scratchy throat and being worried that my voice might not make it through the two-hour show, while this fellow with no legs and one arm had driven over an hour just to spend a few minutes with me before heading back to coach hockey! It was just too powerful to be coincidence or luck. No, INTENTION put him in my pathway to remind me of how good my life is. This INTENTION was called up from a subconscious inner place on my behalf to bring me back down to earth and make me realize the blessings that I have and to remind me of just how grateful I should be. Incidentally when I got back to my hotel room there was a book I had not noticed stuffed into my bag. It was a book by Dr. Wayne Dyer called "The Power of INTENTION." I had left home in a rush and my wife had obviously seen it by the bedside and had stuck it into my case for me.

If you are at a roadblock that is causing you stress in your life, find a corner and a moment to yourself and think of something positive. It's there. Trust me. So look for it. Those of you who believe in and practice the art of meditation certainly have a leg up on those of us who don't. However, look for it, that special thing. It only seems like it's not there. I know it may be difficult right now, but if you have to, go back to when you were a child and life seemed so much more carefree, then feel what that was like. Let that feeling grow within you at this very moment. That child is still in you. That is still you. It is important to find this time. I do not meditate, but I always find time for myself to practice positive thinking. I do it while driving or when working out, or if I manage to get out and go for a relaxing massage.

THE DAY THAT ALAN MEDITATED

Okay, what is my INTENTION here? Oh yeah that's it. I want to rid myself of this stress. Okay, now c'mon Alan, close your eyes, take a deep breath now. Go to silence. Ahhhh, that's it, deeper, deeper, deeeeeeeepppperrr. Now chant softly. Ohmm, ohmm, oohmm, oohhhhmmmm, ohmmmmmmz! ohhmmmmzz! ohmmmzzz! ohmzzzz! zzzzzz! ZZzzzzzz! ZZZZZzzzzzzzzzz!

AND IN THE MIDDLE OF NEGOTIATIONS, YOU BREAK DOWN

I often tell my audiences that if ever they want to see expert negotiators and entrepreneurs at work, then look no further than little children, your own if you have them, but if you don't then little nieces, nephews or bratty neighbour kids will suffice. Watch how relentless kids are when they DESIRE. They begin by asking parent number one for whatever it is they DESIRE. If denied, they simply move on to parent number two. If that fails, they move perhaps to grandparent number one, then, if need be, number two. No luck? Back they go to parent number one, then number two, and again to the grandparents who, by this time, are more likely to break down or at least to take sides against parent number one. The child has already won because they know that the odds are they will get at least part of what they've asked for. They have made ground. If the adult still remains reluctant to give in, he or she will most likely carry the torch on behalf of the child to parent number two, who inevitably says,

"Oh, for Pete's sake, yes!"

Sound familiar? Parents reading this book know exactly what I am talking about.

Children are masters at getting what they want because they ask for it and if they do not get it they ask again, and again, and yet again. I haven't had a full, uninterrupted conversation with my wife for three years in my little daughter's waking hours. Oh sure, you can try the old, "Now sweetheart, Daddy and Mommy are speaking, so be a good girl and wait your turn!" Right, good luck! When they get something in their little heads that they want to ask for or tell you, then forget it. It is a relentless barrage of machine-gun talk until you give up and give in.

Asking for what you want works wonders. So why then do we stop doing it? Simple, because as we mature we become steadily more afraid of the fact that with asking can come rejection and with rejection can come pain and embarrassment. We become more and more fearful to ask. The outcome is never as bad as we think it is going to be, is it? You ask someone for something and they say, simply, no. Then what happens? A lightning bolt strikes you dead on the spot? You read it as a front-page headline in your local newspaper: "He asked and was told no, details page 18?" Of course not. Though you might feel a twinge of embarrassment or hear a nagging voice inside your head say, "See, I told you he'd say no."

So what if you break a heel and go flying, or exit a toilet dragging a roll of single ply. Is it not all just part of life? Of course it is. Why then is asking any different? Tell me, if you ask and you don't get, are you any worse off than you were before you asked? The answer of course is no. At the very least you are still the same. You don't have $20 so you ask Frank for it and he says no. You still don't have $20, but at the very least you might have discovered where not to go in the future to borrow money. Asking is as much a part of success as any other thing in this book, even if you have to take the occasional pie in the face.

People who have navigated the road to success certainly know the power of asking for the things they want and more than just a few of them have taken some pretty big pies in the "clock" on the way there. Yours truly is no exception. So do you want to know how to a get a recording-deal? Ask someone who works for a record company. Want to know how to start a business? Take a successful businessperson to lunch and ask them how they got started. Do you want to improve your golf swing but can't afford private lessons? Ask the best golfer on your street. Want to find out if you have what it takes to work in medicine? Go chat with the head nurse at your local hospital.

Do you want to know how to turn your $100 into $10,000? Ask Donald Trump! I'm serious. You will be amazed at how many people from all walks of life, regardless of social or financial status, will be more than willing to answer your questions. I know this because I have done it, especially in business and entrepreneurship. I have taken extremely successful business people to lunch for the specific purpose of picking their brains. And the best part is that they've known upfront that this is what I intended to do. I asked them ahead of time, and they agreed! Sure, some will decline your request but that's okay. Don't give it a second thought. Just erase them from your list and move on. It takes only one or two and you can have more answers to your questions than you had ever hoped for. One of the greatest topics that successful people love to discuss is how they became successful, so start there. This is useful information on your road to success. Inevitably, as you move forward on that pathway, you're going to have to negotiate at some time or another, and although listening is going to come in pretty handy when that time comes, having the ability to clearly define what it is you want and asking for it is equally powerful and necessary.

After you have successfully mastered the ability to ask for what it is you want from this universe, you will be challenged yet again. It is easy to fall into the trap of just asking indiscriminately for things and stuff and goodies. So be careful. Be selective. Think. We have all heard the term, "say no to the bad and yes to the good." Jack Canfield coined a phrase that raises the bar: "say no to the good and yes to the great!" All teachers of success subscribe to this adage although this kind of doctrine tends to make one fair game for the "easy for you to say" crowd. So be it. It's true and I know that it works.

Try this exercise of saying no to the good and yes to the great and you will be amazed to see how much "great" comes your way. It is the natural law of attraction. However this won't happen before a few tempting "goods" hit your world, for this is a universal truth. When you draw a line in the sand your life will definitely test the theory to see if it is true. Remember, what you ask for you get, and the more you ask for, the more of it you will get. So if you settle for "OKs and goods" then that is precisely what you will get. No matter what level you are at on the social economic ladder, this concept remains true.

ALL GOOD CHILDREN GO TO HEAVEN

My school contained a wide array of characters from brainiacs with IQs off the charts to maniacs with the IQs of farts. As for me, I was always somewhere in the middle. Smart and intelligent enough to get to where I needed to go, yet tough enough that I could swim among the sharks and not get eaten alive.

I learned these skills so very, very, young. Wheelin' and dealin' becomes second nature when the street is your playground, whether by choice or necessity. Here's a lovely little example of what I mean.

At around five years of age, I liked the idea of having money in my pocket and I wasn't one of those kids who preferred shiny coins to bills, just because they glistened and were more fun to play with. No, I liked coins, but I loved bills. Still do as a matter of fact, but even as a child I knew you could do more with bills.

One day, approximately a hundred lifetimes ago, my parents took me to a museum dedicated to the life and work of a famous Scottish explorer called David Livingstone, most noted for being the first European to see Africa's wondrous Mosi-oa-Tunya waterfall, which he renamed (as if it needed it), Victoria Falls after his monarch, Queen Victoria. He also gets credit for locating the true source of the Nile (again as if the Africans knew only of the false one). Isn't it interesting that Africa is the oldest inhabited territory on earth, with many fossils and evidence of human occupation dating perhaps as early as seven million years ago and yet Africans are expected to thank their lucky stars that a European explorer came along to tell them all who they were and where they lived. I mean, they must have been at their wit's end trying to figure that out until a wee "Roman came roamin' over the hill."

First native: "Who are we?"
Second native: "How the hell should I know?"
First native: "Oh thank god, here comes a little white guy in a red dress and gold hat on his way to a parade no doubt. He'll know who we are."
Second native "Go on, ask him."
First native: "Hey! Who are we?"
Roman: "Well, I've decided that you are... Afri's."
First native: "And where are we?"
Roman: "Glad you asked. Since the Roman suffix 'ca' denotes 'country or land', I have decided that you live in... Afri-ca."
First native: "Well I am so glad that you cleared that up for us. I mean we've only been living, breathing, working, screwing, loving, laughing and talking for about a hundred bloody centuries, before your scrawny little white arse got here! But thanks for sorting that out for us."

Now, to a five-year old boy David Livingstone and his memorial was real John Wayne stuff. Looking back on it, it was a tiny space, but to this lad, it held all the treasures of the world and then some. Livingstone's bloody, worn-out uniform hung on the wall, for all to see. His sword and musket, remnants of a savage journey, were encased here. A hand-written letter, the penmanship exquisite, to his Queen, recorded his epic tale in fine detail. And of great curiosity to me, the very bone from his arm, which had been brutally ripped from his body during an attack from a ferocious lion, was also openly on display. It was marvelous. In fact, for a five-year-old, it was magical.

Yes indeed, my RECEPTIVITY to what I had seen in the museum had me consumed. I was equally receptive, however, to the existence of a willing clientele, including my parents, who had spent their good hard-earned money visiting this little gold mine from the Nile. My DESIRE therefore was to recreate it at home, and I had oodles of BELIEF in my ability to do so and in my own ability to sell it to a very captive audience. With unhesitating

INTENTION I took ACTION and here is what I did.

I took my grandad's old boiler suit, which was ripped at the elbows and knees, and smeared it with oil and splattered it with ketchup, then hung it up with a card saying "David Livingstone's Uniform." I wrote a letter to Queen Victoria, stained it with my granny's tea and signed it "Livingstone." I made a sword from two pieces of old wood. I broke the windshield wiper off of our first car (which I paid for later when my dad found out and not, I might add, with money) and I painted it blood red and declared on a card that, "This was the bone from David's arm." A few bells and whistles later and I had turned my grandad's garden shed into *THE DAVID LIVINGSTONE MEMORIAL* of all time. Now all I needed was my clientele.

Around the corner I went to the local pub, where spilling out onto the street was my wonderful old grandad and several of his cronies. The pubs opened at 11:00 a.m. and closed at 2:00 p.m., presumably to give the staff an afternoon break before opening again at 5:00. There was no one in this world like my grandfather (my dad came as close as you'll get); he was a truly unique piece of work. Gentile and caring, it seemed the drunker he got, the more lovable he became. I'll never forget the day several of my pals came running up to me, frantic, with that look on their faces that announced "I can't believe what I just saw."

"Yuh...yo... you ha...haaave to come ssseee this!" one of them said.
"What is it?" I asked. "A de...a dead man, we found a dead man!"
"Where?"
"At the bottom of the road, he's down there," one said as he pointed.
"And he's DEAD!" said the other, obviously excited.
"How do you know he's dead?" I inquired.
"Cuz he's hanging over a wall...he's GOT to be dead."
"Let's go!" I cried, and off we scurried to see the dead man.

Now to a boy some nine years of age or so, the prospect of finding a dead body ranks right up there with the flattened cat with maggots, the poop-in-a bag through the mail box or the stripped naked pal tossed into the girl's gym, so off we ran at top speed to the bottom of my street, and sure enough when we got there I saw the legs dangling over a small wall that he had obviously fallen over upon gasping for his last breath.

I looked all around me, wondering where the sniper was located that had so skillfully taken him out. Perhaps, though, he was a foreign spy who'd been poisoned at a spies' banquet and the drug had just kicked in, right here, at this wee wall on my street. Yes! That could be it. He was passing this wall and BANG! Down he goes, dead as a doorknob. I saw the legs and I stopped in my tracks, for I had never seen a real "live" dead person before, except the ones that John Wayne killed at the Alamo. Deep breath, here we go. Slowly, cautiously, I leaned over the wall to take my first peek. I couldn't see his face for his cap had fallen over most of it. I slowly reached down to remove it so that we might all get a good look at this corpse when suddenly... it decided to make a noise.

"Tccchhhhuh," it said, from that gargly spot in the back of its throat.
"Mammy, Daddy!" cried one of my pals.
"QUIET!" I commanded. "It's ok, I've heard they do that when they're dead."
"Tccchhhuh Too," it warbled again.
And yet again, "Tooch...Tooo."
Slowly, cautiously, defying my years, I reached down to uncover the dead man's face...when suddenly the corpse bellowed,
"TOOT TOOT TOOTSIE GOODBYE,
TOOT TOOT TOOTSIE, DON'T CRY."
"Jesus! It's Al Jolsen!"
"WATCH FOR THE MAIL,
I'LL NEVER FAIL,
IF YOU DON'T GET A LETTER, THEN YOU KNOW I'M IN JAIL," he sang at the top of his lungs.

Oh yes, my dear reader, I may never have seen a dead body up to this point in my life, but I had seen THIS one many, many times before. For this was my grandad. That sweet, loveable old man who adored me, who shared his roast potatoes with HP sauce with me even though he had very few of them on his plate. There wasn't much I couldn't get him to do. So on that day outside the pub, as the curator of the new Livingstone memorial, I knew I would have his full support in my venture.

"Come and see the wonders of darkest Africa!!!" I cried out. "Follow me gents, right this way!"

Now, if you think the real memorial was small, this one was a shoebox, but I kid you not, they filed in one at a time, some even turning around and going back for seconds.

Through my megaphone (a rolled up school notebook) I yelled,

"Come one, come all! Look if you dare!"

Soon other pubs had spilled out and my grandad was calling out to some others. "Frankie! Bob! Jimmy! My goodness, ye have tae see this, it's the bone oot of David Livingstone's arm!!"

I made a killing. It played for three days I think. Critics? They loved it ... even though they were tipsy. And my dad, well he went easy on me for the windshield wiper, but not that easy. Let's just say we cut a deal.

I still create David Livingstone's memorial today, only it's a song you can find on a CD, it's this book, or perhaps it's a concert in your hometown. It can be a speaking engagement or perhaps it's a piece of clothing I design or a painting done by my own hand. But it's all the same thing. The five-year-old entrepreneur, the twenty-five, thirty-five or one day sixty-five year old, they are all the same with the only difference being their circumstance and their ability to ask for what it is they want, while being able to negotiate with their surrounding world by being receptive, by having DESIRE, by believing, intending and taking ACTION, passionately towards the success that will not be denied them.

I love to tell the David Livingstone story. It comes from a time when life seemed so much simpler. Stress? What's that when you're a child? Was that not something your granny tied your grandad's hernia up with?

Think what it would be like to be happy beyond your wildest dreams. Close your eyes and be happy in your mind, body and soul, even if just for a minute. What is it that is stopping you from feeling this way for more than just this moment? The answer is, you, only you. Now I am not diminishing any or all the problems you may be facing, and indeed you may not feel responsible for all of them. However, I am saying that you are responsible for how you handle them and how you respond to them no matter how painful they may feel. If you detest your job, you are responsible for not leaving. If your husband beats you, you are responsible for remaining. If you have cancer, you are responsible for the fight against it. I know this can seem harsh and cruel but it is so necessary to understand and believe this, in order to be able to make different choices, towards different outcomes. Now hear this, if you take only one thing away from this book it is this: you cannot change what you do not acknowledge. If you want 100% of the "say" in your life, if you want 100% of the control in your life, then you must take 100% responsibility for your life. No ifs, ands or buts, period.

We are almost where we need to be. INTENTION is such a powerhouse of force, yet it should be obvious why I call this *THE ACTION SANDWICH*. For without the ACTION of getting up off of my backside and actually doing something like making the sandwich, I will remain hungry. You have to DO to get DONE! So I need to get up and go over to my fridge, gather the ingredients; then and only then will I be on my way to success and have in my possession a delicious sandwich. Remember now, THIS is the moment of truth. For if indeed it is a delicious healthy sandwich I DESIRE, then my ACTION will lead to my success. However, what happens if during my ACTION phase I get unfocused or lost or perhaps just plain lazy and instead I take a quick fix of, say, a large chocolate milk and a big helping of pie...what then? I may have removed that feeling of hunger, but at what price? I'm hungry! Let's talk some ACTION.

TEN STEPS TO INTENTION

1. ORVIL OR WILBUR? - Somebody had to do it, right? Ever wonder how many people said to them, "Hey Orv! Willy boy! That thing'll never fly!" Once you are receptive to your DESIRE and BELIEF, your path is set. Let nothing negative in, ever. Don't doubt your creativity for this is INTENTION'S doorway. Invent your own Kitty Hawk.

2. IT'S MAGIC OF A KIND - There is nothing negative about kindness. One of the synonyms for the word kindness is good INTENTION. Spreading kindness synergistically creates power and positivism throughout the world. Again, *The Butterfly Effect*. By the way, don't forget yourself.

3. MONSIEUR PIERRE SEVERE - "This just in. Thomas Edison has finally given up! There will be no light bulb after all, news at eleven." Can you imagine? INTENTION requires perseverance, the steady persistence, and purpose in spite of difficulties, obstacles, or discouragement. This is non-negotiable. Get used to it.

4. YOU'VE GOT THE WHOLE WORLD IN YOUR HANDS - Try on occasion to think as part of one large mass of energy whose thoughts, choices and decisions ultimately affects the body of the universe as opposed to thinking about just yourself. Putting your thoughts on a grander scale not only elevates your decision-making but also raises the bar on INTENTION asking greater things in return. Elevate.

5. WE ARE EVO - Choose your pathway. Be prepared to evolve. Expand with the universe and you will open your RECEPTIVITY and awareness to an unlimited capacity, thereby

elevating INTENTION. Do this and you will accept that the universe is filled with abundance for all. You are sending out the message that says, "Nothing is beyond my scope. There are no limitations."

6. EMAIL FOR MR. UNIVERSE! - Give equal credence to the energy and power of your thoughts, as you would your arms or legs. Each thought is an email of your INTENTION notifying the universe of what your BELIEF and DESIRE is for any given choice or decision. This is where "I am who I know I am," lives. The universe will believe you and act accordingly. Be careful.

7. WHAT ARE YOU WORTH - If you are a $100 guy do not then accept $99.99 unless by doing so, you can see more than $100 value further down the pipeline. Jack Canfield says, "Say no to the good and yes to the great." You will be amazed what happens if you stay true to your self worth. Amaze yourself.

8. GET COMMITTED -
"I pledge allegiance to myself,
and to the life for which I stand.
One universe indivisible,
with RECEPTIVITY, DESIRE, BELIEF, INTENTION
and ACTION for all."

9. OF FLESH AND BLOOD I'M MADE - Change doesn't happen overnight. If you stray from the core of your INTENTION, go easy on yourself, but not too easy. Be firm in your resolve to evolve and start again. Use any mistakes or failures as guides to where not to go, on your journey ahead. Live and learn.

10. I CAN SEE FOR MILES - Visualize exactly how it's going to look, how it's going to feel, how it's going to be, when you get there. This process of creating internal mental images of how it shall be in the end conjoins you to INTENTION. It declares, "this is where I am, but this is where I shall be." Visualize.

MY SONG
Opus 4

GOD GAVE ROCK 'N ROLL TO YOU

"What are you doing son?"
"Easy, I am aligning my actions with my dreams."
"What are you thinking?"
"Simple, I am thinking about what it will feel like when I am one."
"And what exactly is it that you are going to be?"
"Why, a Rock Star of course."

I'LL TUMBLE 4 YA

I wore a canary yellow suit that night, difficult for the audience to miss no matter where one might be sitting. Difficult to miss even for canaries. I know in my heart that my RECEPTIVITY, DESIRE, BELIEF and INTENTION were in complete harmony with everything that makes me who I truly am and as for my ACTION; well Monday's phone call answered that.

"Alan wake up. Alan, you have a phone call, wake up," said my mother.
"Who is it? Tell them I'm knackered. Tell them to call again."
"It's some man from Capitol Records."

I got up but it was painful for after both performances I was basking in a few minutes of glory with the lads before heading back to my hometown and working the night shift until 6:00 a.m. I remember chuckling at one of my patients saying, "Well, how did it go?"

"It was magic," I said, the sound of the crowd still in my head.

"Good for you Alan," he replied, as he reached beneath the sheets to remove a very full bedpan. Can you empty this?"

I groggily spoke into the phone.

"Hello?"

"You're a star," the voice said.

"Come again," I replied.

"You are a... star," it repeated.

I recognized it as being the voice of Tim Trombley, the A&R representative that had wooed the band from the very beginning. He was second in command to Deane Cameron and had been wounded by the split that had occurred upon my refusal to sign as a solo artist.

"Deane is on the line here with me Alan," said Tim.

"Hello Deane."

"Hello Alan," he replied a little conservatively. Then he delivered a phrase that was to become a defining moment.

"Well," he said gently. "I guess if I want the cherries, I'll have to take the whole pie!"

I stood silently, contemplating my world around me. I sighed deeply.

"Alan, gather up the troops and come on down and sign with Capitol Records."

Finally, a deal, a recording contract, a recoding contract with the label that signed *The Beatles*. Would this mean that I could still meet a Beatle? Can you imagine what it would be like to meet Paul McCartney?

It was a beautiful moment. A moment I will never forget. Yes this was something that should be shared with loved ones yet there I was, alone by the telephone, in my fruit of the loom Y-fronts all one hundred and twenty five pounds of me, with my hair looking like Elsa Lanchester's in the *Bride of Frankenstein,* with my son at school, my father at work and my mother... drunk.

"Thanks Deane, I'll see you soon."
I hung up the phone and crashed.
The following day I met with my hospital supervisor.
"You will always have a job here waiting for you," she said cheerfully.
I couldn't have asked for anything more than that, although I sensed one huge sigh of relief coming from her that kind of said, "Thank God, he's going." I had one last shift in me, one final, hospital gig and then the boy who was never going on the road, was about to do just that for a very long, long time.

SOMEONE SAVED MY LIFE TONIGHT

"CLEAR!!!"
The sound of the defibrillator firing off its electrical surge into the chest of a dying human always made me quiver, no matter how many times I had taken part in resuscitations.

As an orderly I had been part of The Crash Team, which is a small crew responsible for attending situations within the hospital where patients have lost consciousness due to heart attack or stroke and assisted in many of these procedures, performing C.P.R. (think of *Baywatch* without the breasts). What was interesting was in all of my years in nursing, I had never been the one to actually discover the patient at the moment when the stroke or heart attack happened becoming the one to call the "code" that rallies the resuscitation team. This was to change on the very last minute of my very last shift as a member of the medical community.

As a favour I had been given only four patients in a four-bed ward, all of whom had surgery that day. My shift was called doing a "special," whereby I didn't have to work the entire floor but just attend to these four post surgery patients or "fresh bleeds" as we called them. I monitored wounds, measured fluids and blood pressures and up until the last minute of my shift everything had gone smoothly. Just as I was taking the last blood pressure of my nursing career, one of my patients turned deep red and his eyes rolled up into his head. He then gave an enormous grunting exhalation, his last breath before turning blue and spasm-ing violently. I leaned over him and hit the call button.

"Code 99! Code 99!" I screamed.

I dragged his limp body onto the hard surface of the floor and began administering C.P.R., working furiously until the team arrived and the doctor in charge took over. I continued to assist. After it was all over I sat at my desk and filled out the mounds of paper work required when such a thing happens. Unfortunately I had found out first hand a few years earlier what happens when you and your hospital are on the receiving end of a law suit, whether rightly or wrongly, from the family members of a patient who runs into difficulty during his or her stay in the hospital, and it's not pleasant. The administration needs you to do whatever you can to assist in keeping the hospital from being on the wrong end of the judge's decision. Once the hospital is free and clear, you're on your own! A nurse's notes therefore are the key to their ability to recalling the events of the incident in question and so I made copious notes on this one. The very last thing I ever did as an R.N. was to walk over to the Intensive Care Unit and see how the fellow was making out. He was alive, on life support but alive nonetheless.

Now, I was done. Finished. The milk boy who became a clothier who became the shoe salesman who became the tube-cutter, who jumps at the chance to be an orderly, who became a nurse, who did not become a doctor but instead became ... a Rock Star?

But hold on just a minute there Spanky for you're not quite a rock star yet, are you?

I'M LEAVING ON A JET PLANE

The roar of the engine and a sudden burst of speed, so fast that one seems magnetized to the seat can give a guy, especially this guy, a feeling of helplessness, as some 200,000 pounds of steel grinds its way into the heavens and for a brief shining moment, your arse hangs in the balance like a little girl's doll, dangled over a balcony by her mischievous brother. I was on my way to my destiny.

Vancouver, British Colombia has since become one of my favourite places in the world, but back then on the day I made my first trip across this vast land, it was unexplored territory. Coming in over the magnificent Rocky Mountains was a sight to behold for this cheeky wee bastard from Coatbridge, and I smiled quietly to myself as I descended to the relative unknown. I was accompanied by Sam Reid and Al Connelly and it had been decided by Deane Cameron that we fledgling writers would work with a man who has since become somewhat of a legend in the business of song writing, Jim Vallance. Jim rose to fame as the behind the scenes songwriting partner of Bryan Adams as together they penned hit after hit, not only for Bryan but also for some of the biggest recording acts in the world. At the time Jim worked with us he was on the verge of stardom and had decided that he wanted to try his hand at not only co-writing with us but at producing as well. This session in Vancouver was to establish several things. Could we write great songs? Could we co-write with an established songwriter and was he the right man to take the wheel of our first major recording? It proved to be a week that changed my life, for in our first session together that lasted but a few days, we penned the two greatest selling singles of *Glass Tiger's* career: *Don't Forget Me When I'm Gone,* and *Someday.* Vallance was indeed "the man."

"Suit the ACTION to the word,
the word to the ACTION."
WILLIAM SHAKESPEARE

CHAPTER FIVE: ACTION

If I were told I must give a one-word answer to the question, "What is the meaning of life," I believe the first word to leave my lips would be ACTION, for ACTION is the life force of all things. I repeat: You must DO to get DONE! If you're in the race and the starter sounds his gun, you have to run to have any hope of winning. Indeed, in the game of life, if you stop moving, you die. From the tiniest creatures to the mightiest galaxies in our heaven's energy, the pulse of life flows through all things. ACTION is a constant even when motion is not apparent.

"Never confuse motion with ACTION."
BENJAMIN FRANKLIN

IT'S RIGHT IN FRONT OF YOU

Imagine this illustration for a moment. You're hungry, really, hungry. In the fridge you have all the makings of a great sandwich, yet you aren't making one. You're sitting on the couch thinking about how unfair it is that you're hungry. Your stomach is growling. You are actually starting to get a headache.

All physical, emotional and mental indicators point to the need for food, but still you sit there. You call your friends one after the other and say, "Man I'm so hungry."

"Why don't you make a sandwich?" they suggest.

But what do they know really? So you sit there and you start to think about that one time you made a sandwich and it didn't turn out very well.

"I might as well not even try," you say to yourself.

"That was such a terrible sandwich, I must not know how to make one."

"I don't really deserve a sandwich."

"My parents really never taught me how to make a proper sandwich and I failed home economics."

After a few minutes, you start to think some more about how hungry you are. "I could make a sandwich," you think, "but my husband bought the wrong kind of bread. So I guess I'll just have to be hungry." Eventually you die of starvation on that couch.

This may sound pretty far-fetched, but it's all too real for many people in real-life situations. Some people refuse to act because of the reasons I have mentioned, plus a thousand more. Imagine that there is something you really want, but you spend your energy on the reasons why you can't have it as opposed to actually acting upon the reasons you can and should have it. You have everything you need to start, but you don't. Often you have the support of your friends and colleagues, yet you discount their opinions while making excuses and blaming other people, allowing your ideas and dreams to die of starvation.

OOPS SORRY, YOUR MISTAKE

When I was born, the term "politically correct" had not yet entered our vernacular. This, I know today for certain, because I can still remember those sweet, tender father-son moments, when my dad would take me up onto his knee, stroke my golden blond hair, pinch my soft dimpled cheeks, look engagingly into my glistening blue eyes and say, "See you, ya wee shite, you were a mistake!"

Ahh, isn't that special? Oh, now, please don't get me wrong; my father certainly did love me. It's just that in those times and that place, subtlety had also yet to debut in the lingo of Coatbridge. If you had subtlety in my town, someone would probably have gotten you cream for it, I'm sure.

How romantic to think that your dad came home late from the pub one dark and cold Friday evening, jumped into bed with your mother, who succumbed to his belches and farts – sorry, I mean kisses and charms – and, forgetting to wear his condom from the fifties, (which was easier to find than a Goodyear tire), they accidentally create you. How do you know all of this? Because he tells you, that's how. And he tells it to you like he's telling you a story about that other old belcher and farter, Santa Claus, who you know is really your grandfather, because he's wearing your grandfather's ring, watch, working boots AND horn rimmed bi-focal glasses! Isn't it also a dead giveaway when Santa says, "Ho, Ho, Ho, Ho, Gracie! Can you get Santa a wee whisky? I'm dyin' in this bloody suit!"

But what BELIEF I had and fun I shared with those men. The grandfather I speak of was the one on my mother's side of the family, making him my dad's father-in-law, but they were bonded closer than most fathers and sons – my dad loved him dearly, even more than he loved his own father. They were inseparable, and they were wonderfully entertaining.

"Dad, c'mon are you ready? The natives are getting restless out there."
"Hang on a minute son, ye canny rush greatness."
"Alan?"
"Yes, Grandad?"
"Get your grandad a wee whisky, would ya pal?"

And so it would go, time, after time, as my family prepared to once again make its own entertainment in the living room of the small, damp, pre-fabricated, bloody freezing, post-war house that I was born in.

This was 16 Kirkshaws Avenue, home of The Frews. Come one! Come all! My dad is about to enter from the kitchen, but he's no longer Hughie Frew. He's now the Vaudevillian Vagabond Burlington Bertie.

The original song "Burlington Bertie, with the Hyde Park Drawl" was performed in the old music halls of the early twentieth century, by the one and only Vesta Tilley, a male impersonator born in Worcester in 1864. Burlington Bertie was a young man about town, a dandy and a "toff" who stays out all night partying and doesn't get up till ten thirty in the morning. Vesta paid meticulous attention to detail when dressing and always took over an hour to get ready, padding and constructing her figure. Immensely popular with women, who saw her as a symbol of independence, she went on to make as much as £500 a week in the early 1900s! Meanwhile this old bugger, my father, was also taking about an hour to get ready and he wasn't even earning £500 a year – and this was the 1960s! I know I could write an entire book on the subject of my family, and perhaps I will one day. At any rate, he had a slew of characters inside him that he would bring out at random to entertain us. The other one I loved dearly was the "Red Shadow," a character that dated back to the early twenties, when Arabmania was abundant throughout the Western culture and the legendary icon Rudolph Valentino was the golden boy of the silver screen. My dad would dress up as an Arab, complete with the kitchen towel wrapped around his head, and enter singing "My desert is waiting..." from "The Desert Song." But here is the funniest part: my granny, my mother, my Aunt Sadie, Auntie Nan and any other woman who may have been jammed into our wee living room that night would all fight over who got to be his leading lady! True. It never failed to bewilder me. Now you see, if you didn't get to be Esmeralda, you got stuck being a mere dancing girl. Who the hell just wants to be a mere dancing girl when you can be romanced in Rudolph Valentino's arms? But what I am saying is it was really my dad in bed sheets and a towel!

"D-A-D, hurry up!"

"I'm comin', I'm comin'. You know you can't ru–"
"–Rush greatness. I know Dad, I know."

How I worshipped him; I can't explain it in terms that might make any sense for you, because he was not an attentive man per se and he didn't show his love or affection, as I would with my children. He didn't take any interest in how or what I was doing. I never kicked a ball with him. Never shared a bike ride. Never played a game with him and never did he help me with homework. Hugs and kisses were for sissies and I stayed out in the streets until the pitch-blackness of nightfall. I was always just one shout away from him coming to find me and that was never good news for my backside.

When I brought a report card home for his signature it could have read, Mathematics F, English F, Geography F, Everything F and under teacher's comments, "Dear Mr. and Mrs. Frew, Alan continues to exhibit behavioural problems. As a matter of fact, he killed little Billy Potter today with a ruler and a Bic pen and then proceeded to eat him in front of the entire class!" Still my dad would have gone straight to the bottom of the page where his signature belonged, and signed it.

"Right, well done! Keep it up!"
Yet I believed in him, for there was goodness in him. He always trusted people until they gave him cause not to. He always looked for the best in a person. He laughed at life and he always took the time somehow to acknowledge that I was marching to my own drummer, strongly and independently, and he liked that. He saw talent, an edge, a rawness in me that he always encouraged and never suppressed.

During the precious early years of my life, my mother spent an inordinate amount of time at her own mother's. It's just the way it was done. It was my father who became my pillar, my lifeline, and who made me most of my dinners, especially during the workweek. I was, shall we say, a bit of a menace, and so my parents would not allow me the key to the door. They did not want me in the house alone after school, as that would spell disaster. So I was always to play out in the street until one or both of them got home from work, and nine times out of ten that was my dad. I would see his working-cap peek over the crest of the hill and then his head and body would follow. He seemed so tall and straight, so upright and proud, and I would run as fast as I could to him. We had a little saying between the two of us that we would say each time like it was the first.

"Hi ya, scud," he would say.

"Hi ya, bud!" was always the reply.

It was a common event for my parents to catch wind of my mischief as they walked home after work. As they passed the houses on my street, any neighbour who happened to be home would announce from a window or garden something like, "I saw your Alan up on your roof earlier today and.......... it didn't look good."

"Aye, it's not for me to tell tales but I saw your Alan with a large piece of cable tied from your gate to your chimney and that boy is going to kill himself one day!"

"Hello, Gracie. There was a large flame that shot out your kitchen window about an hour ago. Alan ran like the clappers, missing some hair. He went that way."

Often I would "jimmie" the window and basically break in, only to go around to the front door and let a pal or two in the house.

On one occasion my dad came in, gave me the usual warning to "stop breaking in," then immediately proceeded to make my dinner. As usual, Mum was not home. So there was my dad and I sitting having our dinner around 5:00 p.m. when soft, muffled sounds began to become audible and I could see him rubbing his ear as if to say, "Is that a noise?" I'd heard it as well as "Lassie" could hear "WALKIES?" But I said nothing n-o-t-h-i-n-g.

"Mmmph!" says the noise.

Again, "MMMmmph!"

"What the hell is THAT?" says dad. "Do you hear something Alan?"

"No Dad."

"Mmmph! Hello? Mmmph! HELP?" squeaks the sound.

"You don't hear THAT?" he says again.

"Maybe."

"MAYBE?"

"MMMMPH! HEEEEELP!" the voice cries to the heavens.

"What in the name of Christ! WHO IS THAT?"

"John Kerr," I say poking at my dinner plate.

"JOHN KERR? And where the hell IS he?"

"He's locked in your wardrobe."

"LOCKED IN MY WARDROBE? WHAT THE HELL IS HE DOING LOCKED IN MY WARDROBE? Who locked him in?"

"Me."

"And how long has he been in there?"

"Oh, since about half past one. Hey, guess what, the teacher let us out early."

"Half past one? Alan, it's six o'clock. Go and let that poor laddie out of that wardrobe, right now!"

When I opened the wardrobe door, John was staring straight ahead, trance-like and shaking like a leaf. I knew he would be, as I had locked him in it many times before.

"Want a chip, John?"

WE ARE FAMILY

Yes, there was never a dull moment around that wee house and I always believed my dad. I believed him when he told me that he was a World War II Flying Ace who had single-handedly shot down over one hundred German planes, or that he had fought with "Charlie Wingate and his Chindits" deep behind enemy lines within the jungles of Burma, when in actual fact the biggest war he'd ever fought was the one with the sleeve of his jacket when it was time to leave the pub. I found out years later that he had applied to join the army but was denied admission because tradesmen were needed at home to build the machines of war, not die using them. The fact that he never fought in the war always troubled him and he would become incensed if teased about being a coward and not going to battle.

I believed him when he told me he had fought for the Middleweight Boxing Championship of the World title, or when he said to me one time while sporting a black eye, "Don't worry Alan, I'll be all right. By the way, you should see the face on the other guy!" In actual fact he had been walking home from the pub drunk, took a stumble and hit his head on a big red mailbox. But then again, I always believed him.

"Alan, your big brother is coming home from Canada for a holiday. You have a little nephew now and so your brother, his wife and the little boy are coming home to meet all of us."

"Big brother? Nephew?" Waves of confusion swept over me, for I had never been able to get a handle on the concept of having a brother. You see, (and don't ask me why for the life of me), my brother, as a tiny baby, stayed over one night with my mum's parents, and basically that one night became the rest of his life before moving to Canada as an adult. As I said earlier, do not ask me how something like that can happen, but I do know the same thing happened to my father, who was also raised by his grandparents. I think it is based in some old country custom where the firstborn son went to live and help the elders of the family, rather than his own parents, who were younger, stronger and more able to take care of things themselves. And of course more than likely they would get pregnant again and have numerous children. So giving up the first-born wouldn't seem like such a big deal when you expect eight or nine kids.

Anyway, the fact that my brother was older than me by thirteen years meant that by the time I was four or five years old he was already a young man of seventeen or eighteen and since he did not live in my home, I could not for the life of me figure out who the hell he was. I called him Gordon Fleming, which was my grandparents' surname.

So the brother that I did not know came home, and he, my older sister and I were now all under the one roof for the very first time in our lives. At the same moment I got a new brother, I also got a new idol. It didn't take very long at all for me to want to be like him. He took me to see my beloved Glasgow Rangers play their bitter rivals, Glasgow Celtic, who were in the midst of dominating the scene from the late '60s to early '70s. And although they defeated us that night, I still loved it because I was with my big brother. Yes, he grew on me rather quickly.

Still, I was only a boy and my time with him was very limited. He, on the other hand, was a man and spent a lot of time in the company of our father and uncles, drinking, talking, telling tales of Canada, the New World, the Promised Land. It was during this time that he said something to my father that forever changed the course of all of our lives. He said it only in passing, and I am not sure if he was even serious. He said it to my dad, who in another off-the-cuff passing remark repeated it to my mother. I just happened to be on the floor playing with my GI Joes, who had all coincidentally decided that the Secret Agent Man my mother had bought me didn't fit in, and was to be taken out to the back yard some day very soon to be burned at the stake.

So what exactly was it that my brother said to my father just in passing? Five simple words: "You should come to Canada!"

WORKIN' NINE TO FIVE

My father was already forty-nine years of age by this time. Certainly not old by any stretch, but no spring chicken either. He had now worked in the steel mill since the tender age of fifteen, and after thirty-four years a man starts thinking about the possibility of retirement with a nice big severance package, a gold watch, and a big pat on the back. He wouldn't get anything like that in Canada. He'd be out looking for whatever job he could, and at the age of fifty, that just wasn't very appealing at all. Oh yes, one other thing, we were broke.

When the topic of Canada came up he would declare,
"Me? Canada? Impossible. That's okay for younger men, know what I mean?"

This would be repeated ad nauseam any time he had a good amount of drink
in him.
"How in the name of God are we going to be able to afford Canada?" he'd
bellow. "It's just NOT going to happen."

Well, I have news for you Hughie Frew…It already has!

> *"Whatever you can do, or dream you can, begin it.*
> *Boldness has genius, power and magic in it."*
> GOETHE

NO REST

ACTION is impossible to escape and is one of the common denominators of all
living things. ACTION is the response that creates outcome. It determines the
drama of life. This is where the lion and the gazelle play out which one lives and
which one dies. This is where a Mother Theresa completely takes another
pathway from a Bin Laden or where the old saying comes from that the only
difference between a great con man and a great salesman is the outcome of their
actions. Their INTENTION has predetermined the type of outcome we will see.
ACTION puts INTENTION into play. Funny thing is, even if I ask you what
you are going to do today and you answer, "nothing, I am going to be a couch
potato today", well even that takes ACTION. You need to lock the front door,
get the chips and dip, find the clicker, shoo the cat, flick the channels…phew!
Sounds like a lot of work to me. Sleeping? Well, there is still a ton of ACTION
going on within your mind and body. Dreaming, digesting, growing, healing, cell
death, cell birth, and a million other duties being performed at levels we cannot
even fathom. So you see the light never turns off; in fact there is no "off" switch.
You are always "on" to some degree, so why not align this unavoidable ACTION
with your desires, beliefs, intentions and yes, even your dreams?

OUR HOME AND NATIVE LAND

"What are you doing, son?"

"Easy, I am aligning my actions with my dreams."

"What are you thinking?"

"Simple, I am thinking about what it will be like when I get there."

"And where exactly are you going?"

"Why, Canada of course."

My brother returned to Canada in the summer of 1969 not knowing me all that much better than he had for the previous twelve years and ten months of my short young life. But for me it would never be the same. He had changed it forever without even knowing it, for I, this scrawny, scrapping, hand-me-down wheeling-dealing kid from Scotland was going to Canada.

"Right, tie his hands, you there, tie his feet and ask him if he wants a blindfold."

"Do you want a blindfold?"

"No, you bastards! I am braver than all of you guys put together! I don't need your stinking blindfold!"

Executions are always touchy things, aren't they? This one, I'm afraid, was going to be no different. GI Joe was the greatest, and was not only from different areas of the armed forces like the Army, the Marines and the Navy, he also came from different armies, like the German, Japanese and the French Foreign Legion. I had begun with only one GI Joe, that being GI Joe MARINE. However, when you bought accessories for the product you could save up stars that were attached to the box each accessory came in, and after saving the required amount necessary, you could send away for a free GI Joe. Coming from a family with no money, I had proven beyond a shadow of a doubt that what you think about you get, and between my David Livingstone Memorial scheme, my saving up pop bottles for refunds, and my playing the flute for tipsy protestants who only wanted to hear tunes in which mayhem, plague and murder were bestowed upon the Pope and his followers (where I made an absolute fortune because I could play them in my sleep), all of these and more allowed me to have six GI Joes! They looked cool. Their arms and legs were bendable, you could position them, you could dress and undress them in awesome uniforms, and the newest ones would bark voice commands when you pulled a cord in their backs. Yes, I loved GI Joe.

Secret Agent Man, on the other hand, was not bendable. He was stiff plastic and wore a painted-on suit. He had no uniforms, couldn't be positioned, and didn't speak! He just had to go.

They say it takes only a spark to get the fire roaring. Well, I have news for you. It may indeed take only a spark for the fire, but it takes a can of gasoline to get the attention of the local fire service. You see, a spark just doesn't cut it like a fire! So you get the can of gasoline that your father happens to have in the unlocked shed in the back garden, grab the matches, and you're all set. This burning at the stake will be underway very quickly, with just one wave of the can to get things going. I held it to my ear and shook.
"Good. It's almost full."
I unscrewed the cap, got it on its side and with a drum roll and a count I let it go.

WOOOOOOOSH!
"No more darkness, no more night,
Lordy, Lordy, I saw the light!"

Yes indeed, I saw the light all right! I saw it so closely it took an eyebrow with it. I didn't even have time to blink. My instantaneous reaction was to scream and get that can of gasoline up and away from me, saving the rest of my face for another day. The can, however, had further mischief in mind. It hit the side of the shed, my dad's shed, and I know you won't believe this but it set it on fire! It then introduced itself to the plant life.
"TREE'S ON FIRE!"
It ricocheted off of the shed-tree combo, landing next to the fence that was shared with our neighbours, setting it on fire as well. By now you probably know my modus operandi. I am amazed I never had tryouts with the British

Olympic track and field team, for setting fire to your dad's shed, fence and garden is a great training regimen for any young budding athlete. Once again, dear friends, I ran like the clappers around to the front of the house, in through the living room, settling at the kitchen table across from my father, who was engrossed in his newspaper. I looked over his shoulder, out through our kitchen window and observed what was now a full-fledged twelve-foot-high roaring fire.

"Dad?"
"Yes?"
"I'm going to Canada."

Just then a flame shot up in an attempt to kiss the hydro wires.

"That's nice son," he said never looking away from his paper.
"I'm serious Dad, in fact we're...(loud sirens were closing in on us)... we're ALL going to Canada."
"Aye that's good son. What's all that racket?" he said, inquisitively.

I could see several large firemen in our neighbour's yard preparing to blast the raging flames with water. Their siren was very loud indeed.

"What the hell's going on," said my father. "Hmm, there must be a fire somewhere, eh?"
Sherlock Holmes, your job is safe.
"Yes, Dad."

Gallons and gallons of water were dousing the shed, the trees, the fence and a big melted blob of soldiers...oh yes and a spy.

"Dad?"
"Uh huh?"
"Can we go to Canada – right now?"

THREE JEERS FOR THE
RED, WHITE AND BLUE

I have a little diary here at home that I actually found long before I ever thought of writing this book. It's a little pocket daytimer that someone once gave me. I'm not certain, but I get the feeling that it probably came from my mum and it is from the year 1969. Within its pages, written in my thirteen year old scribble, are things like "Going to Canada", "Sold table today", "Only six more weeks to go." When I read it I get such mixed emotions. I feel a sense of pain, sadness and even a little embarrassment for that boy, yet I am also proud, impressed and a little in awe of him. Let me explain.

You see, I didn't set foot on Canadian soil until August 18th, 1972. So why then was this boy writing things like "only six weeks to go" in 1969, and why was he selling off family belongings, much, I might add, to his father's consternation.

Well, it is very simple. I was so receptive, so desirous of, so believing in and so intended on going to Canada that all of my actions were those of a boy who was leaving his homeland, leaving all he had ever known behind and moving to a new world. When I think back on it, it is everything from warm and endearing to hilariously funny, yet painful too, for I had everyone around me convinced – and I mean EVERYONE – that my family and I were indeed leaving. And so everyone in my school, every pal in my street, their families, their friends and so on, all believed that I was indeed going to Canada.

I would pick a date, say, November 28th, 1969, and I would tell everyone that *that* was when we were leaving. I would offer them the chance to buy our couch, our bed, our teacups, even our dog, and come they would, one after another after another.

Man at door: "Aye, hello, I am here to see your couch."
My dad: "See my couch?"
Man at door: "Yes, your couch, the one you're selling."

My dad: "But I'm not."
Man at door: "Not what?"
My dad: "Selling."
Man at door: "Why not?"
My dad: "Because our arses will be sitting on the floor if I do! ALAN!!!"

And this would go on and on and still they came.

Stranger in our garden: "Hello."
My dad: "Hello, and what is it you think you're doing exactly?"
Stranger in our garden: "What does it look like I'm doin'? I'm digging up these here hedges."
My dad: "I can see that, but what do you plan on doing with them?"
Stranger in our garden: "Well, I'll plant what I need into my own garden and re-sell the others."
My dad: "Re-sell?"
Stranger in our garden: "Yes, sell what I don't use, to my neighbour."
My dad: "ALAN!!!!"

The dates would come and the dates would go and I would get tortured relentlessly. Finally, no one believed me. Not a single soul.

"You're not going anywhere! You're not going to Canada! You're a big liar, Frew!"

As I write about it for you, I still get that feeling of distress that was always so present for me during this time. The taunting, the jokes –and yet, never did I change my story. I would simply rub out the date and write in another one. I never changed my ACTION SANDWICH, not for one second. Every idea, every ACTION, every BELIEF and every DESIRE were those of a lad going to Canada.

The following winter my brother thought he was doing a good thing when for Christmas he sent home an anorak, today known as a parka, that not only stood out in a town like Coatbridge, but would have stood out in a town like

ANCHORAGE ALASKA because, my dear reader, it was an ALL FUR parka! Oh, but there's more, much, much more, for this big, hairy, monstrous covering also happened to be RED, WHITE and BLUE! I looked like a polar bear at a Republican convention.

Now, in today's world, Britain is post-revolutionary when it comes to Americanization. Hamburgers, cheeseburgers, fries, Budweiser, words like "yeah", "garbage" and "right on", all of these things have become not only acceptable, they are the norm. Walk down any of Glasgow's main streets and see a guy wearing a Miami Dolphins football shirt with a number sixty-five on it – he will not get a second glance. Television, movies, fast-food chains and especially the Internet have brought mainstream New York and Los Angeles right into the living rooms of London, Glasgow, Manchester or Belfast. It is ALL ONE WORLD.

But this was 1969, and this was Coatbridge, and their world wasn't ready for hamburgers and fries, not ready for sneakers and pop, not ready for a number on a team shirt to go any higher than number eleven, and God knows it certainly wasn't ready for a guy on his way to school in a RED, WHITE and BLUE FURRY COAT!

"Oh God, please, please, if you really are up there, could you do me this one small favour, please…yes…right now. Could you please just send a big ball of fire right here to my house and melt me to death…please?"

"Is it not bad enough that I am a Protestant totally outnumbered in a Catholic town nicknamed 'Little Ireland'? Is it not enough that a coat with a hood has never been invented as far as this part of the world is concerned? Is it not enough that everyone thinks I am a total bloody lunatic because I keep saying I am moving to Canada but never do? Is all of that not enough torture, dear God? How then have you found it within your mighty wisdom to SEND ME THIS F***ING RED, WHITE AND BLUE FUR COAT? ARRRRRRRRRRRGH!"

And so, with not a snowman or even a snowflake around for probably some five hundred miles in all directions, I set off on foot dressed as Frosty the Snowman's wee brother, *in drag*.

It was hard, it was very hard...and yet I believed. Three years had passed and still I filled my diary. Still I shouted it for all to hear, "I AM going to Canada."

But still we stayed. My dad exhausted himself trying to convince me not to do this to myself. And then it happened. He got laid off from work.

"BLOODY HELL! Are they kidding me?" he screamed. I don't think I had ever heard him this angry in my life.

"Eight hundred and fifty f***ing measly quid? Are they daft? And not even a goddamned handshake on the way out the door? Who the #^*@ do they think they are?"

He was seething, for after more than thirty years of service to this company, my dad was being shown the door with only eight hundred and fifty pounds (about two thousand dollars) to show for it. That was it. Done. He was gone and there wasn't a thing he could do about it.

Or was there?

"Well that's it! F***! THEM and F*** THIS PLACE. WE ARE GETTING OUT OF HERE, NOW!"

What had he just said? Was I dreaming? Did he just say that we are going to leave this toilet of a town? Is that what he just said? But to where?

"Where are we goin' Dad?"
"WE ARE GOING TO CANADA!!"

IF YOU WANT TO SING OUT, SING OUT

If I told you that you must do one of the following, either rob a bank or visit children in hospital, the chances are you'd be visiting the children. If I told you that you must either clean the equipment in a fire hall or in a slaughterhouse, I think I know what most would choose. That's because when faced with such obvious scenarios we have little difficulty choosing where to apply our actions, especially when we have an outside force giving us very little choice. But when choice is available, I know that many of us struggle with the idea of the black and white scenario of this vs. that. No one can make these decisions for you. Only you can decide:

Will you work out and watch what you eat, or choose to be fat, unfit and risk a heart attack?

Will you quit smoking or risk an early demise from lung cancer?

Will you save at least ten percent of your income or keep blowing it on junk?

Will you run for city council and try to improve your community, or continue to be an armchair critic, pointing out the flaws of those currently holding office?

Identifying these types of obvious scenarios allows you to "get into the water" without necessarily being able to do the backstroke, but it's eventually doing the backstroke that gives you control over the situation that directly affects you. When I talk with people about this I often hear that it is a lack of confidence that keeps them from taking ACTION. Well, let me say this: do something, try something, attempt something, achieve *something*, and the confidence will follow. Make that a little mantra and trust yourself. How can you not gain more confidence if you are trying, attempting and achieving? They say that "practice makes perfect"; well, it also builds confidence.

ALL IN ALL YOU'RE JUST A...

Why is it that those who are the best at any given skill or talent are not always the ones who succeed? Have you ever played soccer, football, basketball, tennis, darts, Trivial Pursuit or dominoes with someone so talented that it boggles your mind as to why they are not a legend, while some other "what-in the-name-of-God-is-he-doing-on-the-field" is out there making millions?

I have played soccer with guys who were so talented it was beyond my comprehension that they weren't playing professionally. Yet I would watch Rangers, Celtic, Manchester United or Liverpool and scratch my head as to why some "diddy" was playing and being paid pretty well to do so.

How many virtuosic guitar players are selling guitar picks in music stores? How many perfect tenors are delivering mail? How many teens are in detention centres instead of universities? The reason to me is clear. It comes down to choice, and choice is ACTION.

You are every choice you have ever made in your life up to this very moment, so if you are not happy with those choices then you must elevate them. You must make better choices.

A colleague of mine, Cynthia O'Neill, has a company called High Altitude Thinking (www.highaltitudethinking.ca). High altitude thinking speaks volumes to me about RECEPTIVITY, DESIRE, BELIEF, INTENTION and, of course, ACTION. It immediately elevates my attitude. It begs me to function at a loftier level. It commands me to be alert, aware, and receptive; to ask better, more enlightened questions of myself and of those around me. It places my desires on the top rung of the ladder. It says, "I believe in me!" Higher altitude thinking raises the bar on INTENTION and motivates me to take immediate ACTION in pursuing my life's dreams.

That moment, or for some of you *this* moment, is the instant when we run out of excuses and must take responsibility for the shape of our lives. I have not arrived, and I struggle with many of the things you all struggle with and have the same questions and sometimes non-productive solutions that you do. But I have chosen to make each day better than the day before. I guarantee that if you work incrementally towards a better life, you will achieve it. There is no other possible outcome. So it is with those who I mentioned earlier, who have far greater talent yet are not always the ones who succeed. For what I neglected to mention was that I now know why the guys that I played soccer with, who were so highly skilled, didn't make the grade. They did not honour their gift. Instead they chose things like alcohol, anger, an undisciplined training and practice regimes, while those that I so misjudged as "diddies" actually honoured their gift and in doing so practiced all of the discipline required to succeed.

THE LONG AND WINDING ROAD

Let me briefly revisit that moment on my way to the fridge when I must decide how I wish to execute my DESIRE to eat and stay on course with making a sandwich as opposed to grabbing the pie and chocolate milk.

ACTION is where one can really excel or, conversely, derail. In your head you can be as receptive as possible, DESIRE what you know to be true in your heart, believe you deserve, and INTEND until the cows come home, but without the discipline of ACTION, all that has come before is rendered useless.

Take the classic case of a recovering alcoholic who is receptive to the need to stop drinking and yet at the end of rehabilitation, takes the ACTION of heading to the bar and sabotages all of the hard work that *THE ACTION SANDWICH* put into his DESIRE to recover.

THE ACTION SANDWICH keeps fat people fat, poor people poor, rich people rich and so on. However, when applied with positive RECEPTIVITY, DESIRE, BELIEF and INTENTION, it will assist you to ACTION your way from fat to thin, poor to rich, depressed to happy – for it is an all-encompassing formula that I promise you, you cannot escape from. You are doing it regardless...ALWAYS. You are that which you know you are, nothing more, nothing less – the total summation of all of your choices. Use it wisely, my friends, for even ACTION falls prey to time and, as we know, time waits for no one. Use it continuously and thoughtfully, and never assume you've arrived. How many people have I seen in my industry who used the formula to become rock stars and then used it again to become drug addicts or alcoholics?

I like to think of my fulfilled goals and successes as tokens or rewards along my pathway of ACTION. I don't like to think in terms of "Oh, I must take ACTION", but rather that I am in a constant state of evolution, where being and becoming gives me a sense of always striving to move forward on this wondrous journey called life. You cannot strive backwards or even sideways. As soon as I find myself in a state of "being," my brain immediately asks "So what's next?" So here we are finally at the roller coaster of life. This is the holy grail: life in ACTION for the sake of goodness and fun and business and pleasure, loving, family, friends, rewards, good old money, and of course my favourite condiment, PASSION.

Ah, PASSION you're next.

TEN WAYS TO TAKE ACTION

1. A THOUSAND MILLION QUESTIONS - A better question demands a better answer. Your brain knows all the answers. Stop avoiding the truth, accept responsibility and ask tough questions. Ask.

2. LIGHTS, CAMERA, ACTION! - Stop waiting to live. Talking about what you could do, should do, might do, or worse still, could have done, is useless and an unconstructive use of

ACTION. Decide on something, even *one thing* and move. Get going.

3. BEGIN THE BEGUINE - So you don't know how to start the dance of life, okay relax, it's not the end of the world, don't beat yourself up. Choose the steps that look the most appealing, even if awkward, and move. Clumsy feet in ACTION are better than no ACTION at all. Come dancing!

4. DID I TELL YOU THE ONE ABOUT - Your brain is way more important than your brawn so keep it involved constantly. Talk, dream, think, write or even sing about what you are doing, where you are going and how you are going to get there. Doing this only enhances and reinforces that it shall be so. The universe is listening. Speak up!

5. EIGHT DAYS A WEEK - Be prepared to step it up. Accomplishment asks for unwavering resolve and effort. Loving what you have chosen will help, but purpose, sweat and resolve will help you even more. C'mon!

6. POOR, POOR PITIFUL ME - Success evades those who feel unworthy simply because they focus on unworthiness. Keep putting one foot in front of the other no matter how muddy the trail is. Get off the pity train. I mean it.

7. TOMORROW, TOMORROW - Accept the fact that you are every choice and every decision you have ever made. You are the result of all of your yesterdays. Done? Good, move on! Now the good news, you will be the result tomorrow of what you decide today! Rejoice and decide.

8. HAND ME THAT MOP - If you don't love it, want it, use it, read it or care if you have it, then get rid of it. It's hard to take ACTION when you're lugging crap along for the ride physically or mentally. Lighten the load. Clean up your act.

9. ABRACADABRA! - Success isn't a rabbit pulled from a hat, nor is it a letter mailed to your door. Success is the culmination of efforts repeated over and over again. Ask the right question and get the right answer. Now commit.

10. A SIMPLE PLAN - Get up off your arse. You must DO to get DONE. Need I say more?

MY SONG
Opus 5

WE'RE OFF TO SEE THE WIZARD

New York, Paris, London, Madrid, sounds glamorous doesn't it? It is I guess. For the boy who ran away from Father Dickie-bird, and away from his granny and away from a furious band and away and away and away, was now running at these places, faster than he ever could run away. It was a whirlwind, a speeding train without the driver and a rocket doing what a rocket does best. We were hanging on for all we were worth.

The first tour was basically one where just myself and the senior representative from our U.S. label toured the entire continental USA in about six weeks, setting up the soon to be released recording for all of the major American radio stations. Occasionally one of the other lads would come out to join us, which was a great relief, but for the most part it was Jack, the record guy and myself. Never again would breakfast in New

York, lunch in Baltimore, dinner in Philly and cocktails in Chicago sound exciting, for that was achieved all in one day! We have a thing in our industry called "meet and greets" where you shake hands with hundreds of people that you are meeting for the very first time, either working the room or simply greeting fans or contest winners but this trip I christened, "meet and eat," for it seemed like that was all we did. You are repeating the same thing over and over again, trying to win the favour of each of the key players from the various radio stations in hopes that they will add your song to their play-lists. We worked it and it worked. The first release, *Thin Red Line* was a smash hit for the band. We toured and toured and toured, working with the likes of *Journey*, Tina Turner, Rod Stewart and yes, even *Cheap Trick* who had caused me to say years ago, "Now I want that job!"

There it is again. Tell the universe and it listens.

The pace was frantic. It was like going back to the "beans" days, only in a limousine, a jet or in a luxury bus. Having no boundaries, bosses, rules or limits, can be a deadly combination and has been for so many of my kind. Drugs and alcohol aplenty with no one to tell you no, can be a one-way ticket to doom. I had sessions that I look back on and gasp, as I realize how much was consumed without stopping. On one occasion I had tried cocaine, which got me so hyped up that I wrecked my room. The scene at the front desk was "Monty Python-esque" in its darkness and humour.

Desk Clerk: "Yes sir, how can I be of assistance?"
Singer: "Well, I've wrecked my room...your room."
Desk Clerk: "Very good sir, just let me get my note pad, and, okay go ahead then sir."
"Well let's see. I've smashed the telly."
"Very well."
"And the head board."
"Uh huh, got that."
"Smashed a window."
"Gooood."

"And I threw the mattress out onto the street from the 22nd floor."
"Right you are then sir, I'll send someone out to get that right away.
Now if you'll just be so kind sir, to sign here for the damages, I'll have
you on your way in a jiffy sir ... good. Well goodnight then sir, will there
be anything else I can get you?"
"Yeah, ...a mattress."

WRESTLING WITH THE IDEA OF BEING A ROCK STAR

I befriended one of the record reps in America called Terry who was
based out of Atlanta, Georgia, a lovely man, who quickly became a great
pal. We both had a great PASSION for music and an undying love of
movies and movie trivia. He was charming and funny and very quick
with his wit. We had verbal sparring that I loved. One evening he was
entertaining several guests with yours truly when I accidentally knocked
over a candle setting the table on fire.
"Terry I am so sorry," I said apologetically. "I spoiled the moment."
"No you didn't man," he replied. "You simply created another one!"
That was Terry.

On days off, which were few, I would pop out to Atlanta to see him and
together we played hard. He was Mr. Promotion and was always
working to have me be seen as much as possible. On one crazy occasion
he got the two of us front row tickets to the wrestling match, which was
just on the cusp of being the monstrous spectacle that it is today. Hulk
Hogan, Roddy Piper and Randy "The Macho-Man" Savage were all
coming into their own as stars of the ring and on this night I was getting
caught on camera as the behemoths would toss each other out of the ring
and begin battling right in front of Terry and I. In one particular match
up, Ric Flair was fighting a wrestler called the "Iron Shiek," who would
prance about the ring waving the Iranian flag, inciting the Americans
who had long memories and remembered all too well, the Iranian
hostage crisis in which members of the new Islamic regime held 63
diplomats and three other hostages from November 4th, 1979, through
to January 20th, 1981.

The "Sheik" would yell at them, "ME HATE AMEERICA! ME HATE YOOOR COOONTREEE!" and the crowd would go insane throwing beer, pop, ice cream, you name it, and it hit us in the front row.
"Man isn't this great!" screamed Terry with a large ice cream cone lodged on his head.
"That's not quite what I would call it," I yelled back at the top of my lungs.
"What if the crowd gets out of hand and they riot? We could get mangled down here, don't ya think!"
"Man I hope so," barked Terry. "Think of the press!"

Sure enough Ric and the Sheik, brought their battle out of the ring and down to us, causing us to get drenched and caked and caught in the crossfire of a frenzy of abuse laid on the mad Iranian.

After the fight Terry said, "C'mon man, let's go!"
"Go where," I enquired.
"To the dressing room. I know the guys."
When we entered, Flair was the first to speak up.
"Hey Terry what's up man? Did you enjoy the fight?"
"Awesome!" replied Terry still buzzing from the spectacle.
Suddenly the mad Iranian "Sheik" came out of the shower area, looked straight at us and said, "Hey, Terry, long time no see man. What's up?"
"Hey Hoss," said Terry, "that was great man."
"Holy Moly," I thought to myself. What happened to, "Me hate yooooor coontreee?" Where did, "Me hate Ameerica go?"
This guy I swear had a Texas drawl going on.
"Hey thanks a lot guys for getting down beside us, it was great," said my friend.
"Any time T, catch you soon," said the American hater and then off he went.
Those crazy Iranian Sheiks fool you every time, don't they?

Terry asked me to be the best man at his wedding and six weeks later, he made me his pallbearer at his funeral.

It was in his home that I spent my short recovery period after my first knee operation and during that time he woke me up one morning, sparkling like a boy who has just been picked for the starting team. "Dude wake up," he yelled.

I was groggy, not only from sleep but from the after effects of the anesthetic and pain medication that I was on.

"C'mon man, let's go! We are going to Ringgold, Georgia!"

"What the hell's in Ringgold," I asked.

'My bride to be. I'm getting married!"

Ringgold is a city located in Catoosa County, Georgia, which as of the year 2000 census was still showing a population of just over 2000 residents. This story however takes place in 1987 and the little "cowboy town" of Ringgold looked mighty smaller than that. It was like something straight out of an episode of Bonanza. A "Smith & Wesson" carrying Sheriff who was a dead ringer for Gene Autry, the Singing Cowboy, married Terry and his fiancé. The ceremony took place with the Bride, Groom, Best Man (on crutches), Sheriff and a piano playing witness all in attendance in the Sheriff's office. Afterwards I took them both for traditional Wings and Ribs. I had never seen him happier than on that day at his Cowpoke Weddin'.

I left the comfort of Terry's home and set off on tour with *Glass Tiger*. The brace for my leg was now firmly a part of my life while he set off on married life with his new bride. Never, ever in my wildest of nightmares could I have imagined that this was the last time I would ever see him.

My life had already been scarred by tragedy a couple of years earlier while on tour with *Journey*. I was making my regular call home to make sure all was well with my son, when my dad's voice answered in a very strange way.

"Hey Dad, I don't have long, I gotta get going, everything okay?" I asked.

"Well, err, yes, it'll be fine. You err, you go on, and call back af..."

"What's wrong?" I demanded.

"Now it's probably just a scare. Go on and call home right after your performance, okay?"

After unsuccessfully prodding him for answers I reluctantly did as he asked. I did it by going to that place in an entertainer's soul where, "The show must go on" lives. It's a place I have been to, many, many, times.

When I got off of the stage, drenched in my own sweat I went to the production office and called home. My sister answered. She didn't have to tell me what I already knew.

She had fed the baby and put her down for a nap as she had done on any one of the other ninety-some-odd-days her little life had blessed this earth. Baby was still napping when her husband came home from work and after washing up immediately went in to her room for a little peek into her crib. What he found this time though was a blue and unresponsive infant.

Picking her up and screaming to his wife, they rushed this little angel to the nearest hospital only to have her pronounced dead from S.I.D.S. (Sudden Infant Death Syndrome) shortly after their arrival at the emergency department.

I was devastated. I was so devastated.

Now you question the meaning of it all, huh?

Our schedule was such that we had a three-day window coming up during which time we were supposed to hop off this grinding tour in the U.S., get on a plane, fly to Holland, do a live television performance, hop another plane, fly to London, do a breakfast television show, grab yet another plane, fly back to Florida and pick up the tour with *Journey* four days later.

Everyone in *Journey's* camp were incredibly sensitive to what had just happened and since we had two more shows before some time off, they told me they would try and find a substitute band.

I sat up in my room all night, calling home constantly hoping one of my calls might change the outcome of what had just happened. It did not.

In the morning someone from the production team came to my room to tell me that they had a flight for me late that evening, however the bad news (as if any news could be worse), was that they could not get a band to cover both shows, only one. I was being asked if I had the fortitude to get up on that stage just one more time before flying home to Canada for the baby's funeral.

PEPPERONI, BACON AND DOUBLE MUSHROOM

I have never met *Bono*. I don't know *Sting*. I have never had a conversation with *Annie Lennox*. I do however know this. No matter who you are, there are times when as a performer you can be on stage, completely focused on the task at hand, singing your hit songs to the frenzied masses as the words are flowing out with precision and strength, while having a completely unrelated conversation with yourself inside of your head.
For example my mouth can be singing,

"You, you take my breath away, oh,oh,oh,oh,"
"Love, thinks it's here to stay, oh,oh,oh,oh,"

While my inner voice is saying,

"God, I can't wait to get back to the hotel and have a nice warm bath."
And as the crowds cheer, my mouth continues,

"Still so much for me to do,
And I can't stop loving you."

Just as my inner voice is saying,
"I think I'll order a nice, well fired.........pizza!"

Removing yourself mentally from a difficult, stressful, absorbing task is similar to the resting of your heart between beats. You don't have to tell your heart to keep beating, for it knows exactly what it is doing yet that little tiny rest between each beat is as necessary to sustain your life as the air that you breathe, or the water that you drink. In fact the rest period of the heart is considered in many ways, more important, if that's possible, than the beating part.

Great athletes talk of zoning-out or going on automatic, which doesn't mean they are any less focused on the task at hand but I guarantee you they are not saying. "Okay, move that foot, now that one. Good. Left hand up, now, jump." I will bet you Michael Jordan has ordered himself up a few pizzas from centre court while in the middle of some of the most important games of his life. This is how I managed to go onstage that night. This is how, although I knew my baby niece was dead, I managed to sing, gyrate, smile and rock! This is where "The show must go on" comes from.

Late that night I flew out of Miami back to Toronto, where just a few hours later, I was placing a little teddy bear at the side of the dead child. I was now pretty delirious from not having slept for close to forty-eight hours, a trend that was to continue right through this new day and into the evening spent around the kitchen table chatting at my sister's home. My family, like most dysfunctional families, still seem to do funerals and weddings extremely well. At least it brings us all together.

At the funeral I carried my niece's coffin to its resting place as a limo with its engine running, waited for me at the gravesite.

This death had of course brought me home unexpectedly and so I was seeing family, friends and my son, for the first time in weeks. I took him into the limo for a few minutes for a chat and some hugs before having to leave him again. I couldn't help thinking about what it would have been like if the call had come in that he had died, and not my niece. Would the show have still gone on? Would that have been possible? Does the "LOVE AND SUFFERING" infect you that badly?

There was a television show in Amsterdam followed by a television show in London and then it was back to Florida to pick up where we had left off touring America.

The bubble of touring is a well-oiled machine. The chain of command: Manager - Road Manager - Stage Manager - Sound Tech - Lighting Tech and Roadies become your family for out there, they are all you have. I found however, that the external demands put on me especially in the earlier part of our success kept me quite distant from the crew, meaning that usually I was off somewhere else, promoting, via radio and television, just about any time the band had a day or two off.

Once, when we were doing shows for Disney in Florida and California, and living in both locations for a month each time, Sam (keyboards) and I would hop up to Vancouver and work with Jim Vallance on new material for our second release. This pattern of always being somewhat separate from the crew continued for the duration of our band's success. It was on one of those occasions in Vancouver that I decided to pop home to Toronto to see my son. Tragedy had struck again as I learned about Terry.

He had been married about six weeks and was in the midst of a heavy work schedule. Record guys are a special-breed. Their job basically is two fold - schmooze radio guys into adding your band's song on their airplay list and schmooze the band guys when they are in your city. Always keep them happy. Needless to say, this lifestyle requires great stamina. On some occasions you could be out seven days and seven evenings a week working it. This is what he was doing the last week of his life. To add a little salt to his already exhausted wounds that week he was suffering from a bad toothache for which he was taking some prescription painkillers until he could have the tooth pulled. Combined with a substantial amount of alcohol he was unknowingly depressing his central nervous system as that is what alcohol and narcotics do, they slow you down.

On the fateful evening, in the wee hours of the morning his doorbell rang. It was a buddy of his who had just had a fight with his girlfriend and was looking for a place to vent his frustration and lay his head down. Terry welcomed him in and poured each of them a drink. The buddy then pulled out a large amount of cocaine. They snorted some lines of death before Terry's wife awakened and joined them. It was now around 4 a.m.

What happened next was positively creepy.

Terry had lit himself a cigarette as the three of them continued their conversation. In one of those moments where talking subsides and silence ensues Terry's wife noticed that his cigarette was actually burning into his finger without his reacting to it. The buddy started into another conversation but Terry's wife was now distracted by her husband's unresponsiveness to this cigarette burning into his hand.

"Terry, your cigarette, can't you feel that?" she asked.
He sat motionless. Speechless.
She arose and went over to him, putting her hand on his shoulder.
"Terry? TERRY!"
Sitting upright and without a single motion or hint of sound, he was dead.
What happened next must have been so terrifying for her, for the buddy panicked knowing that in a matter of minutes the place would be swarming with paramedics and police officers.
"Man, I gotta get out of here," he cried. "I can't be found with this shit on me, I gotta go!"
"Help me, don't leave, call an ambulance and help me," she pleaded but her plea fell on deaf ears for he was out the back windows, down the fire escape and gone before she had even called for help.

A KODAK MOMENT

"Mr. Frew? There is a telephone call for you sir," said the waiter. What a beautiful day it had been. I had my boy with me for some well-deserved father-son time and we went to a large park that had rowboats. Once on board our little boat we could finally be alone and not be followed by the throng of fans who had gathered to "look" at us. This was a strange time for me, this time of celebrity. Buying gas, going to the corner store, working out at the gym, going to the movies, walking in the park; all normal every day things to do, but I did them with a following.

"Hey man! You know who you are?" says the gas pump attendant, store clerk, bank teller and coffee shop guy.
"No Einstein, you want to say. Tell me, who am I?"
But you don't. You just keep smiling and walking, smiling and waving, smiling and paying, smiling and signing autographs. Everywhere I went the scene that would inevitably develop thwarted everything I tried to do in public. I learned during that time to never stop walking. Stop, and you're dead. Stop, and they've got you. It was very hard on my son because he just wanted to do all of the normal things that boys do with their dads. It didn't stop out on the streets but it made its way into my home on several occasions.

"Hold it up... (CLICK) okay, got it. My turn."
"Hey look at this, is this his?"
"Yes it is."
"COOL, hey! Get a shot of me with this, will ya?" (CLICK).
The strange voices were coming from the living room. I climbed out of bed in just my underwear and Elsa Lanchester hair (morning version) and tiptoed down the hallway to see what the hell was going on. What was obvious to me was that this was a family. A father, mother, son and two daughters and they were in our home. In our home and having tea and posing with my music awards, clothes, shoes and even my soccer ball!

My dad was sitting with them, refilling their cups of tea and topping up the juice for the kids.

"Pssssst! Dad, come here", I said quietly.

My father walked over to me while the family continued posing.

"Dad what the hell is going on? Who are these people?"

"They've come all the way from Newfoundland. The kids were asked what they wanted to do for their holiday and they said, find Alan Frew. So here they are."

I was amazed.

"But Dad, why did you bring them in here? Why did you let them in our home?"

"Well now, they were outside and it's cold and I thought a wee cup of tea and a digestive biscuit would warm them up."

"Dad, they have got to go! This is not right. They shouldn't be in here."

He didn't have the heart to do it. He was putting me on the spot. I threw some clothes on and entered the room.

The girls immediately got very excited.

"Folks you must leave," I said gently. "This is my home. This is where I live and I need a little privacy."

There was a bit of an awkward moment brewing. It was the moment where people cannot see beyond their own needs and desires. For these people it was about fulfilling the desires of their children regardless of how intrusive it may be. For me it was to not look like too much of a jerk and simply get them out of my home and on their way. I posed with the kids for a few shots and they left.

I cannot for the life of me ever imagine spending a vacation with my family trying to find Bryan Adams or David Beckham or even Paul McCartney, no matter how much I admire him and his music.

On other occasions girls gate-crashed my home by baking pies for my elderly mother whose mind was showing signs of deterioration. People camped out on my lawn. Girls conned my son into thinking they were his cousins in order that he would bring them home. Such is life when you step into the public arena. My experiences were mild compared to what *The Beatles* or Michael Jackson or other superstars go through but it left me so sufficiently scarred I cut down on activities that involved having strangers around me.

"Sir, you can take the call over here," said the waiter.
"Thank you," I replied as I followed him to a place behind the bar where the phone was located.
"Hello!" I said into the receiver.
"Alan," said my mother. "You know that friend of yours that you have down in America?"
"Yes."
"Well he's dead and you have to call New York right away. Okay? Bye."

My mother had never met Terry. My mother never knew the feelings I had for my friendship with him. My mother never knew sensitivity. Dead? Terry? Dead? My legs felt like they wanted to buckle beneath me. My stomach churned.

"Hey Alan smile!"

I lifted my head only to find some two-dozen people staring at me like I was the Gibbon at the local zoo. Some were snapping pictures of me. I wanted to scream at them,

"You bastards, don't you know my friend has just died? Don't you get it? Piss off!"

But of course I didn't, and twenty-four hours later I was standing by his casket looking at him, lifeless, gone forever. I wondered what this world was all about just as I had done so many times before while staring at cadavers in the autopsy room.

In my head I heard his voice saying, "Captain, remember the show must go on."
As I leaned over to plant a little kiss on his forehead my leg rubbed against the stigma of a flower that transferred pollen onto my pants, impossible to get out. I could hear Terry's voice from wherever he had now gone, apologizing to me for the stain that I never ever attempted to wash.

"Hey man," he said, "Sorry about that, I'm afraid I spoiled the moment."
"No you didn't Terry, you simply created another one."

What had killed my friend that night was described by the coroner as his heart basically exploding from the contradictory messages that the different drugs sent to it. On the one hand you had alcohol and pain killers telling it to slow down, take it easy and relax, while on the other the massive surge of the cocaine told it to speed up, get moving, put the pedal to the floor. By his estimation death had been swift, instantaneous and painless.

I was back at it within days, picking up the pieces and touring once again. I would miss my friend forever but the train was rolling and he would have been the first one to tell me to get my ass back on.

CHAPTER SIX

6

*"They're not that different than any of you, are they?
There's hope in their eyes, just like in yours. They believe themselves destined for
wonderful things, just like many of you. Well, where are those smiles now boys?
What of that hope? Did most of them not wait until it was too late
before making their lives into even one iota of what they were capable of?
In chasing the almighty deity of success, did they not squander their
boyhood dreams? Most of those gentlemen are fertilizing daffodils!
However, if you get very close, boys, you can hear them whisper.
Go ahead, lean in; hear it?* Carpe Diem, *lads. Seize the day.
Make your lives extraordinary."*
FROM DEAD POET'S SOCIETY

CHAPTER SIX: PASSION

BUT I STILL HAVEN'T FOUND WHAT I'M LOOKING FOR

You did it – congratulations! You were receptive to something that you felt
would better your life, you desired it honestly and you totally believed that
you deserved to have it. You allowed INTENTION to flow fast and furiously
and you got up off of your backside and went out and got it! It's yours.
CONGRATULATIONS, now are you happy? I sure hope so. Let me ask you
this, though. Is it possible to do all of this and not be happy? Can such a thing
exist? Can you really appear to have, or worse still, *actually* have everything a
person could possibly want or need and STILL not be fulfilled? The answer of
course is "yes," and we see it happen all too often. We see the person who
seems to have everything, yet is miserable. Why is this so?

Well, there can be many reasons why someone who apparently has everything is still miserable. It can involve a whole variety of difficult, complex issues from the external world of personal relationships, family dynamics, professional choice and so on. But regardless of these things, if we follow our ACTION SANDWICH strategy, it's my BELIEF that somewhere along the way the miserable, the disillusioned and the disgruntled person is still missing a KEY ingredient. Your sandwich, my friend, needs to be garnished with that special condiment called...PASSION.

Anyone can eat to stay alive – dry bread will get you through – but would you choose to eat nothing but dry bread every day if you didn't have to? Your sandwich is so much more enjoyable, so much more desirable and believable with lettuce or honey mustard, or perhaps mayo, relish or one of a limitless number of other flavourful condiments that you can add. Why then should it be any different for *THE ACTION SANDWICH* - a slice of RECEPTIVITY, a slice of DESIRE...layered with BELIEF, smothered in INTENTION, heaped with lots and lots of ACTION, then topped off with a healthy portion of mouth-watering PASSION!! Mmmmmm, sounds delicious doesn't it?

You see, true PASSION is not a shopping splurge, nor is it fast food. It is not the latest fad, nor is it a quick fix. True PASSION can't be found on the street corner, nor can it be bought in a mall. It cannot be borrowed from a friend, nor loaned out for a price. PASSION is a slow-simmering delicacy that can take from minutes to lifetimes to reach its fullest potential before unleashing a taste so powerful that it can capture the taste buds of streets and towns, cities and countries and yes even worlds. It can build tunnels under oceans and rockets to the stars. It can find cures for deadly diseases and it can feed the starving. It can change the psyche of a generation and it can change the future. PASSION does not live in the external world; rather it comes from the INTERNAL one. Yet when unleashed into the external it can create feats of magical and legendary proportions. Socrates, Michaelangelo, Da Vinci, Shakespeare, Einstein, Chaplin, Churchill and Hawking to name so much less than just a few, all of whom were filled with an unbelievable love of what their true purpose was in the life that each was given, which in turn found its way out to the external world in the form of talent and PASSION, allowing them to live extraordinary lives, each reaching the pinnacle of success.

Now, PASSION doesn't give you a get-out-of-jail-free card, and I am not about to suggest that these people and the many others who reached the same levels of success were trouble-free. That would be a ridiculous notion. But for the moment we are talking about a compelling emotion that we should ALL feel at some point in our lives, for to live a life that has never experienced PASSION is, I fear, to have never truly lived.

Oh yes, and speaking of talent, extraordinary lives and PASSION, what about those four young lads from Liverpool who unleashed theirs on the world back in the early sixties, changing the face of music forever? What was their name again?...Ooooh, it's on the tip of my tongue...wavy lines...waaavy lineeeees.........

MEANWHILE BACK AT THE PRESS CONFERENCE

Suddenly the door opened and the first one in front of me was God, his back turned to me, facing towards one of the Capitol Records' representatives, who upon seeing me spoke up.

"Ah, great here he is, this is one of our nation's top recording artists. Please let me introduce you both. Alan Frew, meet Paul McCartney. Paul, Alan."

He turned slowly in time with my heartbeat. *Bu-Bum*, his head and shoulders move. *Bu-Bum*, he's repositioning his feet. *Bu-Bum*, I can see his face. *Buuu-Buuum*, my God...it IS GOD! And he looks like...

"Hello mate," he said. "Paul McCartney. How're you doing?"

He extended his hand and took mine in a traditional handshake. Alan Frew. Great Communicator. Man of many words.

Orator extraordinaire, replied with...blank stare...silence... nodding...more blank staring...a little muted nodding and just for good measure another nod and a stare. Our hands though were still performing the handshake ritual as he repeated, "I'm Paul McCartney.What's up? Everything going well then, is it?"

The Great Communicator continued his mastery of the English language with the following oratory masterpiece, "Daaa, blaaaa, ummmmm, errrr." Darwin would have been so proud.
Still the handshake continued, for he was now locked in my vice-like grip.

"Listen. You hear that? No? I wonder why? Oh, I see, it's because I'm shaking hands with...PAUL McCARTNEY!!!!"

The Beatle politely managed to pry his hand loose and continued on his way, meeting others in and around the room.

"IDIOT! LOSER!" I screamed at myself inside my head. "This was THE moment of your professional life! Forget the albums, forget the accolades, forget the money, this is Paul McCartney and you blew it!"

Suddenly they were all posing for a photo-op when he looked at me and said, "Alan, come on, get in here beside me."
I pointed to myself.
"Yes you, come on over here and get in the picture," he said in that unmistakable Liverpudlian twang.
I went over, and a second later I was beside the legend himself. Not god after all, just a man.

The photographer snapped a few shots and the group disbanded. Paul was walking away towards his assistant and I hadn't even spoken a single word to him.

Is this what it has all boiled down to for me, was I about to let FEAR decide my fate and not speak to him? Surely I wouldn't, I couldn't let that happen. What did I have to lose? What's the worst that could happen? Successful people understand and accept fear as a factor, not a force. I had nothing to lose. So I went for it.

"Paul?" slipped out of my mouth.
"Yeah, mate," he asked.
I remember thinking at that precise moment how amazing it was that if you said his name, he not only recognized it but he answered!
"I have a poster of you here over on the table, would you be kind enough to sign it for me?"
"Love to," he replied, as though to say, "Oh, you CAN speak."

Shortly after that, and upon recognizing my accent as being from Glasgow or nearby, he got me talking about the city and about soccer and we had an unbelievable few moments together. He was gracious and attentive and I will always remember that. That is all I have to go on as far as my memory of our short time together, for there was no way that my brain could hang on to every word spoken between us, as my mind was racing way too fast. No, the only memory I was to be left with was the experience of speaking to him, and I remember thinking when I was being walked back to the room just prior to our meeting, that I so dearly hoped that he would be friendly and approachable. I was saying to myself, "Please, please, please, don't let him be a jerk." For, you see, I have a lot invested in *The Beatles*. Years in fact. A lifetime, actually. Watching them, listening to them, imitating them, loving them and all of that could have been destroyed in one aggressive, pompous, super-star moment.

What would have happened if he had basically given me a nod then dumped the moment? What would have happened if I had been told "don't look at him, don't speak to him and don't even think of asking for an autograph?" At the peak of my recording career, I have experienced that moment from the other side of the fence. When young fans were meeting me for the first time, it was a very big deal for them. How I behaved and reacted would ultimately be all that they would take with them after the meeting was over. The answer is as simple on stage as it is in life: manners, decency, kindness, listening are all human traits that cost us nothing to use.

Gracious, humble, polite and attentive – that is how I remember James Paul McCartney.

But what would it have really been about had Paul reacted in a way that I felt made him a jerk? How much of that luggage would actually have been mine and not his? Come to think of it, what about those people out there that think I'm a jerk? (Sniff) Hmmm...I smell the unmistakable aroma of burning Ego.

Ahhhh...Ego, that little image of who we have come to believe we are and how we distinguish ourselves from others, based on the input from the outside world, can sure seem to get in the way at times. Why is that, I wonder? And why is it that the more successful one becomes, the more negative the feedback seems to be?

Now it is not my INTENTION to go off on a wild tangent here about something as complex as Ego, but how, I ask you, can I tackle a book about abundance, purpose and great accomplishment and successful lives and NOT include Ego? Am I afraid? Scared I'll get in over my head? Damn right I am. Am I going to do it anyway? Yup!!

So here goes.

LEGGO MY EGO

"Show off!"
"You big-headed bastard!"
"Thinks he's God's gift, that one does!"

I've heard them all in my time and I have to admit that I am guilty in the past of using them too. Come to think of it, is there one of us who hasn't used them? Let's see, show of hands right now, who hasn't used terms like those?

No, Jesus, put your hand down, you don't count.

Society seems to declare open season on so-called celebrities and super successful people, claiming that it comes with the territory. Yet where, I ask, is it coming from if not from the ego of society itself? Wasn't it society's ego that decided to give them celebrity status in the first place? Isn't it fair to say that society feels a need to create them? I mean, after all, they didn't do it themselves, did they? Of course not. They need a leg up, a BIG LEG UP, along the way. Sometimes I find it difficult to see where one ego begins and the other one ends in the celebrity tabloid world. What size of an ego does it take to grab a camera and stick it up the nostril of a movie star because there is a demand to see what his nose hairs look like or, better still, how he'll react to the unwanted photographer? Then there is the magazine publisher, whose ego is bigger than both the cameraman and the celebrity put together, willing to pay a small fortune for shots in order that he may satisfy the even more enormous ego of the collective society thriving on such events, displayed for all to see in the magazines we call the tabloids.

Once we point out the flawed ego of another person, we have merely activated our own by reacting to the messages we have received in an ego-based reality.

Jealousy is ego, but so is gratification.
Envy is ego but generosity can be as well.
Criticism is ego, but so is the need for approval and flattery.
Unworthiness is ego and so is self-importance.
It seems that in the world of the ego no one can win.

But what about poor old PASSION, then? Those who live the ego-less life would surely include PASSION into the ego mix, would they not? Hmm, it's so easy for it all to become very, very confusing when you begin to acknowledge and try to understand ego's role in your own life, and downright difficult when you try to understand it in others.

We certainly don't seem to be born with one, an ego that is. In fact the world at birth seems to be entirely opposite to the concept of self. It seems to be all about *the other*. When my baby daughter entered the world for her first out-of-the-womb breath, she certainly had no ego accompanying her that I could see. On the contrary, it was a moment that seemed more concerned with, "Who the hell are you?" But from that very second when I first met her, she began to receive and internalize feelings and messages that declared her something special, and so began the journey of self-awareness. And with this awareness of herself comes ego.

Two and a half years later it still fascinates me to watch her living life in a state of simply *being*. She has no inhibitions, no self-censorship, no self-consciousness; she simply does what she feels the impulse to do. For her life just *is*, although as each day passes her self-awareness increases and her ego becomes more apparent. Consequently, those of us around her, especially her mum and I, whether consciously or not, begin to define who we think she is, which in turn causes us to define what we will and will not tolerate. After all, the home, like society, requires rules. If she cannot have what she wants, the world according to her is disrupted and all hell can break loose. More and more it becomes a battle of egos as we the parents and she the child clash over the important things in life like another cookie, or teeth brushing or just one more glass of chocolate milk. This is as much a clash of egos as going toe to toe with your boss at work or with the coach of your basketball team or your wife or husband. This is part of the groundwork being laid for how the future will play out. At times it feels like she's saying, "Hey wait a minute here! You've both been telling me since the day I joined you two stressed-out, overworked, un-slept me-worshippers that I am beautiful, that I am clever and that I am an angel. So why then, pray tell, can I not smear this chocolate ice cream all over that plasma television, while one of you cleans up after me and the other runs to get me another one of these things?"

Ego has no problem in joining the party early, but in my generation when a child tried to make a stand for what he or she believed in, they played with the flames of a fire that was very likely to burn them. In the world of my childhood, adults crushed and squashed the spirit of children who tried to express themselves as individuals, especially if it made the adult feel uncomfortable or challenged in any way. Keeping the child in line with the same doctrine that had been hammered into them as children was extremely important.

"It was good enough for me, so it'll be good enough for you too!" was the battle cry of generations. This type of one-dimensional thinking leads to one-dimensional living, but thank God history is full of souls who did not conform, regardless of what the generations who came before them said. They faced the flames, got burned, and faced them again. They got crushed and squashed, but lived to fight another day. They stood up for what they believed in and for the people they believed themselves to be.

Here then lies one of the single most important philosophies on the journey to success.

You cannot possibly be who you or I or even society *says* you are. You can truly only be who you *know* yourself to be, and with that comes the "territory" to be negotiated along the way. This is where a guy like Donald Trump openly tells the world that he knows he is the best at what he does, then does things exactly the way he wants them done and the rest of us can go shit in our hats if we don't like it. But what does it all mean in the end? Well, it would seem to me it's a kind of paradox of nothing and everything depending on who's being asked – Donald or the rest of us. Ultimately though, the responsibility lies with the receiver of the information rather than the giver when it comes to how the response is going to play out.

For example, if I call you an idiot and you crumble and fall and your self-esteem drops off the radar, does that mean you really are an idiot? Of course it doesn't. It simply means that you had a certain response to my calling you one. When Donald Trump stands up and tells the world that he is the best at what he does, we all get so caught up in the drama and flair and audacity of it all that our knee-jerk response is to lash out and call him "big headed" and a "showoff." It's you and I, the "receivers," that seem to have the need to make the big deal out of it, no? I mean, if Donald quietly goes about his mission of making billions and feels the need to let us know that he's the best and our reaction is to take a big yawn and say, "Good for you Donny! Knock yourself out, son," would the drama of it all really rank up there with *One Life To Live?*

I have always prided myself on telling the world that there is not a single name or word that you can use to describe me or to try and hurt me with, that can ever penetrate my self-esteem, my mission, my purpose or my PASSION. And I MEAN THAT! When I fought during my other life, I fought because somewhere inside me I wanted to, not because somebody had thought up some words to rhyme together to insult or hurt me. I responded by fighting because I was a "scrapper," not because I was what someone else was saying I was. Make sense? My calling you a loser doesn't make you one, but punching me in the nose doesn't make you one either. The punch is coming from something and somewhere entirely unrelated to my using the word "loser."

Sometimes I feel sorry for PASSION. Poor old PASSION gets a bad rap way too often. A person's passion and willingness to "let it all hang out" gets misconstrued way too many times by receivers as something negative, causing an outburst and a backlash of unwarranted anger and abuse from those who feel the need to give us their take on it all, hence for example the tabloids.

But then again, only bad news sells right? Would you watch a newscast that began with, "Today in North America 67,352 flights took off from various airports all around the Continent, and they ALL landed safely!"

My God, I mean what would CNN do if at least one of them didn't fall out of the sky and land in a fireball on a school campus that had just been desecrated by a gun-wielding, disgruntled maniac who had just killed dozens of his school mates?

Powerful, complicated, complex stuff, this Ego and PASSION, huh?

Trying to get as close to an ego-less existence as possible is a worthy and noble challenge, and although I'm not there yet, I know the first step on the pathway to a successful and abundant life is that you must embrace the fact that you have an ego in the first place, accept it, and recognize that it is not something that has exclusivity. I've got news for you, Spanky. WE'VE ALL GOT ONE, and that's what makes the job of keeping them in check just that much harder.

So, if I know what is true in my heart, mind and soul regarding who I am and what my purpose is, what does your account of who you think I am mean? Well, I've got another newsflash for you, *nothing*. That's correct, I said nothing.

If I am taking the time and great effort to work towards a more ego-less life which will include my own recognition of the fact that I am not really who my ego thinks I am, why in the world would your ego-driven opinion of me matter? Think hard here, for I know that even writing something like this suggests that your opinion means nothing, stabs your ego in the arm, and makes you want to tell me even more adamantly that I am indeed a bigheaded bastard et cetera, possibly, God forbid, even AN EGOMANIAC!

Hey, blame that Freud dude, for he was the egomaniac.

Conversely, the good news is that what I think of you is equally meaningless. All that truly matters is that you know who you are and what it is that is significant and true to that knowledge. If I had left it up to others to decide who I was and what my future was to be, then my ship would have sailed into other waters, perhaps even dangerous waters, with a very good chance of finding the bottom of the ocean along the way. Now, I have never been adept at marching to someone else's drum and, of course, my ego floats in and out and back in again all along the way. Is this a bad thing? I guess that depends on who is being asked, doesn't it?

Okay, enough already. I said I wouldn't get too heavy, and here I am getting exactly that. I mean c'mon, who the hell do you think I am here? I'm just a simple, plain, ordinary, everyday, run-of-the-mill Rock Star. Gimme a break, will ya? God knows I gotta put up with all of you, talking and yakking and banging and ringing and clanging in my five-karat, diamond-studded ears, don't I? It's enough to make me want to jump into my Porsche 911 Turbo Special Edition and drive immediately to my private spa for a lavender-mocha exfoliation and butternut facial at the hands of a Peruvian goddess named Kalinda, whom I'm dating along with her sister, Dulcemer the super-model. I mean what's a guy supposed to do to get a little attention around here? But I digress. Where was I?

So what does it all mean? If I tell you I know for sure, that would be my ego talking because I know for sure that I don't. Just be aware that the road to success can be a very long one, and a rampant, unchecked ego has a tendency to make it even longer. There is a saying that "no one likes a show-off." Well, personally I like show-offs. To me, Tiger Woods is a show-off. Brad Pitt is a show-off. Michael Jordan is a show-off as is Gretzky, Clinton, Bono and, yes, even that Jesus guy – who else could make those five loaves and two fishes cut it after inviting five thousand strangers to dinner? Showing off or presenting great talent is what successful people do. The ego is merely the platter for that presentation. You're human; it will get away on you every now and again, but that's okay. Just try and remember that when it becomes more presentation and less talent you may become one of the so-called egomaniacs. They usually get found out in the end.

So the celebrity may be fair game, but if you feel the need to tell it to the world by gossip, blog or billboard then I've got news for you, you're a...

"Two fishes huh? What a guy!"

Perhaps living with just a little less of an ego is as far as I will get. I do know that just being aware of it has helped me ten-fold on my journey to a more successful and abundant life, and it can for you as well. It may take to my dying day, but perhaps before I leave this world I will know what it feels like to be ego-less. There I'll be, in the Twin Palms Nursing Home, having just finished a hearty helping of pureed potatoes, bacon and plums, a little drool escaping from my toothless head, having just peed myself; I'll take my last breath, and then head off to the big Rock Arena in the sky.
"Aw, he's gone," the nurse will say. "Poor, old, egoless, bastard. OH WELL, WHO WANTS HIS SLIPPERS?"

I'VE GOT TO GET A MESSAGE TO YOU

Do you remember back at the beginning of this journey when I asked you which of the two guys was a success and which one a failure - the Wall Street dude vs. Mr. Wilderness guy? Well now, if it holds true that success cannot just be about the money and the toys, but rather about how much control or "say" you have in what you do, then what if you have put into play RECEPTIVITY, DESIRE, BELIEF, INTENTION and ACTION, and you get to make all of the decisions and have all of the say in how things are done, but you STILL hate what you're doing and have little or no PASSION for it? Are you still considered successful? I am going to make a bold statement here, and go out on a limb and say – NO. No, you are not truly successful. If life is not fun for you, if it's not enjoyable, then where is the success in that? A successful life is therefore in direct relationship to the joy it brings you, and a thousand or a million or even a billion dollars is not going to solve that for you. Money but misery, houses but no happiness, cars but no caring? PASSION bleeds of TRUTH, for it would seem all but impossible to be passionate about something that you dislike or don't want.

Do what you do because you are meant to do it. Do it because you can, and because you love it. By following the path in front of you and focusing on where you're going rather than where you've been, you are also sowing seeds for the future. This world is not a perfect place, so don't look for it to be. Just honour your personal growth and stay committed to each moment of each day. Try not to attach too much emotion to an imperfect world, or you will lose the energy that you will need to fuel your positive beliefs. Stay attuned to things that affect you and that you can affect. All too often people stress over that which they cannot ever hope to change. Let the outcome take care of itself. PASSION is a true ally of all of the elements contained within *THE ACTION SANDWICH*. It amalgamates, joins forces, and is the true reflection that tells the world that you are making the correct choices. I have tried and tried to get passionate about doing my taxes, but somehow it never seems to work. They get done eventually, but it is a horrible experience for me so I try to stay passionate about how I will feel when someone else does them for me.

Life should not be lived in misery; in fact, it should not even be lived in complacency. Your job and relationships are not meant to make you want to jump out of a window! You can be happy in all things if you remain receptive to that which makes you happy. Don't wait until the movie is two thirds over before buying your ticket. Don't wait until the end of the race to lace up your running shoes. Don't wait until the end to become an expert. Do it now, ALL OF IT, all of the things that make you happy. Go to night school. Learn that second language. Join a band. Take a cooking class. Learn to swim. SUCCESS isn't about the money or the toys..............is it?

Yogi Berra once said, "You've achieved success in your field when you don't know whether what you're doing is work or play."

If you think that this is a rather romanticized notion, let me tell you that I know there is truth to it. Living a life that includes forty hours a week of work you dislike or, worse still, hate, is hopefully harder for you to swallow than Yogi Berra's idea of success.

TEN STEPS TO PASSION

1. ALL YOU NEED IS LOVE - Do you love what you do? If not then why are you doing it? You were not put here to live in misery. If PASSION doesn't live where you work, then make sure it lives where you don't work. Remember no condiment...no flavour. Pass the mustard!

2. I'D LIKE TO THANK MY MOM FOR HAVING ME - Gratitude makes great kindling for a passionate fire. Reminding yourself how lucky and thankful you are for all that you have is tremendous fuel for attracting more of what it is you're grateful for. Always focus on what you have as opposed to what you do not have. Be thankful.

3. OH YES, YOU TOO - When you are handing out all that new found love and gratitude don't forget to pause at the mirror occasionally. Appreciating, loving and crediting yourself, reminds your true essence to shift the power back from the ego to the inner self. Love you too.

4. YOU MEAN LITTLE OL' ME? - Don't force your accomplishments on the world. Let it discover you on its own terms. It is but a short step from self-importance to self-pity. Practice a little humility. Egos shout. Deeds speak.

5. ALL OR NOTHING AT ALL - At some point in everyone's life PASSION asks you for "all or nothing." Why wait to be asked, get out on that stage, give everything you've got and leave nothing behind. Only then can you look in the mirror and say you truly gave it your best. As the song says, "All or Nothing At All."

6. AND THIS ONE IS LITTLE TOMMY - Display your PASSION with the same ease you would pictures of your children. Share PASSION with the fervor one would feel for a new car or the love of a newborn baby. Infect your whole world with it. PASSION, pass it on.

7. DREAMER - Go ahead and take yourself on a wonderful journey to the perfect life you see in your mind. Reinforce continuously the what, why, where, how and when of it all. By the way, you're dreaming anyway so don't hold back. Dream big.

8. PASSION NOT PEDIGREE - PASSION has no bank account, no fast car, no mansion on the hill. It wears nothing, costs nothing and dines nowhere. PASSION is your birthright,

like the blood in your veins and the air that you breathe. No one has exclusivity to it. Take a deep breath.

9. YOU ARE HERE - Don't know what to be passionate about? There has to be something! Is it walking, reading, cooking, checkers, juggling, pogo-sticking? Come on, you're not going to break PASSION so toss it around for a while. It's an environmentally responsible, completely renewable, nonexclusive resource. Do something! Begin from where you are!

10. REGRETS, I'VE HAD A FEW - Even unwavering PASSION can go a bit wobbly at times. Give yourself the freedom to question the direction you have chosen, the understanding that mistakes are made, the forgiveness for those mistakes and then make the changes required to get back on track. Let the record show, you took the blows and did it ...your way.

MY SONG
Opus 6

I AM WITH YOU TONIGHT

By now my relationship with Gary was solidified. It had gone far beyond that of artist and manager and had become more like father and son. There was not a day that passed that we did not speak and if I happened to be off the road we would see each other almost daily. The PASSION we had for what was going on around us was strong. He was equally as driven as I, and although he still had a couple of other bands in his stable, it was *Glass Tiger* that remained his one true love.

He and his wife never had children of their own, so it was his two dogs and yours truly who filled that void for him. He would have done anything for me within reason. He was my biggest fan, my greatest sounding board and by now my closest friend. I kept nothing from him and that was a great feeling for a kid that had never experienced what it was like to have someone to turn to for advice or a shoulder to lean on. He had stood by my side during the death of my niece and of my pal in Atlanta. He took my calls in the wee hours no matter where I was calling from or how trivial the topic may have been. When you are lying in a cot in a Berlin hotel that resembles Stalag 13, with your family and all that you love back in your homeland, you can get pretty lonely. A voice that cares and understands what you are sacrificing in your endeavor can be the difference between calling it quits and understanding that what you are doing is indeed authentic and worthy.

His voice reminded me of home, and reassured me as to why I was doing what I was compelled and driven to do. He traveled with us on numerous occasions, which I thoroughly enjoyed and he always brought with him a voice of reason that could help settle me down especially since I felt the extra pressure of being the front-man of the band.

A bit of a "them vs. me" thing was developing even if not consciously vindictive in nature, but rather a bit of good old fashioned jealousy that can happen when someone seems to get most of the goodies that are going around the table. I seemed to need to fight a bit more for ideas and suggestions that I felt would benefit the band. One particular fiasco comes to mind that shows both sides of that coin. I remember it now as if it was....wavy lines...waaavvvy lliinnness.......

BOTH SIDES NOW

It was July 16th 1988 and I had been invited to attend and sing at "The Great One's" wedding.

Glass Tiger's arrival on the music scene in 1986 coincided with the

Edmonton Oilers solidifying their claim to the term dynasty as they were about to secure their fourth Stanley Cup in the space of five years, led by none other than the greatest to ever lace up a pair of skates, Wayne Gretzky. I had met and become friends with winger Mark Messier a year earlier and through Mark I had spent a fair bit of time around the team, getting to know most of the lads. Many an evening was spent in a bar called Barry T's and little did I know that in that very place, somewhere on the dance floor was the girl who would eventually become my wife and the mother of my daughter.

Athletes, great athletes are enigmas. I have witnessed some of the top sports stars in the world partying long and hard into the wee hours on the eve of a big game, yet without skipping a beat they take the field or the ice and play the game the way it was meant to be played, tough, hard and selfless, perhaps picking up a hat-trick along the way just for good measure. I'm not condoning or condemning it, just reporting it. *The Oilers* could do this as well as most and of course *Glass Tiger* was well versed in this conditioning. So Edmonton became a little bit of a playground for yours truly.

One of the biggest thrills of my career was when I was asked to sing the national anthem at the Stanley Cup Final. I can still remember thinking about how my dad must have felt watching a sports event of that magnitude, hearing my voice over the top of those classic style images of athletes fidgeting with anticipation, the Canadian and U.S. flags flying and the crowd going wild well before the singer finishes his rendition.

Then came the invite to Edmonton's Royal Wedding.

The jabs came fast and furious even if not directly aimed at me. There is no doubt that I was the most recognized member of the band and certainly the most sought after when it came to the media.
Question, what's the drummer's name from the band *Aerosmith*? Ok you get my drift?

So with being the front-man of any popular band the bar is certainly raised and at this particular time when the perks were coming fast and furiously I was asked by the organization known as *Child Find* if I would be their National Spokesperson, to which I said yes.

MacLean's Magazine had voted me one of the top ten most recognizable faces that year and *Child Find* felt that this would add some reasonable clout to their message.

Meanwhile back at the Ponderosa a division was brewing among the ranks.

We were touring when I planned to attend Gretzky's wedding. I was going to fly in and out the same day leaving the guys to get ready for a show on the East Coast. It was also arranged that upon my return I would be picked up by representatives of *Child Find* and taken to visit some homeless kids before going to do a private autograph session signing posters from a shot taken with some of these kids.

I flew into Edmonton for an event that was the very embodiment of extravagance. This wedding ranked as close to the Charlie and Diana event as you could possibly get (without the ears of course).

Movie stars, music stars, sports stars, past and future legends were all in attendance. It was real Hollywood stuff. Many people think to this day that I sang at the church but I did not. It was in fact a fine singer by the name of Tim Feehan, however David Foster and I were to perform a *Glass Tiger* song together later that night. The reception line had other ideas though as Wayne and Janet were tied up taking photographs and participating so long in the receiving line that Foster and I were a little too "jolly" by the time we were to perform, so we passed on that idea for the betterment of all. It was no big deal and after a superb meal, a snuggle from my girl and well wishes from all, I was on a red eye feeling no pain and ready to do my *Child Find* duties.

Two little ladies greeted me at the airport. For the life of me I would never remember their names so for the purpose of my tale we'll call them Agnes and Betty.

Gary had stayed in touch with me the entire time and told me that although the boys were a bit miffed at my gallivanting they were going to do the local promotion and the sound-check at the arena, minus a singer of course (dig-dig).

I should have sensed danger when Betty and Agnes packed me into the back of a Ford Pinto on our way to visit a couple of the half-way houses for runaway, addicted and abused kids.

"So ladies, I am to do an autograph session later, correct?"
"Correct you are," said Agnes.
"And so tell me, what kind of promotion have you had, regarding this event," I asked inquisitively. "Radio ads? Television perhaps?"
"Oh," said Betty, "I must have told at least a dozen people or so and I know Agnes has told everyone she knows, and she knows everybody, believe me."

Instantaneously I knew I was in trouble. I have had autograph sessions with *Glass Tiger* that have been nothing short of riots and I have had autograph sessions with *Glass Tiger* that have been not so riotous at all shall we say. It all comes down to promotion. If you don't tell the public en masse, the public doesn't show up, en masse.

"You did do some radio promotion girls, didn't you?" I asked.
"Um... no," replied Betty in a matter of fact way.

"Don't think you'd need that here, son," Agnes piped in, "word of mouth works wonders here doesn't it Betty?"
"Oh definitely Agnes, why we know everything about everybody around here, don't we? Right, here we are then."

I entered the mall via the front doors thinking I was to be taken to a location perhaps in or near a music store but no, we walked right passed all of them and we kept on walking...and walking...but to where? This was the decoy route right? What elaborate set up had they planned for my presentation I wondered?

The furniture department in Sears is a big place, especially when you have shrunk to the size of Stuart Little. Even the table, pen and especially the posters that I was to sign seemed enormous.

"Can I get you anything?" said Agnes.
"How about a gun or a large bacon, lettuce and cyanide sandwich to go please," were the words that filled my head while "a cup of tea please," were the words that left my lips.

Not only was I in the bloody furniture department, I was neatly tucked in behind the sofas and chesterfields surrounded lovingly by the standard lamps and armoires. Only one thing could have been worse than this and that would be to have it witnessed by *Glass Tiger* or heaven forbid, Wayne Gretzky!

I sat and stood then sat and stretched, then yawned, then sat some more. At one point a little man came along polishing the floors with one of those enormous flying saucer type cleaners that pulls the cleaner-person along as he buffs the floor from side to side. His curiosity was getting the better of him as he buffed closer and closer to me, straining his neck to catch a glimpse of the poster to see if he could figure out who the hell I was and what in god's name I was doing slap-dab in the middle of his flying saucer's buffer zone.

"Aye boy," he said in that unmistakable east coast twang.
"Hello, how are you," said the singer.
"And what do ye have there?" he inquired.
"Posters," was my reply.
"Hmmm and what might they be posters of?" asked the polisher.

"Me...and some great kids," I added with conviction.

Who, I wondered was he going to request that I personalize it to? His wife? Kids? You never know, perhaps he'd keep it for himself.

"Would you like one?" I asked.

Shamelessly, I added, "They're, free."

I was desperate.

He stopped his buffer, stared at the poster, took a deep breath and said, "Nope!"

He then fired up the flying saucer and buffed on his merry way to friggin' Mars I hoped.

"Would you like to keep the posters," asked Betty.

Back at the arena, the guys had not seen me since I left for Gretzky's wedding and of course there was a bit of the "wanderer has returned atmosphere" as I entered.

Some of the crew were mockingly bowing as someone yelled out, "It's the other great one!" Remember this dear reader, they thought I had just come from my own personal Rock Star autograph signing session for the masses. Little did they know I hadn't done one for the masses but for the Mrs.........Betty and Agnes.

Our drummer took the lack of attention harder than anyone. He was popular with female fans and never lacked for their attention but it was the recognition of the music industry and media that he desperately craved. We had several incidents that caused animosity within our ranks. On one occasion Sam and I had flown to New York to do the big stuff like Entertainment Tonight and CNN, leaving Michael, the drummer with the responsibility of doing local press in St. Louis where our next show was to take place.

When I arrived back at the St. Louis airport I was greeted by Gary and Derek who told me I had just enough time to get downtown to do radio and television newscasts prior to show time. It seems that Michael had refused to do it on the grounds that he should have gone with me to

New York. I was livid. I wanted to kill him. He was rooming with me. He moved out.

We performed the show, with me still wanting to kill him. Later that night Derek said that Michael wanted to speak to me and asked me if I would let him back in the room long enough for him to do so. I agreed.

"I would walk over five hundred miles of hot burning coals to get my face on the cover of a teen magazine," he said quietly, "while you get it without even trying!"

At that moment I knew what it all really and truly meant to him. It was about the fame, the adulation and the worship, not the craft...and yet it was the most honest thing a band member had said to me in quite some time.

Michael quit the band in Ireland, but the band had mentally released him well before that. Still we toured. As a matter of fact a very short time after he quit we had to go to Germany for a television show. We didn't panic because the song was "Diamond Sun," which had at its core a "drum loop", a synthesized sound created on the keyboard. We didn't really require a drummer but the Germans weren't buying it. They couldn't get it through the inner mechanisms of their minds that we were now four instead of five.

"Fünf, ja?"
"No not fünf! Vier! We are now four."
"Fünf, ja?"

As luck would have it a Canadian band called *Chalk Circle* were there and we asked their drummer if he would fire on a baseball cap and sit in behind the drum kit to make the number "funf" and keep the Germans happy. He said he would do it for fifty bucks!

He might as well have said $5,000 for just on the grounds of principle alone we told him to stuff it. My wife who was my girlfriend at the time said she would do it. She was deadly serious and so we sat with her showing her the rhythm while assuring her it would be easy. She pulled a baseball cap on as the television guys ran the playback for the first time. When the loop blasted out over the speakers the look of enlightenment was apparent as it dawned on the Germans that this song did not require a drummer, not even for aesthetics.

"Ahhhhh vier, ja?"
"Ja! Ja! Vier! Vier!"

And then, we were four.

I often regret trying to hammer it into them that we didn't need a drummer that day, for it would have been one of the better *Glass Tiger* trivia moments had my now beloved wife been our drummer that day.

The magical mystery tour continued and our third CD was released. The luster was wearing off however and confusion was setting in. I fought a losing battle to have the Rod Stewart duet released as our first single while the remainder of the band and the record company felt that we needed to release a classic rock song called "Animal Heart" which has a mountainous wall of guitars in it.

I had contributed to the song as I had for all *Glass Tiger* songs in the past but the style of this one never won me over. I felt it sent a confusing message and created an even more confusing image similar to the one that we had displayed years prior when we first met up and the drummer sang the rock songs and I the pop ones. Arguments ensued but my pleading fell on deaf ears.

"Animal Heart" was a hit in Canada but the USA wouldn't even release the CD. We began a nightmare tour of Europe opening the show for Swedish sensation *Roxette*, whose road crew treated us very poorly, which added to our misery. The tour as usual was a buy-on. This is when you actually pay them to be on their tour. As part of this arrangement we were to have a catered dinner only on gig days, not thinking for one second that they would refuse us a cup of tea or a piece of toast in the morning or perhaps a hot chocolate in the evening but refuse they did.

They held to the letter even when at night they were throwing mounds of food and drink out into the garbage. What made it most difficult was the fact that the bulk of the tour was in rural areas, which didn't offer us the chance at a late night pizza or sandwich. Who the hell am I kidding, a Swedish pizza?

We were on our own until the sun came up and someone could do a coffee run. Eventually I personally said, "screw this" and went marching in and made myself a bit of toast and poured a cup of tea, daring them to order me out. They never did and thus began a little trend of our guys quietly getting the odd bite of breakfast. I remember phoning Gary back in Canada.

"Get me home! Get us out of this!" I demanded.
"I'm coming to see you," he replied, "I'll be on the next plane."

He brought the band's pal Jimmy with him knowing full well that it would cheer the lads and I up. Jimmy looked after odds and ends for us, nothing overly important but I loved having him on the road with me. We had a lot in common, a love of sports, a love of history and a great love of movies and movie trivia. It was a brilliant move on Gary's part. We stuck it out together and got through it but the end was near.

ALL BY MYSELF

"I'm quitting," I said matter-of-factly in our dressing room in Ottawa. "I'm going to go it alone. I have to."

Surprisingly, the one who seemed to take it the worst and was most insulted was Wayne our bass player. Sam immediately took the stand that it was the right thing to do. Gary, who was not aware of my intentions (I didn't want him to talk me out of it), walked beside me on the way to the stage.

"So what do you think?" I asked at the foot of the stage stairs.
"Well, it's painful but when all is said and done, I'm coming with you," was his immediate reply.

There was never any big announcement that *Glass Tiger* had split. We simply all slipped into a mode of doing our own thing. I was offered a solo deal with EMI and I took it. One of the first things I had to do was, you guessed it, go on the road.

I traveled to London England to do some writing then on to Los Angeles and then back again to England for some more. During a trip to England a good friend, someone who today would have been my brother-in-law, died from cancer. As I stood beside his casket among family and friends, Gary who was again by my side said something that was to be terribly foreshadowing.

"It's always the good guys isn't it?"

GOOD ROCKIN' AT MIDNIGHT

My travels to Los Angeles secured my hiring of John Jones, a talented songwriter and producer to work with me on my first solo project. I literally moved to Los Angeles renting a home in the hills of Hollywood, leaving my son behind once again with family. "LOVE AND SUFFERING" was still driving me and I was unable to resist.

Los Angeles always held a mystical attraction for me. It also seemed to greet me in style for I was there for the O.J. Simpson verdict and likewise for the aftermath of the Rodney King riots. Mud slides? Done that. Brush fires? Been there. During the recording of my CD however, she held a surprise gift for me that still affects me to this day.

On January 17, 1994 at 4:30:55 AM Pacific Standard Time to be exact I was fast asleep in my bed knowing that I had much work to do the next day. Why am I so certain of this date and time? Well let's see, if you are old enough, do you remember where you were when J.F.K. was assassinated? What about when John Lennon was slain? For you younger readers, I bet you know exactly what you were doing and where you were when the Twin Towers came down on 9/11, correct? Well Jan 17th 1994 was a watershed moment for me.

Marcy, my girlfriend, now wife, had been down for a visit and I had taken her back to the airport the previous afternoon avoiding the freeway by traveling down La Cienega Blvd. That morning I had been finishing a vocal for John, when Marcy had entered the house claiming that she thought she felt a rumble beneath her feet while outside on the porch. We dismissed it and set off for the airport. I remember the traffic being so slow and for a few minutes we were at a standstill while under the Santa Monica freeway.

"My God, can you imagine if this thing came down during an earthquake," I said not thinking.
"Don't say that!" she replied.

I saw her off at the gate for her trip back to Canada and returned to work with John until midnight, at which time I called it a night and headed to bed. John left to go stay with his girlfriend that evening as opposed to staying in the little house he had down the hill from me.

My world was about to change.

To this day it still gets referred to as a moderate earthquake. Let me tell you, it might have been many things but moderate doesn't come close to what I experienced some twenty miles from its epicenter.

It had a magnitude they say of 6.7, and yet the ground acceleration was the highest ever recorded in an urban area in North America and to this day it remains the costliest earthquake in U.S. history. Cost doesn't enter your mind when your arse flies out of bed in the middle of a deep sleep, crashing you naked to the floor just prior to your home beginning a dance that causes it to rise and fall and sway and list, several feet in all directions. The thunderous noise is terrifying. It starts somewhere off in the distance and then comes for you. Thud! THud! THUD! THUD!

By the time it reaches you it sounds unlike anything you have ever heard. You are completely helpless, preparing to be swallowed at any moment. I thought my death was imminent. Something happened however at this moment that still amazes me to this very day for I had fallen with a bang onto the floor but I had landed on top of my telephone. I dialed Toronto, all hell was breaking loose around me and I thought I was going to die, so I dialed home. It rang, it connected, and I heard Marcy's sleepy voice.

"Hello."
"Oh! Marcy! Marcy! MARCY! MARRRCY!" was all I could muster.

To this day she tells the story of how for a brief moment she thought I had been stabbed or shot and left to die on the street. Then she heard the creature and its traveling noise.

"Alan don't talk, get out! You must get out!"

Naked I stumbled to my front hallway and out my door. I heard the loudest crash as one of the houses nearby succumbed to the grips of the quake and crashed down the hill. Suddenly it stopped. The silence seemed deafening. I began to yell for help as I was without glasses or contact lenses and blind as a tree stump.

My neighbour flashed a light.
"Alan can you see this?" she called out.
"Barely, but yes," I replied.
"Take your time and crawl towards it."

I reached her and she quickly wrapped a large blanket around my earthquake birthday suit.

"Sorry I didn't have time to dress for the evening," I quipped.

Shortly afterwards I checked her phone and unbelievably it had a dial tone.

"May I?" I asked.

I dialed Canada again and once again got Marcy who by now sounded more distraught than we were. I told her I thought it was over and not to worry. That is when it struck again with its mightiest blow and that was the last time I spoke to home for almost forty-eight hours.

My neighbour and I jumped into my car and we got out as fast as we could, tuning in the radio hoping for word from authorities that knew what the hell we should do. Suddenly it died again and the silence returned. We listened as they told us to stay calm and wait for further instructions. Stay calm? We were not to return to damaged homes, not to light any flames of any kind and to be prepared for the fact that this moderate earthquake might just be a precursor to a massive one.

We sat together for hours. Listening. Waiting. Thinking.

At one point helicopters flew overhead to inspect possible damage to the water reservoir and the dam that we lived beside. Wouldn't that be ironic, to survive Godzilla only to drown on Gilligan's Island?

After several hours I asked my neighbour a very important question.

"Do you drink?"

"Come again?" she said.

"Drink? Alcohol? Do you partake in the occasional nippy sweety?" I asked her.

"I used to enjoy wine," she replied. "But I haven't had a drink in years."

"Well listen up. I have to go get my glasses for I am blind without them. While I'm at it I am going to grab some pants, however, in my fridge, if

I still have a fridge, are six Heinekens and a bottle of white wine. I'm going to get them and we are going to have a little toast, one to survival and two, to kissing our arses goodbye if this thing returns."

"Deal," she said and off I went.

My house felt wounded. Strange creaking noises lurked everywhere. I found my way into my bedroom and found my glasses on the floor. I also recovered a pair of shorts before edging towards the kitchen. I could not see the extent of the damage but my foot hit cans and bottles scattered about. Getting down on my hands and knees I rummaged around, finding the wine and a couple of beers. I also found a large knife and a cup. Where's a corkscrew when you really need one?

Back in the car I opened the beer with the knife's edge and hacked the top off of the wine bottle. What a strange party this was. We drank, chatted and waited until finally it really seemed like it was over.

Around 7:00 a.m. we decided to re-enter our homes. We hugged and went our separate ways. Inside, it was strange how the pathway of death works in an earthquake. Pockets of my home were ruined yet other areas were untouched. My kitchen was devastated yet my living room practically unscathed. My washroom was a mess but my bedroom was fine. A vase full of tulips remained intact on my television, but all the petals had fallen off and the water had leapt out of the vase.

"What about the recording studio," I wondered.

I went downstairs with my eyes half closed for if I had lost over $100,000 of uninsured gear, I wanted to discover it slowly.

I counted to three and opened them. Unbelievably nothing had happened. Even our guitars were still leaning against the wall where we had left them and yet the little studio washroom was destroyed and the wall had caved in allowing you to step right through to the world outside. It was surreal.

Back home they had to contend with the waiting game of not knowing if I was alive or dead. I did not know if John Jones had survived until he walked through my door several hours later. We hugged and breathed a big sigh of relief before he said, "You do know that this is your fault, don't you?"

"What the hell are you talking about you goof!" I replied.

"I am serious," he said, "It's your fault!"

He hit me with a copy of the Los Angeles Times, which is no easy feat if you are familiar with the size of it. Get a grip L.A.; no paper should be the size of a small car and there on the front cover of the newspaper was the headline declaring the death toll and destruction from the previous night. There was also a map detailing the area, the epicenter and the fault lines responsible for the quake. I absorbed the map and read the following: "The quake started about nine miles underground and during the course of the main shock, ruptured upward and northward, spreading both eastward and westward. The northern end of the fault extends under the Santa Susana Mountains.

The Frew fault is one of several that could have been responsible."

"Are you kidding me?" I was dumbfounded. Spooked beyond belief. Even in Scotland my name is not that common. My first earthquake and it has my bloody name?

The death toll was 57, with 9000 people injured. The fact that the earthquake occurred at 4:30 a.m. greatly minimized the death toll. There was $44 billion in damages and $800 billion replacement value on taxable property.

22,000 people were now homeless and 9 bridges collapsed. Yes, the very section that Marcy and I had sat under in the traffic jam collapsed. No one was beneath it at the time.

I remained in Los Angeles to finish my recording, though for many Canadians a mass exodus ensued. Gavin, my son even came to visit and although we had fun, I was never quite the same. I never slept in my bed again, preferring the couch in the living room.

A few months later I had to return to L.A. for some cleanup work, a visit of only one week and I'll be damned but an after shock in the high 5s hit sending me into a state of panic.

The LOVE AND SUFFERING of my PASSION has taken me down many roads and the stories I have told you are but the tip of an iceberg, the size of which even I cannot begin to fathom. I tell these tales for two reasons. First, being a storyteller I hope to offer you a different perspective on what we would normally classify as a motivational book. Simply put, I want you to enjoy the stories. Second, I am attempting to show you that it is all about the journey, from birth to death, from RECEPTIVITY to PASSION, from a question to its answer, from the recognition of the need to change to the actual changing itself. It's trial and error, good and bad, mystical and mystifying, LOVE and SUFFERING, but it is worthy, you are worthy, the journey is worthy.

SO BLIND

I have been tested, retested and tested again. Upon my return to Canada I prepared to launch my new solo project with a revitalized sense of artistry and stamina. Gary and I negotiated a brand new publishing deal for me and I recorded my first solo video. We were pumped and ready for the challenges ahead. We were a team.

My solo name did not have the clout of the *Glass Tiger* name but we were not deterred. Nothing would stop us now. Nothing... except the greatest test of all.

The songs contained on my first solo CD "Hold On" are without a doubt some of the finest I have ever written. The CD is beautifully recorded and the production is second to none. The musicianship is outstanding and includes the exceptional work of Mick Fleetwood, Steve Ferrone, Robin Le Mesurier and Jim Cregan to name but a few. We even had fun when Mickey Dolenz of *Monkees* fame joined in for some singing.

EMI stepped up to the plate and we spent world-class money. I flew to Jamaica to do one of several photo shoots and upon my return to Canada, Gary and I popped out to see Deane at the EMI headquarters in Toronto.

When we arrived at Deane's office he was conducting his business laying flat on his back on the office sofa suffering from a severe bout of sciatica, pain along the sciatic nerve usually due to a prolapsed disc in the lower spine. We talked about the upcoming launch and the never-ending cycle of touring when Gary uttered something new to me.

"I think I have sciatica as well," he said to both of us, "My leg's been giving me some awful pain recently too."

We concluded our business with Deane and headed out.

"You've never mentioned your leg before." I said sounding a bit like the dad.
"Oh, it's nothing, it'll pass."

In what seemed like the blink of an eye, we were in trouble. Both he and his wife didn't know it, but I knew it. I could see small incremental changes in his color, his eyes and his weight. I smelled cancer but could not bring myself to utter the word. I visited him almost daily although demands were coming in from EMI for me to start fulfilling promotional requests from the media regarding the new CD.

"What's the doctor saying?" I would inquire cautiously.
"Oh, not much. He has me booked for a scan in a few weeks."
"And he's not said anything, else?" I pushed.

"No, not really. You know the funniest thing happened to me outside the doctor's office the other day. My pants fell down. Imagine that, just right down they went."
I wish I could say I laughed...but I didn't. My heart sank.

FUNERAL FOR A FRIEND

Progressively he got more and more uncomfortable. His face was gaunt and he had dropped a ton of weight. Still no one was saying the "C" word and I did not oblige in that way either.

My first video was launched and I flew to Calgary to shoot the second one. I was anxious and scattered, trying as hard as I could to stay focused on what we had to do for this new release. I knew in my heart that he was doomed but I couldn't bear the thought. I wanted to pull the plug on the CD but couldn't do that either.
My LOVE and SUFFERING was unbearable.

I would get calls from our office staff telling me that he was there but laying on the floor, in and out of sleep as he tried to instruct them on business. I would tell them to leave him be and that they should call me if they had any questions. Things went from bad to worse yet I was still working the new promotion for the CD. One day during the making of an EPK (Electronic Press Kit) in a studio in downtown Toronto, I was phoned and told that his breathing was very rapid and shallow and it was scaring the staff. I rushed there and was beside myself when I found him. I swear he was literally losing pounds per day. Every time I saw him, he was more and more skeletal.

"What's really going on Alan?" I was asked.
"He has cancer," I said for the first time, the words crushing me.
"He has cancer...and he's dying."

Gary Pring who in his hey day weighed in at about 230 pounds was now in my arms being carried upstairs to his living room. I placed him on the couch and found the number for his family physician. The secretary answered.

"Yes, my name is Alan, I am Mr. Pring's son, let me speak to the doctor please, it's an emergency."

"I am sorry sir," said the secretary, "The doctor is busy."

"That's ok I'll wait," I replied calmly.

"No you don't understand," she said, "He will be too busy to speak on the phone today. Give me your number and I will have him call you."

"No," I said, "I'm afraid it's you who does not understand. Get me the doctor, or I swear I will come down there, kick his door in and speak with him personally."

"Yes how can I help you?" he asked me.

"Doctor what exactly are you doing for Mr. Pring?" I asked, in what I'm sure was an accusing tone.

"Well I have a Cat Sca..."

"NO! I MEAN WHAT ARE YOU DOING FOR HIM?"

I asked him what he thought was wrong with Gary but got medical jargon back for a response. I asked if he'd seen him recently to which he replied no.

I didn't get very far. I did manage to establish that this doctor had booked him for tests but that was all. He never spoke of the obvious with Gary and his wife nor did he say the words to me. I do not know what his strategy was but on the surface, it sucked.

I told him that I had just carried Gary in my arms, all ninety pounds or so of him, wracked with pain up to the living room level of his home.

"What do you want me to do?" he asked me.

Incredulously I replied, "Be a goddamned doctor! I want him in a hospital. Send an ambulance for your patient now!"

When we arrived at the hospital they looked at me like I was an idiot for I had obviously brought a dying man into their world, which was already understaffed, overworked, with a lack of available beds. Gary should have indeed been at home, comfortably in his own bed, with the appropriate medications to keep him that way but we were desperate and he needed immediate help.

A doctor pulled me aside and said, "Why have you brought him here?"
"Because, he is dying and he is in great pain," I answered.
"Anyone can see he is dying," said the doctor almost mockingly. "My question is why have you brought him here?"
I stared him down.

"Because the last time I looked, the sign on your door said Hospital. He is a law abiding, tax paying citizen of this country and I want you to help him!"

He looked at me contemptuously as he said, "I don't think we can help him. Take him home and have his family doctor see him."
"Doc, Listen to me," I answered. "You don't know me and I am fine with that, but what I do for a living gives me great access to the media all across this nation of ours. Now if you turn us away and make me take this poor, ravaged soul back home, put him in his bed and attempt to get his family doctor who hasn't visited with him and who is completely oblivious to his dilemma, out to see him, I promise you that you and this hospital will be front page news before you can complete your backswing! Get me?
I have no choice. Help him."

Entering his room, Gary actually looked like a new man, which I enhanced by giving him a clean shave. Afterwards we chatted about music, Glass Tiger, and our new CD. He was weak and a little confused but all in all he still knew what was going on. Never once did he ever mention his illness or anything to do with dying. Later I said goodnight and told him that I would keep my appointment to finish the EPK that had been started the day before and then I would come see him. Even then he was still giving me support with a little "bossiness" Pring style, thrown in.

It was around 4:00 p.m. the next day and I was in the middle of an interview for the EPK when I was told that someone very upset was on the phone asking for me. I took the call to find Gary's wife on the other end.

"Alan, help us," she cried, "A doctor just left the room after telling us to get our papers in order! He says Gary is dying! He says he doesn't have long to go! My God, help us!"

"I'm on my way," I answered immediately.

Incredible as it sounds neither Gary nor his wife knew up until that moment just how bad this was. Call them naïve but this was the way it was and now it was a shock being told what I had known in my heart for months. Equally incredible was the fact that as soon as he was told, as soon as he heard from a doctor that his time in this world was nearing an end, he immediately deteriorated and by the time I got there some 45 minutes after receiving the call, he was already in the beginning stages of dying.

"Cheyne-Stoking" is when the breathing becomes a raspy panting as the body struggles to take oxygen in while the rest of the body begins the process of shutting down. I had endured over fifteen hours of this with my little granny and it is not pleasant, in fact it is down right horrible to witness. Gary had an oxygen mask on and was panting like a dog to keep going. I began a crusade to get the doctor to start a morphine drip on him that would make him comfortable while assisting his body to shut down. They fought me on this one and for the life of me I do not know why they persisted in attempting to give him medication orally. The long haul began. I had left him talkative, comfortable and clean-shaven just 12 hours before and now he was in the clutches of death. At one point after watching him struggle I lost all control of my emotions and in the arms of Jim from our office and Sam from the band my heart caved in and I sobbed, with gut-wrenching sobs, uncontrollably. Still he fought, still he hung on, still the hours passed.

By now it was impossible to know if he could hear us. His breathing was machine-gunning in the shortest of pants. He was sweating profusely and his pupils were pinpoints. Finally an order had come to begin a morphine drip. I was on his left side holding his hand as the nurse prepared to insert the catheter into a vein in the back of his right hand.

Suddenly he gave my hand a squeeze and we made eye contact.

"He's going to go now," I blurted out, "Grab Ilona, he's going now."
The nurse stopped attempting to start an intravenous and stepped back
to allow his wife to be on the opposite side from me.

I had witnessed the actual moment of death many times in my medical
life and as sad and morbid as it can seem, witnessing life exiting this
world is every bit as miraculous, equally as wondrous and just as
humbling as witnessing its entry. I felt his power and energy pass from
his hand into mine, traveling up and across my chest, into my body and
my soul. His eyes rolled and he gave an enormous sigh.

"We love you Gary! We are all here with you and we love you!"
And then he was gone, but to where?

I will leave it up to you to decide. He has been given the answer to
something that for me remains unanswerable. However I know his
energy was honest and worthy, positive and good and it would serve him
well on his new journey wherever that may take him. His death altered
my life forever. I will miss him for the rest of my days and as painful as it
was to lose him, I remain so grateful and I am a better man for having
known him, this father and friend who showed up in my life when I
needed him most.

I loved him.

A note on GRATITUDE
TO WHOM MUCH IS GIVEN

Almost 20 years ago I blew my knee out, badly, in what was supposed to be a
fun, charity soccer match with a bunch of North American Rock 'n Rollers
against a group of our counterparts from the UK. Not only was it a

devastating blow to me in the short term but it also became life altering from that point on.

When the game began I was already tired from having to do a video shoot the night before, which lasted right up until one hour before taking the field. My body was exhausted and to this day I believe that I damaged my knee making the video and just did not realize it. But I had played this game all of my life and thought nothing of it. How wrong I was. I tore my anterior cruciate ligament, my medial cartilage and my medial collateral ligament...in layman's terms, "the big three." My leg spasmed uncontrollably and the pain was excruciating, but here comes the best part. The very next morning I was to fly to Atlanta, Georgia to begin a three-month tour of America working with British legends *The Moody Blues*.

As I lay on the hospital gurney the attending specialist whom I knew said, "Well Alan I am pretty sure you have torn your anterior cruciate but I won't know the full extent of the damage until I get in there and look around."
"You can't go in there," I said tentatively.
"What are you talking about?" he asked.
"Doc I gotta be on a plane tomorrow to the States. I am starting an American tour tomorrow."
"Are you nuts? Your leg is all but gone, I must go in and repair it."

I begged him for an alternative. Reluctantly, he acquiesced and gave me one.

"You have got to be kidding," was the general consensus.
"It'll be fine," I said, "Trust me."

I had arrived at the airport not only on crutches but I was also in a full length, groin-to-ankle fiberglass leg cast and still groggy from mounds of painkillers.

What followed was night upon night of relentless agony as I hobbled on stage in one hundred degree weather through Georgia, Florida and Texas, hundreds of miles night after night trying as best as I possibly could to keep my poker face on and give it my all. Some nights I would wear shorts so the crowd would know that I had a disability. On other occasions when I wore jeans, I would hit the microphone off of my leg, producing a loud thud throughout the stadium just to let them know that my funny walk was due to a leg cast and not because I had shit myself during the previous song. It was a nightmare. What I did not know was that the pain was getting increasingly more and more unbearable due to the fact that I was hemorrhaging tiny amounts of blood continuously into my knee cap, putting tremendous pressure on my knee now locked firmly inside a cast. Ironically word came back from Canada that the footage from the video we had shot weeks before at the time of the soccer match was mostly unusable and that the director wanted to re-shoot the band's scene entirely. A surgeon was hired to cut the cast off of my leg and assist me.

What a mess lay under that smelly old cast. It was revolting. The doctor told me he should look inside my knee. The leg was a weak, shriveled, and an emaciated mess, so I agreed.

They propped me up for the video re-shoot and I never moved. They simply panned a camera back and forth in front of me to capture the shots. I hated it and to this day I still hate the video and anything to do with the song.

I agreed to let the doctor at least take a look inside my knee. That evening we did a show in Memphis with me in a heavy leg brace followed by a flight back to Atlanta for my surgery. They opened my leg, cleaned things up a bit then recovered me from the throes of anesthetic to show me inside my leg on a video monitor while we discussed my options for repair. High as a kite, I was watching the old PAC-MAN video game as this little creature ate up all the bits of stuff inside my kneecap. The doc then proceeded to tell me what the plan for my leg was and how long the recovery process would be.

"Eighteen months," he said nonchalantly.

"Are you joking? Am I still under anesthetic and I'm only dreaming that I'm awake?"
"Doc I have got to be back on tour in four days!"

Once again I asked for an alternative and once again I got one.

Four days later I was on stage in Buffalo, New York in a leg brace that would have held Dumbo the Elephant up. I was again plodding across the stage like Lurch and this is how it continued for months on end. Even our triumphant return to Canada for two sold-out performances in Toronto were marred by the fact that my leg was useless and it was not being given the chance to repair properly nor was it receiving proper therapy. What they had done for me in Atlanta was minimal repair for that is all I would allow. The anterior cruciate ligament was hanging by a thread, which snapped completely a year later, and three more surgeries followed. Months and months were spent on crutches and my leg to this day has never been the same. A poorly functioning leg leads to poor posture and the favouring of one side over another. Night after night onstage and you get the picture. A bad back, sore ankles, sore shoulder and I'm thinking, "God, I've become my grandfather and I'm only thirty-five!"

Now here I am at fifty and I must admit to you that it has been such a drag all of these years living with pain and a pretty useless set of legs. Yes, the other one has since joined the party. So what do I do about it?

Well for starters, I give thanks for what I do have! I give thanks that I have legs! I am very grateful that I can still ride a bicycle and I am not in a wheelchair! I am happy to play golf even though I cannot kick a ball or run anymore. I used to laugh at golfers years ago when driving past the courses, but now I admire their skill and stamina, and am thankful for just having legs, albeit not the best! I am thankful that my voice is strong and that I am singing better than ever.

Be grateful for all that you have as opposed to bitter for what you do not have. No, it is not easy, and I am not professing that it will be. Sometimes it's tough to accept that you don't have what you most DESIRE but I promise you if you focus on what you don't have then you will keep on getting more of what you don't have. Conversely if you focus your thoughts on being thankful and grateful for what you do have, no matter how small or seemingly trivial, then you will start to invite more of such things into your life until more becomes a lot more. Successful people know this and apply it everyday to their endeavors.

Think of it this way. When you give someone a gift that makes them light up with joy and you witness just how happy you have made them, what is one of the first things you decide you want to do?

Give them another one right? You want to experience making them happy again.

So it is with ourselves. Being in a constant state of gratitude will not only empower us but it will bring us more of that which we are grateful for and we know gratitude is not just about the money or the toys either, is it? Of course not.

By all means if you have a lot of money and a big house and several beautiful cars then be very, very grateful, however what good are they without a strong beating heart, or healthy lungs or being cancer free? What good are they without loved ones and friends? While you're at it be thankful for your children, your wife, your guitar, your dinner and your dog, your eyes, hands, mind and yes... legs!

I am thankful that I am still able to take my sore legs and get myself up on stage to perform. Besides if I have to, I'll learn to walk and perform while standing on my hands.

"Oooh! Edith, look at that lead singer, he's singing out of his arse!"
"No love, 'e's not, the microphone's on the floor, see look, there's his head right down there where his willy should be."
"Oooh, he's not very good lookin' at all is he Edith?"
"Well 'e's upside down love, isn't he?"

Try to improve yourself constantly. Retire each night knowing you are a little better today than you were yesterday. It is invigorating. Take full mature responsibility for living your dream every moment. Find projects that make you proud and the rest will fall into place. If you do not love what you are doing, someone else will, and they'll love it with PASSION and be truly successful while you sit by and wonder why they can do so much more than you. Be grateful. Say, "Thank you", more.

Remember my last shift ever as an R.N.? The man whose life I helped save before leaving medicine behind forever? Let me share with you quickly one of the most memorable moments of gratitude that I have ever witnessed.

COMING AROUND AGAIN

One day, at least two years or so after that last fateful shift I was rehearsing with *Glass Tiger* and I was taking a break and walking with Michael to a coffee shop when a lady and man were coming directly towards us walking in the other direction. The woman had the man by the arm assisting him on his obviously paralyzed side as he helped himself by using a tri-pod walking stick on the other. He had the classic look a person has after suffering a major stroke.

A curled, shriveled paralyzed arm and hand. Similarly with leg and foot, dragging as he struggled to propel himself forward, face and mouth drooping on one side. About six feet away from me he stopped dead in his tracks and started to shake and display a high level of emotion as our eyes met. He was incapable of speech but made loud groaning sounds, which were obviously upsetting his bewildered wife. She hadn't a clue what he was saying. But I knew. I knew what he was saying. For he and I were bonded.

Now dear reader you must realize something. Back on that eventful night in the hospital this man was almost a silhouette to me. I mean at no time was the room brightly lighted nor did we make close contact. He had after all only been post operative some eight hours prior to becoming my patient and was still extremely groggy and sore and so for his part, he spent most of my shift quietly sleeping in almost total darkness.

When he had his stroke at the end of the shift all hell broke loose and I paid little or no attention to his face. If I had been asked to pick him out of a line up the next day I would not have been able to do it and I can honestly say that he never saw my face with even the remotest clarity that night.

So how then could this be happening? I mean two years had gone by since I last had anything to do with this complete stranger and it had all gone from zero to one hundred in the madness of a blink of an eye.

I asked Michael to go on ahead without me and I approached the couple. Tears were streaming down his face. His poor wife was beside herself trying to figure out what was wrong for she and I had never met.

I got close.

"May I?" I asked his wife as I gestured for her to leave his weakened side to let me replace her. She moved aside letting me in.
"It's okay, I understand," I said gently. "I understand and I need you to know that I was just doing my job."
He sobbed and sobbed as I held him.
He was thanking me. He recognized me, he knew me and he was thanking me. Here he was, paralyzed and aphasic, emotionally wounded, a shell of his former self yet thankful to be alive.
"I was his nurse that night," I told his wife. "More importantly, I was the last living face he ever saw as he began to crossover to the other side."
Then I said, "He is thanking me."
"But how could he possibly have seen your face? He was having a stroke. He was *dying*," she asked astonished.

It was all rather implausible but yet here we were two years after the event and he did recognize me.
"He saw me," I replied. "Perhaps not with his eyes but he saw me."

Why be grateful for what you have? Well, incidentally I met them both again about a year later and once again he picked me out of a crowd and this time he was no longer aphasic and though slurred, he had the power of speech. Still somewhat paralyzed on one side he shuffled over to me without assistance from his wife and threw an arm over my shoulder only this time he took great pleasure in saying the words out loud... "THANK YOU."

Even when he had suffered terribly and was left as a bit of a shadow of who he used to be he was still nonetheless grateful and by showing that gratitude to the universe the universe was in return giving him more of what he was grateful for... life. He was mending.

Why did I tell you this story? I'm not sure really. I know how it makes me feel about the true power in all of us but yet it borders on the spiritual at such a level that it actually goes way beyond what the essence of this book is about and so I prefer to not attempt to share with you now my feelings about how this man could possibly have known me, for I am not qualified enough, I fear. I hope however, that it makes you think deeper about the connection between all of us, and with the universe both in life and in death.

A bit "spooky" huh? But it sure makes you think doesn't it? And you *are* thinking...aren't you?

CONCLUSION

So there you have it, the *ACTION SANDWICH (a six step recipe to success, doing what you're already doing)*. Thank you for reading my book, which of course is now our book, for we are bonded if even just by the fact that together we know the content of these pages. We can bond further by implementing the strategy, by practicing the principles, by frequenting the same roads on our individual journeys, perhaps even crossing paths along the way as we have with this publication. It has been an arduous task writing this book, and an honour sharing it with you but now the true test begins. If when you started the first chapter you were unable to answer the questions I posed to you regarding your life, then I ask you them again.

Who are you?
What do you want?
What do you really, really, want?
Do you know? If so, do you now know what you must do to get it?
I have great BELIEF that you do.

At a certain point in life you just have to take stock of what this world has offered you. More importantly, however, there comes a time when you must take stock of what you offer this world in return. You must take responsibility for where you are today, no matter how painful it seems. You must look yourself in the mirror and take charge, which begins by taking responsibility. When you do, a remarkable thing will happen.

WHAT ABOUT BOB?

Say hello to Bob. He's a regular guy, with a regular job, a growing family (four children and one on the way), a hefty mortgage and a maxed-out line of credit. His credit cards are so fed up with giving him five-minute majors for fighting that he's now been given a game misconduct and can't use them anymore.

RECEPTIVITY: Oh, he's got it all right, but unfortunately he is more receptive to what is happening in the lives of those on *Survivor* than in his own. He remains grossly overweight and is extremely unhappy with his job.

DESIRE: Sure he desires to lose weight, but right now it's just a word. His time is not his own and it just seems impossible for him to ever find the time to exercise. As for all those diet plans, well they just never work, now do they?

BELIEF: He believes he could have owned his own business as a chartered accountant if he hadn't listened to those around him telling him to get that crazy notion out of his head and go get a real job!

INTENTION: He wonders why he seems to be the unluckiest guy in the world. He tries focusing on bad things all the time to see if he can bring about a change, but the more bad things he focuses on, the more they seem to happen. He wonders why that is.

ACTION: Sure, successful people make their money work HARD for them, but Bob works HARD for his money, in fact he's the hardest working guy he knows. Is that not enough?

PASSION: Now what the hell does he have to be passionate about? He just can't win, can't get a break. His one true PASSION, owning his own business, was taken away from him when he listened to others, so why be passionate?

He is so stressed these days he cracks at the slightest provocation or challenge. His wife has taken to hating him, and his actions are so aggressive that she is fearful for her safety and for the safety of their children. She is planning to leave him shortly. Bob gets drunk way too often. He is sickly. He is rapidly losing all sense of self-respect and the respect of others. He seems only passionate about one thing, telling everyone who will listen what's wrong with the world. In Bob's eyes it continues to get worse.

People at work avoid dear old Bob at all cost, for to put it mildly, he's a downer. After his family runs for the hills, leaving him alone with his misery, Bob complains endlessly that he just can't go on. And of course now that he has to pay child support he will never be able to attend the necessary night school accounting courses required for him to be who he really wants to be. The sad thing of course is that it's not his fault. Don't believe me? Just ask him. It sounds like Bob's *ACTION SANDWICH* has some pretty skunky ingredients in it if you ask me. But Bob isn't asking me. The bigger question is "what is he asking of himself?" For I say again, he already has been using the formula of *THE ACTION SANDWICH* to put himself in the position he is in, and no matter how dark the scenario seems (and it can and will get even darker if he does nothing about it), he can use what he has already been using to get himself back in the game of life again.

Easy? No.
Doable? Absolutely!

CH CH CH CH CHANGES

As we know from our first ingredient, if Bob does not show RECEPTIVITY for the need to change, then nothing will change. If he continues on this spiral towards the bottom of the well then, it's game over. If he continues behaving like a victim, the universe will support him and his cause by keeping him one. But say for the sake of argument that Bob has hit rock bottom and now realizes he needs to make a change. We have all heard it so many times before, but let's look at this old adage once more: you didn't get fat overnight, so you won't be thin overnight either. In other words, you didn't wreck your marriage, or give up on your dream in one day, you didn't lose the love of your children or the confidence of your friends and co-workers overnight, nor did you get to the level of debt that you have reached in the blink of an eye. So it will take longer than that to recover.

The good news is that Bob can decide right now to change his self-destructive behaviour, and then the improvement he seeks will follow. Now, if you are reading this and relating to Bob in any way, then also relate to the following: for this is a massive moment. This is the defining moment. This is the moment of truth and it must be non-negotiable. If Bob does not recognize the need to change, then I might as well stop writing about him right now, for he's finished. You must take 100% responsibility for your actions, and recognizing the need to change is the single greatest ACTION that Bob or anyone in his position could possibly take. Bob's decision to change is his and his alone.

Of course, help is just around the corner if he asks for it and seeks it out. But what must an alcoholic do prior to being helped by AA? Everyone with that problem must accept the fact that they are alcoholics, and they must decide that change is their only option. They must take responsibility.

So for the sake of not ending my book right here with old Bob on his way to hell, let's say that he looks himself in the mirror and says the magic words: "I must change." He tells himself and the universe that he wants to come back. Just like the patient who came back from the clutches of death, he must take his RECEPTIVITY and DESIRE, BELIEF, INTENTION and apply his greatest ACTION fueled by a PASSION that says, "I am going to change!" They cannot just be words. They must be the truth. The universe, like you, always knows the truth about you.

Now folks, I could make you an enormous shopping list of the various things that Bob can do, but quite frankly it could take a book on its own just to write them for you.

Things like calling the local AA, beginning the 12-step program. He could look into joining a men's group to assist not only with anger management but also with the need to be understood by other men who have been where he is at the moment socially, mentally, economically and morally. He could find a mental health practitioner, and if he cannot afford one then he could ask friends, his boss, his family including perhaps even his wife to help him with the cost, for I am sure they would all be ecstatic to know that he was willing to take such measures towards change and recovery. The opportunity exists to mend all things. Remember that.

He could decide to start eating twenty percent less at every meal. He may not be able to afford a gym, but walking costs nothing. He could start there. He could call the adult education centre in his community and ask about upgrading his skills or beginning night school or correspondence courses. Are you following me? It is endless and it is not easy, but it is doable, if you're willing to take responsibility. Stop blaming. Stop the excuses. Stop the old bus and get off. Like all of us, Bob is today what he put into play yesterday (consciously or otherwise) and so in order to have a better tomorrow, he needs to make changes now.

When he decides to make a change he will see that he needs a plan. He must begin by tackling his relationship with himself first. He must begin to respect and nurture the relationship he has with his own heart, mind, body and soul. From little changes come big effects. You'll be amazed at how they compound. You do not need to solve it all in one profound motion. The thousand-mile journey really does begin one step at a time.

It's really common sense though, is it not? Life is about small incremental changes every day. It's about undoing the damage you've done, one layer at a time, then improving your life systematically. If you make the conscious effort for little changes every single day, your confidence will begin to flourish and your relationship with yourself and the world around you will improve tremendously.

It's all about knowing when it's time to stop the "justs." That is to say, just thinking about it, just talking about it, just reading about it, perhaps even just complaining about it – start doing whatever "it" may be. It's allowing our sixth sense or our gut feeling to have a say, and not always squashing it because it makes you feel uncomfortable, stressed or frightened. It's a very simple concept, but it's not easy.

What *is* easy however, is to say that you'll start soon, or tomorrow, or perhaps next Monday, or after the holidays, or after you've lost twenty pounds or saved a little more money. Wrong! Its gotta be now! You must stop giving precious energy to excuses and procrastination and give as much as you can to making the changes necessary to turning things around and beginning to live the life YOU DESIRE.

When you take responsibility for your choices and their corresponding results you are given a fresh start, a new life so to speak, a point from which change can emerge, allowing you to let go of what was, accept what is, and embrace what will be. Sadly, for some this may not happen until it is almost too late, and that is a great human tragedy. That's sort of like convicted criminals who after exhausting all appeals for a stay of execution suddenly find God. What have they got to lose?

But where, I ask, was this faith, this BELIEF when they had the choice to live the best life possible? Why wait until you're another year older, or a month, or even a minute? Why wait until you are faced with a crisis situation before making a change?

It is never too late to rise above the pack and take responsibility for the position you may find yourself in. Not tonight or tomorrow or next January, and especially not when you're knocking on heaven's door, but now. Lives are changed, permanently altered, even lost in split seconds. Choices are no different. It truly is like turning one light switch off and another on, or like changing lanes on a highway. You simply need the willingness to do so and you will move forward like never before.

The tales held within the pages of this book are not those of a man who has arrived, but rather of one who continues the journey. It has taken me most of my life so far to reach the point where enlightenment and true self-awareness and understanding are things I DESIRE to pursue. Yet in doing so I have left myself exposed, vulnerable and open to attack, and you will too. This Achilles' heel seems somewhat less perilous when you realize that you are not alone on this journey. I know that this book was not written by a perfect man and I feel it is safe to say that it will never be read by a perfect reader, yet in that beautiful imperfection we are all bonded. Life is not easy, just look around you. When you read about its beginnings and middles and its yesterdays, you discover that it has always been hard, brutally so at times, and we are still not anywhere near bliss or nirvana. Hopefully that future lies ahead for generations to come. We are in the midst of a world changing at speeds beyond our comprehension. What is relevant today is becoming passé and obsolete by tomorrow. Ask any musician or even record company representative over the age of thirty to make sense of the music industry today and they will scratch their heads dumbfounded. Record companies are vanishing before our very eyes at an alarming rate. Websites like YOUTUBE and MYSPACE are driving nails into their coffins with no apologies. We are the generation witnessing the beginnings of changes that will have profound, everlasting effects on our planet and society's future. We all know that global warming is here, most likely to stay, and although I truly believe that each and every one of us must try our utmost to not contribute to its genesis, what is more important is how future generations will prepare to deal with it. Change scares us but I have great faith in our ability to handle these changes even if we must go through severe hardship in doing so.

I did not bring this book to you. You brought this book into your life and only you can decide if it feels true and meaningful to you. For you see, it's all about you. No one is defining what lies ahead for you. Only you are. Your life will be as satisfying as you design it to be. Your future is the future you have chosen to give yourself. When you are receptive to all of the abundance in this universe, and you identify what it is you DESIRE, when you believe you can have it and intend to bring it to yourself, when you act on it with PASSION, you truly can live a remarkable life. Use the simple *ACTION SANDWICH* to remind you to bring yourself happiness and joy. In this state of being alive, INTENTION thrives and you will manifest all that your heart desires.

IMAGINE ALL THE PEOPLE LIVING FOR TODAY

So what are you going to do? Do you DESIRE the best possible life you can have? Are you important enough to obtain all that you want? To live the best life you can takes courage and stamina. You have to speak out, stand up, hold on, be strong, chase after, fall down and get back up again because that, my friend, is life. That is real. That is living.

In the movie *Braveheart*, William Wallace tells his love, "Every man dies, but not every man truly lives."
I offer this slight alteration to that beautiful line:
"Everyone exists but not everyone truly lives." For I fear that it is a far greater crime to just merely exist than it ever is to die. Don't just exist. Don't live a life that just happens to you. Make it happen. You have to DO, to get DONE!

Get up and do it! Make that sandwich. Smother it in PASSION. Live and enjoy the very best life you can.

Thank you, dear reader. Peace.

For Gary,

Alan

THE END

EPILOGUE

Her name was Lettie, Lettie Douglas, "Sweaty" Lettie Douglas, and she was popular, very popular indeed, because without hesitation and for the measly sum of two cigarettes or one bright shiny sixpence, she would let boys look down her blouse for a whole thirty seconds, undisturbed, in a ritual that took place behind Mrs. McDougall's shed with great regularity. For you see, Lettie was a chain smoker. The Seven Wonders of the World may have belonged to the ancients but numbers eight and nine belonged to Lettie!

The problem I had every time this sacred communion would come around was simple. First of all, I was only seven and didn't smoke, and second, I never had a sixpence. And if I did, it would surely have gone into something that found its way into my stomach. But I sure wanted to see those wondrous hidden treasures that seemed to be worth so much to so few, for so many... pennies that is, six of them to be exact.

I would get in line behind the older boys in hopes that she would take pity on a boy whose hem on his trousers was taller than he was, and whose shirt originally belonged to her brother but alas, pity wasn't in Lettie's bag of tricks. I tried giving her a penny wrapped in silver paper once. It was a little trick I learned from my old granddad, who passed the occasional penny-wrapped shilling off at the local off-track betting shops as his wager. But he had my dad as an accomplice, for he worked in the shop and was the one who took the bet from him!

Lettie didn't fall for that and I only succeeded in getting a cuff 'round the ear from her and sent once more to the back of the line, though she kept my penny of course.

What does a boy have to do to witness such wonders, I thought to myself. What can I come up with?

Then the lights went off!

"Simmit" is an old colloquial term in Scotland used to describe a singlet or man's undershirt, while "drawers," on the other hand, as I am sure most of you know, is a word referring to boxers, briefs or underpants. I tell you this because these undergarments became the mainstay of my father's epithets in lieu of using really foul swear words at home; he would take the names of his, or perhaps even your, underwear in vain.

"Och! SIMMITS AND DRAWERS! Not again!" he'd yell out. But of course by then it was too late and we'd all be rooted to the spot in the pitch darkness of our home, waiting for him to spark a match and guide us all in, like moths to a street lamp. As mentioned earlier, I was born and grew up in an old post-war pre-fabricated home that had no central air conditioning system for summer or furnace for the winter. Now summer was no problem because Mother Nature looked after that by not giving us a summer. As a matter of fact, the four seasons in Coatbridge to this day remain rain, sleet, heavy rain and of course, "Cold Enough To freeze the 'Niagara Falls' off you!" So summer was taken care of, but winter, well that was like the planet Pluto with four paper-thin walls surrounding it.

Coal was not only scarce at times around our neighbourhood but also expensive, way too expensive to burn indiscriminately, and so on many a winter's night or morning, the little kerosene heater became your best friend, providing of course that you had kerosene. If not, a candle started to look pretty darned friendly. Barring that, the next best place was your bed with your clothes still on. The best however is yet to come, for you see the reason our lights would go off is quite simple. Our electricity, our only source of any and all the power that ran through the veins of our little home, was coin operated! That's correct, in order to have lights and power to any electrical outlets in our home, we had to put coins in a meter. Shilling coins, to be exact, before inflation pushed it up to two shillings! This process of your lights going out and a coin having to be put into the meter occurred approximately every four hours and it was common practice for families to keep jars of the much-needed tokens near the meter. We, however, opted for having a little stack of them on the mantle of our fireplace, and I use the term "stack" loosely, for that stack got raided continuously and on many an occasion provided the necessary loot for a fish supper when it was better to eat in the dark, than not to have eaten at all.

For me to raid the coin stack usually wasn't worth the risk, for they were almost certainly counted, and my arse just couldn't take that chance. But here comes the pièce de résistance, for you see the meter was attached to the wall out in our small hallway, next to our bathroom. But it also had a sort of cupboard built around it. Access to this meter meant that you had to open the door of the cupboard, which was around shoulder height for an average adult. I, on the other hand, needed a chair if I was asked to put a coin in. Now, if a coin happened to fall from one's grasp it did not fall onto the floor but rather down into the bottom half of this cupboard, into the darkness and into a space that was impossible for even the smallest of adults to squeeze into. Retrieving a missing coin was always a last resort and I will tell you, dear reader, exactly why.

If we had no money at all and our lights went out close to bedtime then off to bed we would go, for it was not worth wasting a coin that you couldn't get your complete four hours out of. However, if the lights went off when we needed light, this is usually how it would play out.

(Blink)...(Darkness)
"SIMMITS AND DRAWERS!"
(Spark)...(Moths fly to the light)

"Alan, run to Maggie next door and ask if we can borrow a shilling. If she says no, go across to the McDougall's and ask them. If they say no, come straight back here, okay?"
"Okay, right Dad!"
(Maggie's door)...(McDougall's door)...(our door)

"Dad! No luck."
"Right then", he'd say, "we're goin' in!" (James Bond, eat your heart out.)

We would then head to the cupboard where the meter was.

"Okay, Alan, you know what to do," he would say.
"Yes, Dad."
He would then hand me a match and have me sit on the floor so he could grab me by my ankles and lift me straight up in the air, turning me completely upside down.
"Now remember, don't waste your match. Wait until you're nearly at the bottom before you strike it, got that?"
"Right, Dad!"

And so it was that he would lower me down into the bottom of this hole for wayward coins, chasing away spiders and any mice who might get the wrong idea because I, my friends, had fire!

Have you ever lit a match while hanging upside-down in your father's hands? It's not easy. The flame rises up towards you and when you are in a cramped space like the hole for wayward coins, it's downright next to impossible not to burn your lip or your cheek or even your hair. But then the lights went off right in the middle of the football match, someone had to do it and that someone was wee, I mean, me!

Days passed since I last saw Lettie, but nothing happened to our lights. As a matter of fact, the meter inspector had been around to empty it and as always the family was given a little rebate of around five pounds. So for a few days after the big payday we were like millionaires, having chops or stew or something equivalent for dinner, instead of soup and bread. We were living the high life but I needed a disaster to strike soon or I might miss my chance forever, for Lettie might come into full bloom and get married, or worse yet, give up smoking.

"C'mon ACTION SANDWICH! This boy is receptive to, desirous of, believing in and fully intended on seeing those wonders of the world and God knows he is ready to take all the ACTION needed"...and then, it happened.

The stack had vanished. My mother as per usual was at her mother's. My dad and I were watching the big match on our wee black and white television. It was a fantastic game, 2-2 with fifteen minutes to go when–Blink!

"SIMMITS AND DRAWERS." And we had no coins.

THE GOLDEN GLOBES

Waiting my turn at the end of the line, behind Mrs. McDougall's shed seemed to be taking unusually long.
"Were there more lads here than usual?" I wondered. "Nah, perhaps I am just extra-impatient today."
Eventually I stood before the buxom Lettie who was already looking at me distainfully, expecting my usual pleading to give me a flash without paying.

"So what do you want?" sneered Lettie.
"I want to look," I replied.
"Where's your sixpence?" she bellowed.
Much to her amazement, I held up not a sixpence but rather a bright, glistening brand-new 1963 shilling.
She paused for a moment, obviously quite taken by the fact that indeed I had a coin for her.
"Ok, come here then," she ordered.

She bent over as I raised myself up onto my tippy-toes for my first glimpse of any womanhood that didn't include my mother or my sister, the most exciting thirty seconds of my young life. If you can believe it, she actually counted your seconds down out loud. "Thirty! Twenty-nine! Twenty-eight! Twenty-seven..."

The British monetary system prior to the Decimal system coming into effect in 1971 was nothing short of a "wack job."
6 pennies = sixpence
12 pennies = one shilling
20 shillings = one pound
240 pennies = one pound. Absolutely no rhyme or reason to any of it.

But wait! Look again. A sixpence contains six pennies but a shilling has twelve or in other words, two sixpences.

"Oh, what bliss. Hallelujah! Sweet 'simmits and drawers', that means that whatever you can buy for one sixpence, you can buy two of for a shilling!"

"Three! Two! One! Okay that's it, you've had your money's worth," said Lettie, pushing me back as she readjusted herself to fit those rolling hills back from whence they came.

"Right then," she said, as tough as any boy, for those perks of voluptuousness certainly belied any hint of femininity, "your money, now!"

As she held out her open palm I placed the coin in the centre of her hand. We both stared at it for what seemed like eternity before she took a coin, half its size, and placed it aside my shilling. This was my change, my half-shilling, my sixpence. We continued staring for a moment when suddenly she broke the silence.

"What's your problem? Take your change, why don't you?"

For a brief moment thoughts of my sixpence had donuts, with soft powdery icing sugar dancing in my head, accompanied by a big box of Smarties, washed down by a gallon of cream soda. A boy could do much with sixpence in 1963. Suddenly her gulder awakened me from my candy-coated daydream. "Hey…what do you want then?"

With both my hands I reached out to her opened palm, and began to turn it into a fist, wrapping it around my sixpence and what was now her shilling. I felt a little smirk form in the corner of my toothless mouth.

"What are you doing," she asked. "What about your sixpence?"

"Keep it," I replied.

"Keep it, but why?" she quizzed me.

"Because whatever you can buy for one sixpence, you can buy two of for a shilling! I'm goin' in again!"